PLATO'S EPISTLES

A Translation, with Critical Essays
and Notes, by

GLENN R. MORROW

Professor of Philosophy, The University of Pennsylvania

. . . .

The Library of Liberal Arts

published by

THE **BOBBS-MERRILL** COMPANY, INC.
A SUBSIDIARY OF HOWARD W. SAMS & CO., INC.
Publishers • INDIANAPOLIS • NEW YORK

D74/71

PREFACE TO THE REVISED EDITION

The present volume is a revised edition of *Studies in the Platonic Epistles*, published by the University of Illinois in 1935. The principal changes are found in the translation of the *Epistles*, which has been thoroughly revised. The intervening twenty-five years have given me a greater feeling for the nuances of Plato's style, as well as a better understanding of the manuscript tradition on which our text depends. I have retained Burnet's text as the most convenient basis of reference for English readers, though my departures from it are now more numerous thanks to my study of the text of Souilhé and frequent consultations with Professor L. A. Post, whose monograph *The Vatican Plato and its Relations* appeared while my first edition was in press. I have also adopted two or three plausible emendations of Pavlu, whose work was unfortunately not known to me when I prepared the earlier version. The numbers in the margin of the translation refer to the corresponding pages in the edition of Stephanus (Paris, 1578), which is the commonly accepted basis for citations of Plato.

In the introductory studies the only change of any consequence is in the chapter on the *Epistles* and the historians, where I have introduced a more adequate discussion of Ephorus' failure to use the *Epistles*. The other changes, though numerous, are chiefly editorial and bibliographical in nature.

The first edition was dedicated to Daniel Shaw Gage, my first teacher of the classics and classical philosophy. I dedicate this second edition also to him, as a memorial to a great teacher and a dearly beloved friend.

July, 1961   G. R. M.

PREFACE TO THE FIRST EDITION

Our knowledge of the Platonic letters has been enormously advanced in recent years by the labors of Ritter, Wilamowitz, Taylor, Post, Hackforth, Harward, Novotný, and others. My indebtedness to these men who have gone over the ground before me will be abundantly evident and is hereby sincerely acknowledged. The special attention given in the following pages to the philosophical—particularly the political—content of the *Epistles* and to the relation between them and the ancient historians of Sicily will, I hope, make the following studies a real, though modest, addition to our present knowledge of these documents.

For personal advice and assistance during the preparation of the manuscript, I wish to thank especially Professor W. A. Oldfather, of the University of Illinois, and Professor George H. Sabine, of Cornell University, neither of whom, however, is to be held responsible for any views here expressed. The editors of the *Philosophical Review* have kindly granted permission to reprint here the major part of an article of mine on the theory of knowledge in the *Seventh Epistle* that originally appeared in Vol. XXXVIII (1929) of the *Review*. My thanks are also due to the Director of the University of Illinois Press for assistance in editing and proofreading. Finally, my debt to my wife, for manifold encouragement and assistance during the preparation of these studies, is hereby thankfully recorded.

G. R. M.

Urbana, Illinois
May 27, 1935

CONTENTS

. . . .

PLATO'S EPISTLES

INTRODUCTORY CRITICAL ESSAYS

INTRODUCTORY CRITICAL ESSAYS

THE QUESTION OF AUTHENTICITY

There are good reasons why the writings that have come down to us as the letters of Plato should be viewed with grave suspicion. We have no decisive evidence of the existence of any of the individual letters nor of the collection as a whole prior to the Alexandrian Age. And they belong to a department of literature which seems to have flourished under peculiarly favorable conditions during the postclassical period, as evidenced by the voluminous remains that have come down to us. With the founding of the great libraries at Alexandria and Pergamum and the systematic effort of their librarians to collect and preserve all the writings of the great age of Greek literature, an obvious mercenary inducement was offered to the production of forgeries of all sorts, and of letters in particular. We do not know how strict the librarians were in excluding doubtful works, nor how careful in their scrutiny; but in any case it is certain that many spurious compositions found their way into the great libraries. The incentives to forgery must have been stronger in the case of letters than in any other department of literature. A letter does not require the sustained effort that a longer composition demands; and the fact that it is ordinarily written for a private purpose and to a single individual makes it more difficult to judge of its genuineness than would be the case with a "published" work.

But there were other more innocent reasons for the production and preservation of spurious letters. It was a common practice in the schools of rhetoric that flourished from the fourth century onward to construct speeches or letters appropriate to historic personages. The students in these schools seem to have found a keen satisfaction in composing speeches

3

in the style of Demosthenes, or constructing letters that could have been written by Socrates to Plato or by Aristotle to Alexander. There is but a thin line, if any exists at all, dividing the rhetoricians in this respect from the historians. The precedent for the construction of more or less fictitious speeches and letters had been set by no less a person than Thucydides himself; and we may be sure a Timaeus or a Theopompus would follow the precedent without qualms.[1] Thus there were numerous circumstances favoring the production and the preservation of fictitious letters, and this necessarily creates a presumption against the authenticity of any letters that have come down to us from Alexandrian times. The extant remains of this type of composition are extensive,[2] and judging from the references to letters we hear of that are no longer in existence, what we have constitutes only a fraction of the epistolographic treasures of the postclassical age. There is almost no person of consequence in antiquity to whom there are not some letters attributed, either in Hercher or in some one of the ancient collections we know to have existed. Therefore we do well to look about us carefully before admitting to authenticity any of the contents of this vast literature.

Yet most certainly not all these letters are spurious. The very existence of such a popular form of literary composition shows that the writing of letters was a common event in real life, and given the industry of the philosophical schools and the librarians at Alexandria and Pergamum in collecting and preserving literary works, it is inconceivable that a number of authentic documents should not have been preserved in this collection. Authentic letters must have existed to serve as

---

[1] There is extant an enlightening criticism of Polybius directed at Timaeus, not for putting speeches into the mouths of his chief personages, but for the triviality and inaccuracy of the remarks he attributed to them. Cf. Polyb. XII, 25.

[2] They have been collected in Rudolph Hercher, *Epistolographi Graeci* (Paris, 1873). See Joseph Souilhé, *Platon: Lettres* (Budé edn.; Paris, 1926), pp. xvii-xix, for the vogue of this type of literature in Hellenistic times.

models for imitators, whether of the dishonest or the romantic sort. The task of criticism therefore only really begins when we have recognized the a priori grounds for skepticism.

The Platonic *Epistles* have fared better than most of the letters in this collection, for they seem to have been generally accepted as genuine until modern times. Cicero refers unmistakably to the *Seventh* [3] and *Ninth* [4] in terms that leave no doubt as to his belief that he is citing genuine writings of Plato. Plutarch's life of Dion is based to a considerable extent upon the material of the *Epistles,* and makes specific citation of the *Fourth, Seventh,* and *Thirteenth* as Platonic letters.[5] Dionysius of Halicarnassus makes general reference to the *Epistles* of Plato.[6] Among later rhetoricians, grammarians, and historians the references to the *Epistles* are even more numerous, not only to the letters previously mentioned, but also to the *Second, Third,* and *Sixth.*[7] The Greek Fathers were glad to appeal to the *Second, Sixth, Thirteenth,* and even the *Seventh* for anticipations of Christian doctrine.[8]

But more important than these references is the fact that the *Epistles* are listed both in the canon of Platonic works drawn up by Aristophanes of Byzantium toward the end of the third century B.C., and also in the canon of Thrasyllus, dating from the first century after Christ. Diogenes Laertius tells us (III, 62) that one of Aristophanes' trilogies consisted of *Crito, Phaedo,* and *Epistles;* but unfortunately we do not

3 *Tusc. Disp.* V, xxxv, 100; *De Fin.* II, xxviii, 92.

4 *De Fin.* II, xiv, 45; *De Off.* I, vii, 22.

5 See pp. 19 f.

6 *De Adm. Vi Dic. in Dem.* 1027 (ed. Reiske).

7 Aristides II, 90, 92, 104, 106, 107, 268, 269, 373 (ed. Dindorf); Stobaeus, *Anthology,* 4, 114; 14, 25; 25, 4; 44, 22a; 45, 24; 46, 105; 47, 23; 48, 59; 62, 49; 79, 40; 93, 28; Athenaeus XII, 527c; XV, 702c; Galen X, 465 (ed. Kühn); Lucian *De Lapsu in Salut.* 4; Demetrius, *On Elocution,* 234 (49, ed. Radermacher); Aelian, *Varied History,* XII, 25; Timaeus, *Platonic Lexicon,* Preface; Plotinus *Enneads* I, 8, 2 (cf. V, 1, 1-8); Julian, *Oration VI,* 189b.

8 Clement of Alexandria I, 72, 228; III, 51, 83, 134 (ed. Dindorf); Eusebius, *The Preparation of the Gospel,* XI, 13, 16, 20; XIII, 13; Origen, *Against Celsus,* VI; Cyril, *Against Julian,* VIII, 271.

know how many letters were included under this head, nor whether they were the same as those in our present collection. With regard to the canon of Thrasyllus, however, we have more explicit information. From Diogenes (III, 61) we learn not only that it contained an item called Ἐπίστολαι, but also that these letters were thirteen in number and identical with the members of our present collection. Thus we know (1) that there existed a collection of letters at the end of the third century B.C., a little more than a century after Plato's death, which were included in the Platonic canon; and (2) that our present collection was in existence in the first century after Christ and received the stamp of Thrasyllus. There is, it is true, a notation appended to the *Twelfth* in our manuscripts indicating that its authenticity was regarded as doubtful by some ancient editor; and if this comes from Thrasyllus it only emphasizes his belief that the others are genuine. The only other doubt we hear of in antiquity is recorded by Olympiodorus, who says that the "divine Proclus" regarded the *Epistles* as spurious, διὰ τὸ ἁπλοῦν τῆς φράσεως.[9] But since he records in the same passage that Proclus also rejected the *Republic* and the *Laws,* we need not ascribe much importance to this evidently garbled tradition.

The favorable judgment of antiquity was almost completely reversed in modern times with the rise of critical historical methods. Ficinus in the fifteenth century and Cudworth in the seventeenth regarded the *Thirteenth Epistle* as spurious.[10] The general condemnation began with Meiners[11] in 1783, was continued by Ast[12] and Socher,[13] and reached its culmination in Karsten's comprehensive work.[14] The view

[9] *Proleg. in Plat. Phil.*, xxvi.

[10] Ralph Cudworth, *Systema Intellectuale* (1678), IV, 23. *Epistle XIII* was omitted in Ficinus' translation of Plato.

[11] C. Meiners, *Judicium de Quibusdam Socr. Reliquiis* (*Abh. der Göttingen Gesellschaft*), V, 51.

[12] Friedrich Ast, *Platons Leben und Schriften* (1816).

[13] Joseph Socher, *Über Platons Schriften* (1820).

[14] H. T. Karsten, *Commentatio Critica de Platonis quae feruntur Epistolis* (Utrecht, 1864).

that all the *Epistles* are spurious might be said to have become, during the latter half of the nineteenth century, the orthodox position of Platonic scholarship as represented by Zeller; though opinion was by no means undivided, and there remained eminent scholars like Grote,[15] Christ,[16] and Reinhold [17] who contended for the genuineness of most of the letters, and others who, in a more cautious spirit, attempted a partial justification of individual letters on the ground that they were written, if not by Plato, at least by someone in the Academy shortly after Plato's death. The literature on the subject is immense, and it can serve no useful purpose to go into details here. Already we are sufficiently remote from the period to recognize the inadequacy of many of the considerations most relied upon in the controversy. Thus Grote's argument for the genuineness of the Thrasyllean canon in its entirety on the ground that Plato's works were doubtless preserved complete in the library of the Academy after his death and must have been referred to by the Alexandrian librarians and later by Thrasyllus to determine which were the genuine works of Plato, is of even more doubtful value with respect to the *Epistles* than with respect to any other writing in the canon. The important point, as has often been remarked in criticism of Grote, is whether it would not have been possible for a spurious work to be received into the library of the Academy, especially after the death of Xenocrates. There is no reason why later scholarchs should have been convinced beyond a doubt that all the Platonic writings had been deposited in the Academy; and there being this ground for doubt, we have all the circumstances required to make possible the intrusion of doubtful works. This consideration is especially pertinent with respect to documents like the *Epistles,* which from the very nature of the case would not be preserved in duplicate in the library—except

15 George Grote, *Plato and the Other Companions of Socrates* (1865).

16 Wilhelm Christ, *Abhandlung der bayrischen Akademie, Phil.-Hist. Kl.,* XVII (1885), 477 ff.

17 *De Platonis Epistulis Dissertatio* (1886).

possibly semipublic documents, like the *Seventh*—but would be admitted gradually as the importance became realized of preserving all traces of Plato's literary and personal activity.

On the other hand, the critics of the *Epistles* argued no more convincingly that the *Epistles* must be spurious because of apparent contradictions with the historical tradition, without attempting a thorough inquiry into the genesis of the accounts contained in the extant historians, and ignoring the fact that at least from the time of Plutarch, and in all probability earlier, these very letters had helped to mold the historical tradition. A great deal was made of the difference between the style of the *Epistles* and that of the more familiar Platonic dialogues. That was in the days when the *Laws* was grudgingly admitted to be Platonic, and there was no appreciation of the changes which Plato's style had undergone between the *Republic* and the *Laws*. Again it was said that the *Epistles* showed everywhere traces of "borrowings" from the dialogues, as if such parallels in thought and expression could not be used equally well to suggest identity of authorship, especially since in the one case we have private or semiprivate documents which might be expected to contain reminiscences of thought or language that the writer had already used in a published dialogue. In fact it would be most unnatural if in a body of genuine Platonic letters there were no echoes of the thought and language of the dialogues. The same ambiguous results follow from the criterion of consistency, as commonly used by these critics. Certainly if the *Epistles,* all or any of them, are to be accepted as genuine, they must be shown to be consistent with the dialogues. But there is a kind of consistency which may rightly be regarded with suspicion; just as there is a kind of inconsistency which no forger would have fallen into, and which may well be taken as affording a presumption on the side of genuineness. How unsympathetically and inadequately this criterion of consistency was employed in the nineteenth century is shown by the fact that the *Parmenides, Sophist, Cratylus,* and *Philebus* were regarded as doubtful, or distinctly spurious, by these same critics of the *Epistles;* and the *Laws* would most surely have been condemned if it had not been expressly vouched for by Aristotle.

It is therefore hardly surprising that the Platonic scholars of the last thirty years have been increasingly inclined to disregard the unfavorable verdict of the nineteenth century. It may almost be said that the orthodox position at present is not only to accept such relatively unimpeachable documents as the *Seventh* and *Eighth Epistles* as authentic writings of Plato, but even to look with indulgence upon even the most suspicious members of the collection.[18] This marked change of opinion that has taken place is no doubt partly due, as Apelt [19] suggests, to a greater willingness to believe, an increase in historical faith, which has succeeded to the over-critical attitude of the last century. That hypersensitive philological conscience which could admit as *echt Platonisch* only nine of the dialogues has given way to a more sympathetic attitude toward the Platonic corpus; and the picture of Plato presented in the *Epistles* is one which makes a peculiar appeal to the men of our own generation, threatened, like Plato, with the imminent dissolution of their civilization through internecine quarrels.

But this is not the chief explanation of the change in attitude toward the *Epistles.* Contemporary scholarship has not abandoned critical historical methods in favor of sentiment. On the contrary, it makes far more serious and effective use of the instruments of philological criticism than did Grote and Karsten; it has merely found that these instruments, when used more precisely, lead to a presumption of authenticity with regard to many of the letters.

[18] Thus Eduard Meyer seems to regard all the *Epistles,* with the possible exception of *I* and *XII,* as coming from the hand of Plato. This is surely more straightforward, as he points out, than to proceed as have many modern historians of Greece by pretending to derive from Plutarch what really comes from the *Epistles* (*Geschichte des Altertums* [Stuttgart, 1902], V, 502, 504, 509.)

[19] O. Apelt, *Platons Briefe* (Leipzig, 1921), p. 12.

Perhaps the most decisive of the factors that underlie the present favorable attitude toward the most important of the *Epistles* is our knowledge of the stylistic peculiarities of Plato's later writings. All the *Epistles,* with the exception of the *Ninth,* profess to have been written after the year 367, and some of them, including the *Sixth, Seventh,* and *Eighth,* during the very last years of Plato's life. Therefore in judging whether or not the style of the *Epistles* is Platonic we must compare it with the style of those dialogues written during the last twenty years of Plato's life. Thanks to the linguistic researches of Campbell, Dittenberger, Schanz, Lutoslawski, Ritter, and others, during the last half of the nineteenth century, the main features of the chronology of the Platonic dialogues are now fairly clear. It is generally agreed that the *Sophist, Politicus, Philebus, Timaeus, Critias,* and *Laws* constitute a stylistic group differentiated in certain rather marked respects from the rest of the Platonic dialogues. Since the *Laws* is certainly later than the *Republic,* we may take the whole group as relatively late compositions, and the stylistic peculiarities they have in common as marks of Plato's later style.[20] It is to this group of dialogues we must therefore look when judging the style of the *Epistles;* and not to the *Republic* and *Phaedrus,* which belong to the middle or transition period of Plato's style, still less to the *Protagoras* and other dialogues of the earliest stylistic group.

The consequence is that philological investigators have found the claims of some of the *Epistles* confirmed, rather than invalidated, by traits of style that were formerly pointed to as evidences of spuriousness. Thus Ritter, who has probably done more than anyone else to formulate accurate linguistic tests, declared as early as 1888 [21] that the style of the *Seventh* and *Eighth Epistles* is identical with that of the

20 For an authoritative account of this phase of Platonic investigation and a defense of the stylistic criterion, see C. Ritter, *Platon* (Munich, 1910), I, 232 ff.

21 C. Ritter, *Untersuchungen über Platon* (Stuttgart, 1888), pp. 105-9.

Laws; and this judgment he reiterated eight years later.[22] Later he declared that the *Third* also is genuinely Platonic in style and diction.[23] Rudolf Adam brought forward additional linguistic evidence for the Platonic character of the *Seventh* and *Eighth,* though on other than linguistic grounds he rejected the *Eighth* as spurious.[24] Raeder's inquiry into the use of hiatus in the *Epistles* led to the same result with regard to the *Seventh* and *Eighth,*[25] though his conclusions from the use of rare words in the *Epistles* do not carry the same degree of conviction. Still more recently Wilamowitz has defended the *Sixth* also on stylistic grounds, as well as the *Seventh* and *Eighth.*[26] Thus with striking unanimity the philological researches of the last forty years have confirmed the claims to genuineness of at least the *Seventh* and *Eighth Epistles.*

A similar recognition of the intellectual interests of Plato's later years, and the special form which "Platonism" assumes in the later dialogues and in the unwritten teachings, has led to a more favorable opinion as to the philosophical content of the *Seventh* and *Eighth Epistles.* The unwarranted discrimination against the *Laws* in most expositions of Platonic thought has worked to the detriment of the *Epistles.* It needs no lengthy examination to discover that the ethical and political doctrines of the *Seventh* and *Eighth Epistles* are the doctrines of the *Laws* and *Politicus;* and the discrepancy between the *Epistles* and the earlier dialogues with respect to these doctrines indicates, indeed, the authenticity of these

[22] In the Appendix to his *Kommentar* to Plato's *Laws* (1896), pp. 367-78.

[23] C. Ritter, *Neue Untersuchungen über Platon* (Munich, 1909), pp. 399 ff.

[24] Rudolf Adam, *Die Echtheit der Platonischen Briefe* (Berlin, 1906); "Über die Platonischen Briefe," *Archiv für Geschichte der Philosophie,* XXIII (1910), 29-52.

[25] Hans Raeder, "Über die Echtheit der Platonischen Briefe," *Rheinisches Museum,* N. F. LXI (1906), 427-71, 511-42.

[26] Ulrich von Wilamowitz-Moellendorff, *Platon* (Berlin, 1919), II, 278-304.

letters rather than their spuriousness. Even the epistemological digression in the *Seventh* (though a stumbling block to
Ritter, who accepted the rest of the letter as genuine) is clearly
Platonic, if we include within "Platonism" the thoughts and
teachings of the last twenty years of Plato's life. The doctrine
of Ideas is there, the contrast between opinion and knowledge,
and other familiar Platonic doctrines; and the unfamiliar
form in which they are presented becomes intelligible if we
remember that it is now the author of the *Sophist* and *Philebus*
who is expounding them. Likewise there are evidences of the
growth of a technical vocabulary, and of increasing attention
to the niceties of exact thought, that thoroughly accord with
the logical preoccupations of Plato's later years. In fact, if it
were not the custom to ignore the letter, this passage would
long ago have been regarded as of great importance for our
interpretation of Plato's later theory of knowledge.[27] Thus
when the *Seventh* and *Eighth Epistles* are judged in the light
of Plato's later thought, the seeming inconsistency with
Platonic doctrine disappears.

Likewise if we consider the formation of the historical tradition concerning the events in Syracuse which is preserved
in Nepos, Diodorus, and Plutarch, we see how superficial it is
to condemn the *Epistles* because they disagree with the historians. It is clearly illegitimate to regard the *Epistles* as historically inaccurate until after we have inquired into the
genesis of the historical tradition with which they disagree.
Thus Susemihl condemned the *Seventh* and *Eighth Epistles*
because of "their arbitrary treatment of the actual historical
relationships"; [28] and Adam rejects the *Eighth* because "it
confuses the events of Dion's time with those of Timoleon." [29]
But what precisely were the events of Dion's time? And what
were the actual relationships between Plato, Dion, Philistus,

[27] See A. E. Taylor, "The Analysis of ἘΠΙΣΤΗΜΗ in Plato's
Seventh Epistle," *Mind*, XXI (1912), 347-70; Wilamowitz, *Platon*, II,
293-98.

[28] Franz Susemihl, *Geschichte der griechischen Literatur in der Alex-
andrinerzeit* (Leipzig, 1891-1892), II, 584.

[29] *Archiv*, p. 33.

Dionysius, Hipparinus, and the rest? Any discrepancy between the *Epistles* and the historical tradition may prove the inaccuracy of the tradition rather than the spuriousness of the letters. Until this spuriousness has been otherwise made probable it would seem that the presumption is all on the side of the *Epistles*. For the *Epistles* are older than the accounts in Nepos and Diodorus; and if linguistic criteria are decisive, some of these letters are older even than the sources which Nepos and Diodorus used. We must also remember that these letters claim to be firsthand accounts, whereas our extant historians rely in the main upon the histories of Timaeus, Ephorus, and Theopompus, none of whom was an actual spectator or participant in the events at Syracuse. The implicit reliance upon the historical tradition that has usually characterized both those who accept and those who reject the *Epistles* sets the problem of their authenticity in a false light. We must examine the historical tradition itself and determine the sources from which it is derived before we can fairly convict the *Epistles* of historical inaccuracy. In the following chapter I have attempted to discover the sources of Nepos, Diodorus, and Plutarch; and if the results to which I have been led are sound, the authority of the *Seventh* and *Eighth Epistles* as historical sources far outweighs the authority of the source from which is derived the divergent tradition that on certain points contradicts the statements of these letters. And furthermore, if it is true, as I have attempted to show, that these letters were a basic part of the tradition that derives from Timaeus, the use of them by a competent historian like Timaeus leads us to believe that they were written, if not by Plato himself, at least by some well-informed member of the Platonic circle, at a date very shortly after the death of Plato.

Again, in dealing with a collection of documents such as the Platonic *Epistles* it is essential to recognize that each letter must be examined on its own merits, and its claims to authenticity must not be prejudiced by the manifest spuriousness of some of its companions in the collection, unless of course it is clearly dependent upon these spurious companions.

There is a natural tendency to think of the Platonic *Epistles* as a whole as spurious or as genuine. Just as in the nineteenth century the prevailing adverse judgment made little distinction between such manifest fictions as the *First* and the more creditable *Seventh* and *Eighth,* so now the turn of the tide tends to bring into favor not only the *Seventh* and *Eighth,* but also the suspicious *Thirteenth* and the even more suspicious *Second.* Even the *First* has found an occasional defender among recent critics.

On the other hand, while avoiding this tendency to accept or reject *in toto,* we must still take into account the evidences of interdependence among the letters. Considering that seven out of thirteen deal with Plato's relations with Syracuse, we should expect to find similarities of thought and expression, as well as contradictions and inconsistencies, between certain of these letters. These relationships between the letters are of great significance, as every student in modern times, even Karsten, has recognized. But the interpretation put upon these facts will be affected to a considerable extent by the order in which the letters are examined. It is necessary to begin with the letters that can most plausibly be regarded as genuine, and thus secure a *point d'appui* for the examination of the rest.

Now of all the letters in the collection the *Seventh* is preeminent, for its length and for the richness of its historical and philosophical content. The greater interest it affords to the philosophical or historical reader makes it a natural starting point for the inquiry. More than that, a long composition is less likely to be a forgery than a short one; and if there are any genuine letters in our collection, it is a priori more likely that the *Seventh* is genuine than that any of the others are. We know of no forgery in the field of epistolography, I believe, of corresponding length. Again, the *Seventh Epistle* is an open letter, a semipublic document, and a writing of this sort is far more likely to be preserved than a strictly private letter. A duplicate of it would certainly be kept by the writer, and it is probable that more than one copy would be put into circulation. For all these reasons the examination of the *Seventh Epistle* must logically precede the consideration of any other. The pre-eminence of the *Seventh* was recognized clearly even by those who once regarded the entire collection as spurious. Karsten, for example, who rejected all thirteen, nevertheless held that the *Seventh* originated first in time, and that most of the others were dependent upon it. For one who is not committed to the spuriousness of the entire collection, this pre-eminence of the *Seventh* makes it necessary to deal first of all with that letter alone, unprejudiced by the thought that all its companions may be spurious. And if its claims to genuineness can be established, it then becomes an indispensable instrument for judging most of the others. The other Syracusan letters will clearly stand or fall according as they can or cannot be harmonized with the contents and the style of the *Seventh Epistle*. And even with respect to the letters not written to Syracuse, the *Seventh* may possibly provide criteria of a more general sort that may be decisive.

Lastly, there are certain special criteria applicable to the problem of the *Epistles* that have not always been given the consideration their importance deserves. Unlike most published literary works, a letter is written to a particular person or group of persons, apropos of definite external circumstances, and for a specific purpose. This fact gives rise to a fundamental canon of literary criticism with respect to compositions of this kind. A letter which cannot be dated, at least approximately, whose destination is uncertain, which makes no reference (or if it does, refers inaccurately) to contemporary events and persons, and which has no clearly defined purpose, is strongly suspect; whereas a letter which fits naturally into the situation it implies, and in its reference to events and persons is consistent with what we know otherwise regarding them, bears strong marks of genuineness. Are the feelings the letter expresses those that the supposed writer would naturally feel under the circumstances? Are they expressed with sincerity? A forger is almost certain to betray himself either by

the conventional emotions he attributes to his writer, or by
the trite or stilted language in which he clothes them. Are
the contents of the letter relevant? A forger is likely to introduce meaningless chatter, pointless anecdotes, or thinly
disguised and irrelevant borrowings from the accepted works
of the author. Lastly, are the traits of character expressed in
the letter consistent with what we otherwise know of the
character of the author? The application of these criteria is
seldom easy; but any letter which satisfies them, and at the
same time agrees in thought, style, and diction with the
acknowledged works of its supposed author, and has moreover the weight of the literary tradition in its favor, must
certainly be accepted as genuine.

When judged by these standards it has seemed, to the great
majority of modern students, that some of the letters, particularly the *Seventh* and *Eighth,* must be accepted as
genuine letters of Plato. The literary tradition of antiquity
ascribed them to Plato; they conform in thought, style, and
diction to the known works of Plato written at the time these
letters are supposed to have been written; and furthermore,
their relevancy to the situation they presuppose, their accuracy in referring to events and persons, the naturalness of
the feelings they express, the appropriateness of their contents to the purpose of the letter in each case, and their conformity to the character of Plato as we know it from other
sources, all point to their genuineness. These points will be
critically examined in the following pages; but the very fact
of such widespread agreement upon the genuineness of these
two letters indicates strikingly the sharp reversal of attitude
that has taken place with regard to the *Epistles*. Once these
two letters are generally believed to be genuine, the likelihood is increased that some of the others will also come to be
accepted. And most important of all, we have at least two
documents of almost priceless importance for constructing a
picture of Plato's relations to the practical politics and statesmen of his age.

THE EPISTLES AND THE HISTORIANS OF SICILY

The discrepancy at certain points between the *Epistles* and the ancient historians raises some critical questions that have not hitherto been properly explored. It has usually been assumed that the word of the ancient historians, when they differ from the *Epistles*, is naturally decisive.[1] On the other hand, modern historians have usually made full and confident use of the *Epistles* as historical sources, at least on all those points which are not contradicted by the ancient historians. But with what right can we reject the statements of the *Epistles* on certain points without impugning their general accuracy? And the fact that none of the ancient historians except Plutarch refers to the *Epistles* is legitimate ground for asking whether they are trustworthy sources at all. Eduard Meyer expressed the view that the *Epistles* had entered into the historical tradition and were a constituent part of the historians whom Nepos, Plutarch, and Diodorus Siculus followed.[2] I have not found that he gives any reasons for believing this, other than the a priori probability that documents as ancient as these *Epistles* (some of them, at least) must have been noted and used by the early historians. Nor, so far as I can discover, has any attempt been made to ascertain by what steps the *Epistles* entered into the historical tradition, if Meyer's view is correct. Such an attempt seems worth making for a double reason. First of all, it will help to elucidate the various sources of our knowledge of fourth-century Sicily, and thus enable us to judge of the relative trustworthiness of the *Epistles* and these other sources. And in the second place, it will throw light on the literary history of the *Epistles,* or some of them, in the Alexandrian period. As has been noted in the preceding chapter, we have so far discovered no decisive evidence of the existence of our

---

[1] E.g. by K. Steinhart, *Platons sämmtliche Werke* (Leipzig, 1873), VIII, 390, n. 27. See above, pp. 8, 12 f.

[2] *Geschichte des Altertums,* V, 502 ff.

present collection, nor of any member of it, prior to the first century after Christ, when the canon of Thrasyllus was constituted. Though we know the canon of Aristophanes of Byzantium drawn up in the third century B.C. contained an item called *Epistles,* we do not know what members of our present collection were contained in that group. The early history of the *Epistles* is therefore most obscure, and it would seem that if this obscurity is to be relieved, one of the most promising lines of inquiry is to examine the formation of the historical tradition; for the historians, more than any other writers of the Alexandrian period, must have known and made use of the *Epistles* if they were then in existence and were believed to be authoritative.

Plutarch and the Epistles

Apart from the *Epistles* and a few fragments of ancient historians, our only sources for knowledge of the revolution in Syracuse in the fourth century are Plutarch's lives of *Dion* and *Timoleon,* Diodorus Siculus' *Bibliotheca Historica,* and Cornelius Nepos' lives of *Dion* and *Timoleon.* Of these three, Plutarch is the only one who cites the *Epistles.* The failure of Nepos and Diodorus to do so will scarcely seem significant to one who knows the characteristics of these writers. Both seem to have been content to rely on the secondary accounts current in their day, without making any effort to go back to original sources. On the other hand, we are scarcely justified in taking Plutarch's use of the *Epistles* as proof of their genuineness. To be sure, Plutarch used some discrimination in putting together his materials and was undoubtedly widely acquainted with earlier writers. But four centuries had elapsed since the death of Plato, and it is at least possible that he was mistaken in his judgment upon what were even for him ancient documents. We may even appeal to Plutarch against himself; for there are discrepancies between his account and the *Epistles,* and on one very important point he deserts the *Epistles* and follows a divergent tradition.

This fact suggests that the greatest help Plutarch can afford us on our problem is to indicate the character of the historical tradition current in his own time. That he follows the *Epistles* in the main, even in passages where he cites other ancient authorities besides them, indicates the existence of a tradition that was at least in conformity with them. On the other hand, his pages give evidence that there existed in his day a version or versions differing from the *Epistles,* since he occasionally departs from them and cites his authorities for doing so. We must then examine Plutarch's narrative to see whether we can determine the nature of these historical traditions current when he wrote, and the identity of their authors.

First let us note the evidences of Plutarch's use of the *Epistles.* The *Seventh Epistle* is unmistakably referred to in *Dion* 4, 11, 18, 20, and 54, though in none of these passages does Plutarch give it any name or title, simply introducing his reference by some such phrase as "Plato tells us." The *Fourth Epistle* is referred to in more definite terms in 8 and 52, and the *Thirteenth* in 21.[3] But these explicit references constitute only a small part of the evidence of his reliance upon these letters. There are several other passages in the *Dion* that are clearly derived from the *Epistles,* though there is no explicit reference to them. Dion's exhortation to Dionysius (10) to develop himself in virtue so that he may by his justice and moderation be the instrument of great happiness to himself and all his subjects clearly comes from the *Seventh Epistle* (321c, 331e, 332d), though Plutarch has embellished the advice with a little Stoic phraseology. Again the account (16) of the relations between Dionysius and Plato after the banishment of Dion needs no other source than *Epistle VII,* 333ab, and is most naturally explained as coming from it. Plutarch's statement (16) that Dionysius was ready to entrust Plato with the chief management of his affairs upon

---

[3] Plutarch refers to *Epistle IV* also in *De Adul. et Amico* 29, to *Epistle XIII* in *De Vit. Pud.* 11 and *De Cohib. Ira* 16, and to *Epistle III* in *De Aud. Poet.* 14.

condition that Plato give him in return the chief place in his friendship looks like an inference of Plutarch's own from *Epistle VII*, 330ab, perhaps supported by the *Third Epistle*. The dismissal of Plato at the end of the same chapter is told in almost the same words as those of *Epistle VII*, 338ab. The reasons Plutarch ascribes to Plato (22) for not joining in Dion's expedition against Syracuse are the same as those set forth in *Epistle VII, 350c*. And there are many other verbal reminiscences and echoes of the language of the *Epistles*.

Plutarch's dependence upon the *Epistles* is also shown in a more subtle fashion by his general attitude toward the events and personages of the revolution in Syracuse. When reading Plutarch's *Dion* we are seeing the intrigues at the court of Dionysius from the same point of view as when reading the Platonic *Epistles*. Plutarch looks upon Plato's philosophy as the primary cause of the revolution. It was no mere struggle between rival politicians, but a contest between the philosophical and political idealism of Plato and Dion on the one hand, and the conservatism, self-interest, and jealousy of Dionysius and his courtiers on the other. The same admiration for Dion that Plato expresses repeatedly in the *Seventh Epistle* is reflected, though in a more circumspect and apologetic setting, in Plutarch's account. Dion is in a real sense the hero of his narrative. Though admitting candidly the faults of harshness and inflexibility of temper that the author of *Epistle IV* had pointed out, he uses every occasion to describe Dion's virtues and the favorable impression he produced upon the Greeks during his exile from Syracuse (7 and 17); and unlike Nepos he draws a circumspect veil of silence over Dion's actions when he was in supreme power after the death of Heraclides (52 and 53).

But Plutarch uses other authorities beside the *Epistles*. Those whom we can identify are Ephorus (cited in *Dion* 35 and 36), Theopompus (in 24), Timaeus (in 6, 14, 31, 35 and 36), Timonides (in 31 and 35), Athanis (cited in *Timoleon* 23 and 37), and almost certainly also Philistus, who is named frequently as an actor in the events described in the *Dion,* and whose history Plutarch must certainly have known. These were, so far as we can judge, the standard histories and documents bearing on the revolution in Sicily. The fact that Plutarch uses the *Epistles* as well as these standard authorities permits us to draw one very important conclusion. The reader of Plutarch is familiar with his habit of noting discrepancies between his sources, and we may be sure that if there had been a wholesale divergence between the *Epistles* and his other authorities we should hear more about it. He does occasionally note a discrepancy (*Dion* 20); [4] but for the most part he seems to employ the *Epistles* merely to embellish his text with additional details not contained in the historians, or to lend additional authority to his narrative by citing what he believed to be the ultimate source from which it was derived. All of this presupposes the existence of a trustworthy tradition in general agreement with the *Epistles*. But the discrepancies he occasionally notes between the *Epistles* and his other authorities, as well as the discrepancies among his other authorities, indicate that there were other versions not so reconcilable with the *Epistles;* and these passages in which he cites such discrepancies will be particularly important for disentangling the threads of the historical tradition. But before carrying further our examination of these particularly important passages, let us attempt to ascertain the identity and something of the characteristics of the earlier historians of Sicily.

The Ancient Historians of Sicily

These earlier histories now exist only in fragments scattered through later authors; but it is possible, by means of these fragments and the indications given in Diodorus, Nepos, and Plutarch, to ascertain to some extent their contents and characteristics. It will help our inquiry if we list these earlier

---

[4] Possibly also the reference in *Dion* 11 to Plato's motives in going to Syracuse indicates a disputed point on which Plato's word would for Plutarch be final.

historians of Sicily so far as we can make them out, beginning
with the eyewitnesses and contemporaries of the revolution.

Philistus of Syracuse, like Dion and Plato, was a major actor
in these events. He wrote a history of his native island in
thirteen books, the last six of which dealt with events of
the reign of Dionysius I and the first years of the reign of
Dionysius II, i.e. down to about the year 362.[5] Philistus was a
loyal and able champion of the house of Dionysius and of
the institution of tyranny, and he was the chief obstacle to
the reforms that Plato and Dion wished to introduce.[6] His
history must have contained valuable information regarding
the political crosscurrents at the court of Dionysius, and we
can guess that Plato's ideas were none too sympathetically
portrayed.

Athanis (or Athanas, according to Diodorus) was also a
native of Syracuse, and it is thought that he was one of the
generals ($\sigma\tau\rho\alpha\tau\eta\gamma\omicron\iota$) chosen with Heraclides at the time of
Dion's withdrawal from Syracuse in 356.[7] If so, he was like-
wise an eyewitness of the events of the revolution. According
to Diodorus (XV, 94, 4) he wrote a *History of Dion* in thirteen
books, the first book taking up the account of events where
Philistus' history left off and continuing to the year 357, the
other twelve presumably dealing with the career of Dion.

Timonides of Leucas, one of the members of the Academy
who joined Dion's expedition, is said by both Plutarch (*Dion*
35) and by Diogenes Laertius (IV, 5) to have written to
Speusippus an account of Dion's expedition. Timonides was
evidently an able and trusted soldier, for Dion delegated his
command to him on one occasion (*Dion* 30). Plutarch probably uses Timonides as his chief authority for the interesting
and intimate details that his narrative contains at this point,

---

5 Diod. XIII, 103, 3; XV, 89, 3.

6 See pp. 169 f. On the political principles of Philistus see the statement
of Nepos *Dion* 4, and on his partiality to Dionysius in his history,
Pausanias I, 13, 9.

7 Theopompus, Fr. 194, from Felix Jacoby, *Fragmente der griechischen
Historiker* (Berlin, 1923-1958).

since, as Plutarch says (*Dion* 35), "he was present with Dion in these events from their beginning." [8]

Ephorus of Cyme, about whose life we know little except that he was probably a pupil of Isocrates and that he died in 330, wrote a history of the Greek world in twenty-nine books, the last two of which dealt with the history of Sicily from the King's Peace in 387 to the capture of Syracuse by Dion in 356.[9]

Theopompus of Chios, another pupil of Isocrates, who was born about 378 and died some time after 324, wrote a work entitled *Philippica* which among its numerous digressions contained an account in three books of the history of Sicily from the accession of the elder Dionysius to the expulsion of Dionysius II.[10]

Timaeus, a native of Tauromenium in Sicily, wrote a history in thirty-eight books of the Greeks in Sicily and Italy from the earliest times to the year 264.[11] The dates of his birth and death are uncertain; it can be said only that he was born about 330 and died some time before 250. Exiled from his native city by Agathocles in the late fourth century, he spent fifty years in Athens [12] presumably working on his history.

The first three persons in this list were eyewitnesses and participants in the revolution; but of these neither Philistus nor Timonides could have used *Epistles VII* and *VIII*, the basic documents in our collection, since their accounts precede the date at which these letters profess to have been written. Athanis could have known them and should have used them, if they were in existence, since they are peculiarly relevant to his history of Dion. But he seems to have sided with Heraclides against Dion (see the fragment of Theopom-

[8] There is a good discussion of these "letters" of Timonides and their influence upon Plutarch's *Dion* in J. Harward, *The Platonic Epistles* (Cambridge, 1932), pp. 53-59.

[9] Diod. XVI, 14, 3; 76, 5; Schwartz, in Pauly-Wissowa, *Realencyclopädie der classischen Altertumswissenschaft*, art. Diodorus, col. 681; Jacoby, *Fragmente*, 2A, 106 f.

[10] Diod. XVI, 71, 3.

[11] Polyb. I, 5, 1.

[12] Polyb. XII, 25d and 25h.

pus referred to above), and the fact that his history is explicitly a continuation of Philistus' makes it highly probable that it was written from the perspective of Plato's opponents; and if so he would not be one of the inner circle of Dion's party to whom these letters are addressed, and hence might not have known them.

But very soon these letters must have been in the possession of the Academy, if they were written when they claim to have been, and either Ephorus, Theopompus, or Timaeus—writing in a later time—could have made use of them. Ephorus' account of Sicilian events after 387 was contained in the last two books of his *Histories*. It is therefore probable that he was at work on the narrative of the events with which the *Epistles* are concerned shortly before 330, the date of his death. The *Philippica* of Theopompus was written after his *Hellenica,* and the digression on the history of the Dionysii occurred in the last third of the *Philippica,* which suggests that it was written towards the close of his life. And Timaeus' account of these events must have been prepared at least a quarter of a century later.

But were these writers diligent and conscientious enough to seek out and consult such sources of information as these *Epistles*? As for Ephorus, he is known to have employed not only the great histories of the past, but also numerous minor works of special historical or geographical interest. Wachsmuth calls him "der erste Gelehrte unter den griechischen Historikern." [13] It seems also that he was more than an uncritical assembler of materials, as evidenced by the praise that Polybius and Strabo give him.[14] Theopompus seems to have been equally learned; his travels were extensive, he had a wide acquaintance with the public men of his time, and his histories contained a mass of information on the geography, the customs, the legends and products of the various parts of Greece. He was, however, a man of haughty and intolerant

13 C. Wachsmuth, *Einleitung in das Studium der alten Geschichte* (Leipzig, 1895), p. 501.

14 Polybius is quoted in Strabo IX, iii, 11. Cf. Wachsmuth, *ibid.,* p. 422.

disposition, and his capacity for sober critical judgment has been questioned.[15] We know that he was openly scornful of Plato's philosophy as contained in the dialogues.[16] There is no telling whether or not he would have been interested in such Platonic documents as the *Epistles*, or if he was, what use he would have made of them. Finally, the history of Timaeus was recognized in ancient times as a monument of industry and scholarship.[17] Like Ephorus he consulted all available documents and inscriptions; and since he lived for half a century at Athens he had abundant opportunity to learn of and consult the *Epistles*. His father Andromachus had been tyrant of Tauromenium, but so moderate in his rule that he was an adherent and ally of Timoleon, whose advent from Corinth put an end for a time to the civil strife in Syracuse; and he retained his position at Tauromenium until banished when Agathocles became tyrant of Syracuse in 317. The moderate political principles of Timaeus' father would have prepared him to sympathize with Plato's political teaching, and his firsthand acquaintance with Sicilian affairs would have enabled him to understand fully the situation presupposed by the *Epistles*. These early experiences seem indeed to have given him a hatred for tyrants that colored all his writing. Polybius (XII, 3, 28) takes him to task for his unfairness to Dionysius and Agathocles, and Plutarch (*Dion* 36) rebukes him for the malice he displays in his account of the death of Philistus, Dionysius' most loyal adherent. Though this hatred of tyrants and of Dionysius in particular may have affected the impartiality of his history, it would undoubtedly predispose him to seek and use such documents as the *Epistles*, if they were then in existence.

Thus if the Platonic *Epistles* are genuine it is hard to believe they would not have been consulted by one or more of

---

15 Wachsmuth, *ibid.*, pp. 537 ff.

16 Arrian *Epictetus* II, 17, 5; Athen. 508cd.

17 On the qualities of Timaeus as a historian, with especial reference to the criticisms of Polybius, see C. Clasen, *Untersuchungen über Timaios von Tauromenion* (Kiel, 1883).

these Sicilian historians and thus have entered the tradition utilized by Diodorus, Nepos, and Plutarch. This should have happened, if the letters are genuine. Did anything like it actually happen?

The Dual Tradition Regarding the Revolution
in Syracuse

Of the relatively numerous fragments of these fourth-century historians, very few, unfortunately, refer to the careers of the Dionysii and Dion, and none of them is concerned with the events described in the *Seventh* and *Eighth Epistles*. It is therefore impossible to determine from the fragments what the attitude of these historians was toward the *Epistles*, or even their general interpretation of the course of events in Syracuse during this period. Our only recourse therefore is to scrutinize the accounts in Plutarch, Diodorus, and Nepos, in the hope that they may afford indirect indication of the characteristics of these various narratives, and tell us whether or not their authors used the *Epistles*.

Let us first ask, however, if there is any way of recognizing the influence of the *Epistles* upon the historical tradition. There are many details in the *Seventh Epistle* that would have been of interest only to the biographer of Plato or the historian of Plato's teaching, and a historian of the Sicilian revolution might easily leave them out of account. But what a historian worthy of the name could not fail to note from reading the *Epistles* is the importance of Plato's personal and philosophical intervention in the affairs of Syracuse. Plato himself says that his having come to Sicily and expounded to Dion his views of human welfare was the ultimate cause of the downfall of the tyranny (326e-327a); and no one who used the Platonic *Seventh Epistle* could escape this interpretation of the revolution.

Let anyone, with this point in mind, compare the narrative of Nepos' *Dion* 1-5, with the corresponding passages in Diodorus (XV, 7, 74; XVI, 5, 6), and he will be struck by the divergence between these two accounts. Nepos gives us a briefer version of the story familiar to us from Plutarch and the *Epistles,* beginning with Plato's first visit to the court of the elder Dionysius, his influence upon Dion, the continued loyalty of Dion to Plato's principles, the second coming of Plato to Syracuse for the purpose of converting the young tyrant and reforming his government, the recall of Philistus, and the growing dissension at the court caused by Philistus' personal jealousy of Dion and his opposition to the political doctrines of Plato, culminating in the banishment of Dion. Diodorus gives us little, if anything, of this. He tells us of Plato's first visit to Syracuse (XV, 7, 1), but seems altogether ignorant of the effect of his visit upon Dion, and Plato does not come into the story again. He does not even tell us of the recall of Philistus. In order to appreciate the striking contrast between the narratives of Diodorus and Nepos it is sufficient to compare their respective accounts of the banishment of Dion and the events immediately preceding:

DIODORUS XVI, 6, 1-4	NEPOS *Dion* 3-5
In the year when Cephisodotos was archon at Athens and Gaius Lucinius and Gaius Sulpicius consuls at Rome, Dion, the son of Hipparinus, one of the most eminent citizens of Syracuse, was banished from Sicily; and the splendor of his character brought about, through the following circumstances, the liberation of Syracuse and the other Sicilians. . . .	Dion continued to importune Dionysius to summon Plato from Athens and make use of his counsel; and as Dionysius in all things wished to imitate his father, he granted his wish. At the same time he recalled to Syracuse Philistus, the historian, a person who loved the institution of tyranny no less than he loved the tyrant himself; but of him I have already said a great deal in my book on Historians. Plato, however, obtained such ascendancy with Dionysius, and his eloquence was so powerful, that he persuaded him to make an end of the tyranny and give back their liberties to the Syracusans; but Dionysius was de-

Now Dion was a man of considerable attainments in philosophy, and far superior to his fellow citizens in courage and military skill. The nobility of his birth and the splendor of his character made him an object of suspicion to the tyrant, who thought he saw in him a man capable of overturning the tyranny. These fears determined Dionysius to get rid of the man by seizing him and putting him to death. But Dion was warned of the danger and hid himself for awhile with some friends. Later he escaped from Sicily to the Peloponnesus, accompanied by his brother Megacles, and by Heraclides, the commander of the tyrant's army.

terred from this by the counsel of Philistus, and began to rule somewhat more severely. Now when Dionysius saw that he was inferior to Dion in natural ability, as well as in the respect and affection of the people, he feared that if he allowed Dion to continue in power with him he would be inviting his own downfall. So he gave him a trireme to carry him to Corinth, declaring that he did this for both their sakes, in order that in their mutual distrust neither might take advantage of the other. After Dion had reached Corinth and had been joined by Heraclides, the former commander of the cavalry who had also been exiled by that same Dionysius, they began with all their might to prepare for war.

Diodorus' account, it will be noted, is not only a superficial one, as compared with Nepos' version, but is even irreconcilable with it. Furthermore, Nepos' version is less in accord with the usual behavior of tyrants, and any historian, I think, would look upon it as prima facie a more trustworthy account of what actually happened than the shorter and more conventional version of Diodorus.

It will be made even more evident that Diodorus and Nepos are relying upon different sources if we compare their accounts of the death of Dionysius the Elder, an event which is darkly hinted at in the *Seventh Epistle* in a strange periphrasis (327b). Diodorus (XV, 74) describes Dionysius' death as having been brought about by a drunken revelry in which he indulged upon receipt of the news that he had won the tragic prize at Athens. Diodorus then recounts that this event fulfilled the prophecy of the oracle that Dionysius would die only when he had overcome enemies superior to himself, a prophecy that Dionysius had always interpreted as referring to his warfare with the Carthaginians, but which was now shown to have meant his contests with the Athenian poets. Nepos, on the contrary, makes no mention of the literary victory, but tells of the attempt of Dion, when Dionysius was ill, to gain an interview with the tyrant in the hope of securing some portion of the kingdom for the children of Dion's sister; and how this attempt was frustrated by the physicians and the younger Dionysius, who had such a strong sleeping potion administered to his father that it carried him off before Dion could gain access to him (*Dion* 2). This is the same story as that told by Plutarch (*Dion* 6).

There can be no question, then, that Diodorus and Nepos are depending upon two quite different sources. One of them, that utilized by Diodorus, shows little trace of the *Epistles;* but the other source—the common source (for these passages, at least) of both Plutarch and Nepos—was one that had many points in common with the *Epistles* and could have been derived in part from them. And this second version is the more circumstantial and on the face of things the more trustworthy of the two.

Just as striking as the disagreement between Nepos and Diodorus is the agreement between Nepos and Plutarch. Upon those points on which Nepos disagrees with Diodorus, Plutarch corroborates Nepos, usually giving a fuller and more circumstantial account of the same events. Plutarch, like Nepos, makes the philosophical interests of Dion and the influence of Plato upon him the chief causes of the revolution. His account of the death of Dionysius the Elder and of the banishment of Dion are in perfect agreement with what Nepos says. But what is more convincing than anything else is a general and sustained parallelism between their two accounts. Plato's first journey to Syracuse, his influence upon Dion, Dion's favor with the elder Dionysius and his responsible position at court, his initial ascendancy over the younger Dionysius, his attempt to make a philosophical ruler of him, his success in bringing Plato to Syracuse a second time, the recall of Philistus, Plato's initial success, the opposition of Philistus, the banishment of Dion, the sending of part of Dion's property to the Peloponnesus—all these stages in the development of the crisis are portrayed in the same order in the two accounts, and force upon anyone who compares them in detail the impression that both Nepos and Plutarch are following a single tradition.[18] It is possible, of course, that Plutarch is following Nepos; but that is not very probable, since Plutarch's account is the more detailed, and he does not refer to Nepos at all. The parallelism between them instead strongly suggests the conclusion that Plutarch (in *Dion* 1-21) and Nepos are following a common source. That this source is in general agreement with the *Seventh Epistle* is clear enough from the ease with which Plutarch uses it together with the epistle; but that it is a source other than the letter is also evident from the fact that it includes events and circumstances, such as the recall of Philistus, and the nature of his political views, that are not given in the *Seventh Epistle*.

This common source is generally agreed to be Timaeus.[19] The two most striking points of divergence between the accounts of Diodorus and Nepos are in connection with the death of Dionysius I and the banishment of Dion. Now on both these points Plutarch's account, as we have seen, agrees with Nepos', and in both cases Plutarch distinctly says he is relying upon Timaeus (*Dion* 6 and 14). As for Nepos, he often relies upon Timaeus elsewhere in his *Lives*, and we have no evidence of the use of any other authority in his *Dion*. A negative verification of this view is afforded by considering the discrepant source employed by Diodorus in the passages in question. Diodorus' authority was certainly not Timaeus,[20]

[18] For a fuller discussion of this parallelism between Nepos *Dion* 1-4 and Plutarch *Dion* 1-21 see Hugo Müller, *De Fontibus Plutarchi Vitam Dionis Enarrantis* (Greifswald, 1876).

[19] Müller, *ibid. passim;* Clasen, *Untersuchungen über Timaios,* p. 67.

[20] As was maintained by C. A. Volquardsen, *Untersuchungen über die Quellen der griechischen und sicilischen Geschichten bei Diodor XI-XVI* (Kiel, 1868). Volquardsen's extravagant thesis that Timaeus is the sole

for with regard to the two events above mentioned, the death
of Dionysius I and the banishment of Dion, his account is
quite different from that in Nepos and Plutarch, and in both
cases Plutarch says he is following Timaeus. Furthermore, his
account of the death of Philistus is different from that given
in Plutarch (Diod. XVI, 16; Plut. *Dion* 35), and here Plutarch
not only tells us that his own account is in general agreement
with Timaeus (though he cites Timonides' ἱστορίαι to
Speusippus as the final authority), but also gives Ephorus'
variant version, and this is the one we find in Diodorus. We
may conclude, then, that Ephorus is the source Diodorus
draws upon for this portion of his *Bibliotheca Historica*.[21]
Further reasons in favor of such a supposition are that
Diodorus' account of the struggle between Dion and Dionysius ends abruptly at the year 356, in the midst of the conflict; and this was the year at which Ephorus' history ended.[22]

___

source of the Sicilian portions of Diodorus' narrative is critically examined and rejected by A. Holm, *Geschichte Siciliens* (Leipzig, 1874), II,
367-74.

[21] It must be borne in mind that our inquiry here has to do only with
the passages in Diodorus mentioned in the text, viz. XV, 7 and 74, and
XVI, 5-6 and 9-20. It is doubtless true, as Clasen maintains (*op. cit.*, pp.
57-66), that Diodorus' chief authority for the greater part of the reign of
Dionysius I was Timaeus, though even here he occasionally employs
Ephorus. For the latter part of the reign of Dionysius I and the reign
of Dionysius II Clasen admits that Diodorus is drawing from a different
source. The exposition is markedly short and inexact as compared with
the preceding, and is full of rhetorical reflections. Even Volquardsen
(*ibid.*, pp. 101 f., 105 f.), in spite of his thesis that Timaeus is "die einzige
Quelle" for the Sicilian portions of Diodorus, admits that XVI, 5-6, 9-11
are drawn from Ephorus.

[22] See n. 9 above. Volquardsen (*ibid.*, p. 106) remarks further that the
description of Dion's expedition in Diodorus XVI, 9-11 suggests the
rhetoric of Ephorus, as contrasted with the more prosaic statements of
Timaeus given us through Plutarch (*Dion* 25). I fail to agree, however,
with his view that Diodorus in the middle of chapter 11 suddenly changes
to Timaeus and follows him to the end of chapter 20. The discontinuity
he alleges in the narrative at this point cannot be made out; and in view
of the fact that Diodorus' narrative breaks off (20) just at the point where
we know Ephorus' history ended, and that he gives the version (16) of

Thus we know of the existence in antiquity of two quite different historical traditions bearing on the revolution in Syracuse. One of them, most certainly Ephorus, shows little trace of the influence of the *Epistles;* the other, which has so much in common with the *Epistles,* is most certainly Timaeus, and this is the authority followed by Plutarch and Nepos. It is natural to conclude at once that the version of Timaeus, in view of its general and specific agreement with the point of view and the details in the *Epistles,* is derived from them; but this conclusion cannot be accepted without first inquiring what other sources Timaeus used.

The Sources of Timaeus

It may seem futile to attempt to determine the sources of an author who is known to us only by fragments and references in other writers; but it will be found that the question within the limits that concern us here is not by any means a hopeless one. Our principal reliance of course must be upon Nepos, for Plutarch's use of the *Epistles* makes it impossible for us to decide, when we find in his narrative evidence of the influence of the *Epistles,* whether this influence comes directly, or through the work of Timaeus; and it is only in Nepos, for the most part, that we can be sure we have the characteristics of Timaeus' history alone, unmodified by any later use of the *Epistles.* One of the first things that strikes us about the account in Nepos (and of course in Plutarch also) is that it gives every evidence of being an "inside" account. Nepos' history, as we have shown, makes Plato's political teaching and personal influence an important factor in bringing about the crisis. It comes evidently from someone who was in a position to have a clear understanding of the differences between Plato's political aims and those of his opponents at Syracuse; and this, it may be assumed, was not something gen-

the death of Philistus that Plutarch (*Dion* 35) ascribes to Ephorus, the conclusion seems inescapable that he has followed Ephorus throughout. For confirmation of this criticism of Volquardsen see Holm, *op. cit.,* II, 374.

erally appreciated, considering the climate of secrecy, mis-representation, and intrigue of the court at Syracuse.[23] We have also seen that it is more circumstantial, at such critical points as the banishment of Dion, than the other tradition, and seems at times to come from someone who knew of things from the inside. It is safe to infer that the account Nepos is following, namely the history of Timaeus, is based ultimately upon the testimony of the chief actors in the revolution or of someone closely associated with them in the government at Syracuse.

One source of inside information that Timaeus could have used was Philistus. Diodorus (XV, 89, 3) tells us that the history of Philistus included the first five years of the reign of Dionysius the Younger; and a passage in Plutarch shows us that it continued at least as far as the banishment of Dion.[24] Knowing what we do of Timaeus' industry as a historian, we should expect that if this history was available he would make full use of it. That he did so is clear, not only from certain general considerations,[25] but also from the indirect testimony of Plutarch himself. The passage in Plutarch describing the banishment of Dion contains clear evidence that Timaeus, whom Plutarch follows, derived an important part of his information from Philistus:

> A letter was produced which Dion had secretly written to the Carthaginian agents, advising them that when they

[23] If on other grounds we find reason for accepting the *Third Epistle* as genuine, it will confirm the above interpretation. We learn from it how much confusion there was in the public mind at Syracuse and elsewhere as to what was going on behind the walls of the citadel during Plato's visits. Plato is trying to keep his name from being associated with the arbitrary policies of Dionysius, a misconception that would be natural in view of the public acclaim with which Dionysius had received Plato. The *First Epistle* also, though spurious, bears testimony in its own way to the misconceptions that prevailed in the fourth and later centuries as to Plato's connections with the government.

[24] *Dion* 14. This incident certainly comes from Philistus, through Timaeus.

[25] Clasen, *op. cit.*, pp. 59 f.

came to negotiate with Dionysius concerning the peace they should conduct their negotiations through him, for in this way they would more surely obtain all they wanted. *When Dionysius had read this to Philistus, and consulted with him, as Timaeus relates,* he overreached Dion, etc.[26]

The inference that Timaeus got his information on this point from Philistus is corroborated by what Plutarch elsewhere (*Dion* 36) says in criticism of the delight Timaeus displayed in describing the death of Philistus and the indignities visited upon his body. Those who write history, says Plutarch, and have been in no way wronged by the man, and *have received assistance from his writings,* should not upbraid him for his misfortunes. There can be no doubt, therefore, that Philistus' history is a basic ingredient in the narrative of Timaeus.

But is it the only source used by Timaeus? Nepos' account reveals considerable sympathy with Dion and Plato. Philistus is characterized as the protagonist of tyranny, and Plato as the champion of liberty. Plato advises Dionysius *tyrannidis facere finem libertatemque reddere Syracusanis* (Nepos *Dion* 3). Of course we know that Timaeus was a bitter opponent of all tyranny, and we should expect him to take the side of the "liberals" in this controversy. But how would he know that Plato and Dion—at this early stage, at least—had "liberal" aims? Of firsthand accounts, besides the Platonic *Epistles,* he would have, so far as we know, only the history of Athanis and the letter of Timonides. Both of these narratives dealt primarily with the later stages of the struggle between Dionysius and Dion. The history of Athanis began, we are told, where Philistus' history left off, viz. about the year 363 or 362; and even though it may have contained some sort of an introduction explaining what the struggle was about, we can hardly expect that Athanis, who as we know was an adherent of Heraclides, would present Dion in such an idealistic light. Of all the documents we have or hear of relative to the struggle at Syracuse, the Platonic *Epistles* are the most likely source of Timaeus' information as to the principles of Plato and

[26] *Dion* 14. Italics mine.

Dion at this period. And it is very probable that the *tyrannidis facere finem libertatemque reddere Syracusanis* of Nepos is an echo of the numerous passages in the *Seventh Epistle* describing the aim of Plato as the liberating of the Syracusans, and the conversion of the tyranny into a kingship (324b, 331d-333a, 336a).

Even more telling is the striking reminiscence of the *Seventh Epistle* in Nepos' account of Plato's visits to Syracuse. On Plato's first visit, Nepos says:

> Dion was so taken with admiration for him that he gave himself to him completely; and Plato was not less delighted with Dion, so much so that although he had been cruelly outraged by the tyrant in being offered for sale in the slave market, *he nevertheless returned to Syracuse later in answer to the prayers of this same Dion.* In the meantime, Dionysius fell sick, etc.[27]

Note that Nepos interrupts his narrative, and leaps over a period of more than twenty years, in thus referring to Plato's return. The reason for this interruption of the narrative is found in *Epistle VII,* 327a-e. Here the description of the intimacy established between Dion and Plato on his first journey is followed immediately by the account of Plato's second journey, and the "prayers" that Dion addressed to him to return. These prayers are given at some length in this passage of the letter, and make an unforgettable impression on the reader. Nepos' reference to them, taken together with the interruption of the narrative, seems to show the influence of the *Seventh Epistle.*

Again, in the language Nepos uses in describing Dion—he had, among other gifts, says Nepos, *ingenium docile, come, aptum ad artes optimas (Dion* 1)—we may venture to find an echo of the corresponding passage of the *Seventh Epistle* (327ab); for the point which Plato most emphasizes is precisely Dion's εὐμάθεια. In general the favorable attitude toward Dion exhibited in the earlier part of Nepos' life tends to confirm the belief that Timaeus' history was based upon documents written

[27] *Dion* 2. Italics mine.

by persons capable not only of sympathizing with Dion's principles, but also of feeling admiration for his genius and force
of character. Likewise the attitude of Timaeus toward the
young Dionysius is favorable, in contrast to his judgment of
the elder Dionysius.[28] He is pictured as a young man of good
intentions, suffering from lack of education and experience,
naturally weak in character, and led astray by the flattery and
insinuations of the court party led by Philistus. This is in
thorough accord with the *Seventh Epistle,* and it is very hard
to explain Timaeus' drawing this sort of picture unless he was
influenced by this letter, and possibly others in our collection.
If we take all these facts into consideration, it becomes fairly
certain that the *Seventh Epistle* at least was a basic ingredient
in the history of Timaeus.

Since Timaeus was the creator of the historical tradition
followed by Nepos, we can readily understand why Nepos'
account of Dion's brief period of power after his second rescue
of the city is so unsympathetic. The reader is startled by the
rapid conversion of Dion from the hero to the villain of the
tale. Nepos (and presumably Timaeus) paints Dion's actions
in dark colors. He unjustly put Heraclides to death, he confiscated and squandered the possessions of his enemies, he
even laid hands on the property of the nobles friendly to himself in order to pay his soldiers, and he employed his mercenaries against the people when they arose in protest (*Dion* 6-7).
This sounds like the behavior of a typical tyrant of the fourth
century. Without going so far as to say that this portrayal of
Dion is not founded on facts, we can at least understand that
Timaeus, with his confirmed hostility to tyranny, would not
be inclined to soften his interpretation of Dion's motives.
Besides the natural misinterpretation to which a strong policy
like that of Dion's would be subject, we must remember that
the only firsthand account of these events that Timaeus
would find available was that of Athanis, who, as we have seen
above, probably belonged to the party of Heraclides. The
ἱστορίαι of Timonides must have been written shortly after

28 Clasen, *op. cit.,* p. 69.

the capture of the citadel and the departure of Apollocrates,[29] and would therefore not contain any information regarding the later events of Dion's reign. Thus Dion's career in power was recorded first by one of his chief political opponents, and this account was incorporated in the historical tradition by one who we know was temperamentally inclined to see the worst side of the tyrants he portrayed. Only a few sentences in Plato's *Epistles VII* and *VIII* (335e, 351a ff., 357a) remain to show the other side of the picture. Plutarch, relying upon Plato's estimate of Dion's motives throughout this later period, but lacking detailed confirmation of it, had no recourse but to pass as quickly as possible over this part of Dion's life.

The Early History of Epistle VII

The results of our inquiry into the genesis of the historical tradition may conveniently be put in a diagram.

Epistle VII
Philistus
Timonides (?)
Athanis (?)

$\longrightarrow$Timaeus$\longrightarrow$Nepos' *Dion*

Timonides
Epistles IV, VII, XIII, III(?) $\longrightarrow$Plutarch's *Dion*

? $\longrightarrow$Theopompus

? $\longrightarrow$Ephorus$\longrightarrow$Diodorus Siculus (XV, 7, 74; XVI, 5-6, 9-20)

These results have some very interesting bearings upon the literary history of the *Seventh Epistle*. If Timaeus used it in the writing of his history, this fact provides us with the earliest information we have with regard to the existence of this letter. Timaeus' history was written while he resided at Athens during the fifty years immediately following the rise to power

---

[29] So we may fairly infer from the fact that Plutarch's account loses its detailed and circumstantial character at this point (52).

of Agathocles at Tauromenium. Since Agathocles' tyranny
began about the year 317, this would make Timaeus' resi-
dence at Athens extend to about the year 267. Thus we have
evidence that the *Seventh Epistle,* and perhaps others in the
collection, were in existence by the year 267, at the latest. In
view of the scantiness of our information about the early history of the *Epistles,* this is an important bit of fact. There is
no other external evidence of the existence of the *Seventh
Epistle,* or of any other in our collection, at so early a date.[30]
Not even the fact that the canon of Aristophanes, drawn up
toward the close of the third century, contained an item called
Epistles affords any decisive external evidence of the existence
of any of the letters in our collection. But knowing that
Timaeus made use of the *Seventh,* we can be sure that it was
included in Aristophanes' canon. More than this, Timaeus
was one of the most careful historians of antiquity. And since
his history was written at Athens, where he would have abundant opportunity for inquiring into the authenticity of the
letter, the fact that he made use of it establishes beyond a
doubt its historical accuracy, and also creates, I think, a very
strong presumption in favor of its being a writing of Plato's.
In any case it is an extremely significant fact that this letter
became an integral part of the historical work of Timaeus,
the work which, if we may judge from the extent to which it
is quoted and referred to by later writers, became recognized
as the most authoritative account of Sicilian history.

But the results we have reached bring us face to face with
another difficulty, perhaps the gravest of all difficulties affecting the acceptance of the *Epistles.* If Ephorus, who so far
as we can see was as careful and industrious a worker as
Timaeus, failed to use these documents, so relevant and so im-

---

[30] Adam (*Archiv,* p. 37) finds a reference to *Epistle VII* in Aristoxenus
(Euseb. *Praep. Ev.* 15, 2), where πλάνη is used, as it is in *Epistle VII.*
350d, to denote Plato's voyages to Syracuse. If Adam's inference is valid,
we have evidence of this letter's existence perhaps earlier than the date
suggested above. But πλάνη in this sense occurs frequently in other
writers, and Adam's inference seems somewhat precarious.

portant if they are genuine, have we not good reason for suspecting not only their authenticity but also their reliability
as historical sources? At the very least the presence of two
traditions regarding the revolution in Syracuse, one dependent
on the *Epistles*, the other not, the former traceable to
Timaeus and the latter to Ephorus, requires us to seek some
explanation of the discrepancy between them. Ephorus was
a pupil of Isocrates, whose school is usually represented as
the jealous rival of Plato's: but this would not *ipso facto*
debar him from access to materials in the Academy. In fact
there is clear evidence of the influence of the *Minos* and the
Laws on the contents of the early books of Ephorus' *Histories*.[31] If Ephorus knew and was influenced by these Platonic
writings, his failure to use the *Epistles* is indeed a significant
fact.

But this fact may not be as prejudicial to the *Epistles* as it
might seem at first sight. There is evidence of disagreement
between Ephorus and Plato in their political principles and
in their evaluation of the causes of political events. In
Ephorus' account (in the first book of his *Histories*) of the
decline of the early Dorian kingdoms of Argos and Messene,
an account which parallels Plato's in the third book of the
Laws, Ephorus blames the peoples for this decline, whereas
Plato blames the kings.[32] Again Plutarch (*Dion* 36) criticizes
Ephorus for his overweening praise of Philistus, a criticism
which indicates that Ephorus' sympathies were with the opponents of Plato at Syracuse, and probably also that he accepted Philistus' version of the events with which the *Epistles*
deal. In justice to Ephorus' qualities as a historian, however,
there are other circumstances to be mentioned. His account
of Sicilian events after 387 was contained, as was said above,
in his twenty-eighth and twenty-ninth books, the last to be

[31] See my *Plato's Cretan City* (Princeton, 1960), pp. 23 f., 71, *passim*.
[32] Isocrates (*Archidamus* 22) gives an interpretation of Messenian history similar to Ephorus'. Since the *Archidamus* belongs to the year 356,
it antedates Ephorus' handling of this theme in his *Histories* and suggests
the source of Ephorus' views.

written before his death in 330. It is even probable that the
twenty-ninth, which must have dealt with the career of Dion,
was left unfinished when he died, for it seems to break off
suddenly with the re-entry of Dion into Syracuse after he had
been driven out by Heraclides, with no mention of later
events which are an inseparable part of the story.[33] It is therefore clear that Ephorus was working on the history of Dion
at the very close of his life. We do not know where he lived
during these last years; it may have been far from Athens.
He was an old man—more than seventy, if we accept the
tradition in Suidas that he was born during the troubled
times at the close of the fifth century—and may have lacked
the energy, and perhaps also the inclination, to re-examine
an interpretation of the revolution which he had long held,
especially since it was the interpretation of Philistus. Hence
he recorded only the somewhat conventional and perfunctory
account that we find in Diodorus. Timaeus, on the other
hand, was a much younger man (since his history extends to
the year 264 he must have been working on these events of
360-350 long before his death), and besides had a special interest in seeing what the opponents of tyranny had to say.

33 Furthermore, Diodorus (XVI, 76, 5) says that Ephorus' history extended to the siege of Perinthus, an event that occurred in 341 and is
quite unrelated to Sicilian history. This is puzzling, for each of Ephorus'
books seems to have had a unitary theme (Diod. V, 1, 4), and Philip's
war against Athens has obviously no proper place in this twenty-ninth
book. The passage in Diodorus may therefore best be taken as evidence
that Ephorus left behind him sketches of events to be dealt with in future
books, and that these fragments were incorporated by his posthumous
editor into the unfinished twenty-ninth book. This supposition is confirmed by another statement of Diodorus (XVI, 14, 3) that Ephorus' son
Demophilus wrote a thirtieth book dealing with the Sacred War, "which
his father had omitted"—a statement that would be difficult to understand if its originator, whether Diodorus or Demophilus, was thinking
only of the unfinished Sicilian history and not of the conglomerate that
later came to be called the twenty-ninth book.

The Discrepancies Between Plutarch and
The Epistles

We are now in a better position to understand the occasional passages in Plutarch that show discrepancies with the account in the *Epistles,* and to judge of the relative trustworthiness of the *Epistles* and the historical tradition Plutarch followed in these passages. These discrepancies have doubtless played a large part in creating an attitude of mind that renders difficult the acceptance of the *Seventh* and other letters.

Clearly, of course, these discrepancies can be adduced as evidence against the authenticity of the *Epistles* only if they prove that Plutarch deliberately rejects the testimony of the letters in favor of a variant historical tradition, and that with respect to matters about which the statements in the letters, if they were written by Plato, would obviously be final—such matters, for instance, as the details of his relations with Dionysius. But a careful examination of the discrepancies between Plutarch and the *Epistles* fails to establish any such thesis. Most of the discrepancies are quite unimportant; and all of them, with one exception, can be explained as the result of carelessness or oversight, not as a deliberate rejection of the authority of the letters. Plutarch doubtless did not always have the letters before him while writing, but relied upon his memory of them. Below is a list of these discrepancies, so far as I have been able to detect them:

(a) Plutarch's account (*Dion* 20) of Plato's final dismissal from Syracuse disagrees in several respects with the version in *Epistle VII,* 349e-350b. Plutarch says that after Archytas had intervened in behalf of Plato, Dionysius gave him elaborate entertainments to disguise his secret hatred for Plato; whereas the *Seventh Epistle* says that from the time of Plato's banishment from the palace garden Dionysius invited him no more to the palace. This seems to be the only instance in which Plutarch is aware that he is departing from the narrative of the *Seventh Epistle;* he explicitly states that Plato's own writings do not altogether agree with this account. The reason why Plutarch chose the version he did is quite clear: it gives him an opportunity to recount a nice bit of Platonic repartee; but this story, like most anecdotes of the sort, is probably apocryphal.[34]

(b) In describing the first invitation of the younger Dionysius to Plato in 367 (*Dion* 11), Plutarch adds details that Plato gives in connection with the *second* invitation in 361 (*Ep. VII*, 338-339). Plutarch here has simply and naturally confused the two occasions. Since he cites the *Seventh Epistle* in this same chapter, it is evident that he is relying upon it as his authority.

(c) In *Dion* 18, Plutarch says that Dionysius put a stop to Dion's revenues before Plato's third journey; whereas the *Seventh Epistle* (345c) says that the revenues were stopped a short time after Plato's arrival in Syracuse, and with this the *Third Epistle* seems to agree (318a). Plutarch could easily fall into this error, as the order of events is by no means sharply emphasized in the *Epistles*.

(d) In *Dion* 21, Plutarch says that Plato wrote to Dionysius that he had talked with Dion about "the matter" (which Plutarch takes to mean the projected marriage of Dion's wife to Timocrates) and that it was evident he would deeply resent it if Dionysius' plans were carried out. In the passage to which Plutarch refers (*Ep. XIII*, 362e), Plato says he has *not* spoken to Dion, but has learned indirectly that he would be much displeased. This is a trivial point, but affords additional evidence of Plutarch's unintentional inaccuracy.

(e) The most troublesome point is the discrepancy between Plutarch's account of the death of Dion's son and the references to this son in the *Seventh* and *Eighth Epistles*. Plutarch says that this son committed suicide shortly before Dion's assassination (*Dion* 55), whereas the *Seventh Epistle* probably

---

[34] Steinhart (*Platons sämmtliche Werke*, VIII, 390, n. 27) finds other points of disagreement here, but his objections seem to arise from the astonishing assumption that two accounts are contradictory if one contains anything whatever that the other does not contain.

(324a) and the *Eighth* certainly (355e) imply that he was alive after Dion's death. Some interpreters have argued that there is no contradiction here; the son referred to in *Epistle VIII* is not the same son who is said to have committed suicide. But I consider this hypothesis untenable, for reasons which will be given later.[35]

These are, I believe, the only discrepancies of any consequence between Plutarch and the *Epistles*. In only one of the cases listed—the first—can we say that Plutarch was conscious of having departed from what he regarded as Plato's account. The second, third, and fourth discrepancies can easily be explained as the result of carelessness or faulty memory and create no presumption against Plutarch's confidence in the *Epistles*.[36] Even with respect to the death of Dion's son we can be fairly sure that Plutarch was not aware of his divergence from Plato, else he would have mentioned it. He could easily have overlooked, misinterpreted, or forgotten the references to this son in the *Epistles,* especially if he had before him another version which he regarded as authoritative, and none of the other historians he used made any mention of this son. This variant tradition comes, if we have correctly interpreted the evidence, from no less a person than Timaeus himself. There is reason to believe, as I shall show later, that this story of the suicide of Dion's son is a fabrication devised for political purposes by the enemies of Dion.[37] Though invented for a particular occasion it could easily have come to be accepted later, especially if this son died shortly after the *Eighth Epistle* was written, without having done anything worthy of record. Timaeus then, like Plutarch later, could easily have overlooked or misinterpreted the references to this son in the *Eighth Epistle*. Even if he was aware of these references, he could have assumed, as have

---

[35] See p. 84.

[36] Another example of Plutarch's occasional carelessness in citing the *Epistles* is to be found in *De Vit. Pud.* 11, where a passage at the beginning of *Epistle XIII* is cited as occurring at the end.

[37] See pp. 84 ff.

some recent defenders of the *Epistles,* that the author of the letters simply had not heard of the death of Dion's son; therefore, Timaeus' divergence from them on this point is compatible with his general acceptance of them as authentic and reliable documents.

EPISTLE VII

This is not only the longest of all the letters in the collection, being equal in length to all the others combined, but is also by far the most important, both for the historian of Sicily and the student of Plato and Plato's philosophy. If it is genuine, it gives us information of considerable value about Plato's political views, his connection with Athenian politics, and his relations with the Dionysii and Dion. Few historians have been so self-denying as to make no use of the contents of this letter, though their reliance upon it is sometimes masked by an ostensible dependence upon Plutarch.

We have seen reason to believe that the *Seventh Epistle* was in existence by at least the early part of the third century and was used by the historian Timaeus. The case for this letter appears even stronger when we take into consideration the philological evidence previously referred to, showing that in style and diction it has the traits of the *Laws* and other dialogues of Plato's latest period. Since the characteristics of Plato's latest style have become known and the *Epistles* examined from that point of view, the condemnation of the *Seventh Epistle* because of its stylistic divergence from the *Republic,* the *Protagoras,* and the *Phaedo,* for instance, has been fairly thrown out of court. Even Richards, whose estimate of the letter on other grounds is exceedingly unfavorable, admits that "there is nothing in the style properly so called or in the grammar and vocabulary that is at all inconsistent with genuineness."[1] There is now general agree-

[1] H. Richards, *Platonica* (London, 1911), p. 279.

ment that on this count the *Seventh Epistle* is above re-proach,[2] and such unanimity on a point so important as this may well be the decisive consideration involved in the question of the letter's genuineness.

There remain, however, certain difficulties connected with the form and purpose of the letter. At first sight it would seem to be primarily a letter of political advice, written in reply to an appeal for help that has come to Plato from Dion's friends and followers in Syracuse. The situation it presupposes is not difficult to make out. Dion has been assassinated; and from the frequent and poignant references to this event we infer that Plato is still under the shock of the first report of it. Dion's followers, moreover, are still in Syracuse. The message to Plato must therefore have been sent before the flight to Leontini recorded by Diodorus (XVI, 36, 5), in other words, very soon after the murder of Dion. The references to the civil strife raging in Syracuse (336de) also suggest the period of turmoil and confusion immediately following the murder of Dion, before Callippus had consolidated his power.[3] We may confidently say, then, that the request for advice was sent out very shortly—possibly within the first few days—after the murder of Dion in 354.[4] How long it took Plato to compose this letter in reply we have no means of knowing; but it would seem reasonable to assume that the letter was completed by the end of 354 or the beginning of 353.

But the *Seventh Epistle* is more than a letter of political advice to Dion's party at Syracuse. It is clearly intended for a larger public than the persons to whom it is addressed, and

2 See pp. 10 ff.

3 Franz Egermann, *Die Platonischen Briefe VII und VIII* (Berlin, 1928), pp. 9-16; see below, pp. 81 ff.

4 The objections of G. Hell to this dating of the appeal for help seem captious ("Zur Datierung des 7. und 8. Platonischen Briefes," *Hermes,* LXVII [1932], 298 f.). It is true that for their immediate task, the overthrow of Callippus, they needed no advice from Plato, nor could they profit by his help; but they were concerned also with the long-range policy to be adopted.

is also clearly intended to serve as a defense of Plato's relations with Syracuse and of the political philosophy he held. This apologetic purpose is unmistakable, and at times it completely overshadows the professed aim of the letter. For this reason the letter has been looked upon with suspicion, either because of an alleged lack of unity resulting from the attempt to combine in one composition the two purposes of political advice and apology, or because it is felt that the apologetic purpose points to a later attempt by a disciple of Plato to clear the reputation of Plato and the Academy. The second point deserves to be considered first, because it bears more directly upon the question of the relevance of this letter to the historical situation for which it purports to have been written.

There are abundant traces in later literature of criticism directed against Plato and the Academy. A good account of such critics and their criticisms is given by Karsten,[5] who concludes rather hastily that this letter was written by a later Academic apologist. But it is of course possible that Plato himself might have thought it worth while to reply in a semi-public document to those attacks upon himself and his school which were current before his death. Some of these attacks are purely personal in their character, such as the charge of Plato's ill nature which Athenaeus develops at length. These may be dismissed at once as irrelevant to the present question, since even supposing that they were current in Plato's day and that Plato thought them worthy of notice, the present letter would not afford a good opportunity for a reply. The accusations which are relevant here are those pertaining to Plato's relations to the court of Dionysius, and in general the participation of the Academy in the political life of Greek states.

We know that there were frequently very intimate relations between the Academy and the rulers, some of them tyrants,

---

[5] *Commentatio Critica*, pp. 226-40. For a fuller statement of these criticisms without special reference to the *Epistles* see Geffcken, "Antiplatonica," *Hermes*, LXIV (1929), 87-109.

of Greek cities.[6] Money and prestige were to be gained at the courts of these enemies of democracy; and it is hardly possible that the members of the Academy who visited them, even with the most disinterested motives, could have escaped criticism and slander. Athenaeus declares that most of Plato's pupils were of a tyrannous and calumnious disposition, and that many of them became tyrants themselves. This is almost pure gossip; probably all there is in it is a reflection of the well-known fact that members of the Academy were frequently found at the courts of tyrants. It is of course possible that some of them were not above feeling the force of the motives that led Aristippus and others to Syracuse during the reign of the Dionysii. Aristippus openly admitted that he sought the favor of Dionysius for mercenary reasons, and seems to have thought all others had equally interested motives. "I want money; Plato wants books." [7] This remark is closely related to the story current in later days (perhaps also in the time of Plato) that Plato purchased some Pythagorean books with the money Dionysius had given him.[8] Diogenes the Cynic criticized Plato for his love of Sicilian luxury; and Epicurus is said to have called the Platonists Διονυσοκόλακες.[9] There is a keen thrust in the epigram of Molon, a contemporary and enemy of Plato: "The surprising thing is not that Dionysius should be in Corinth, but that Plato should be in Sicily." [10]

More serious than this sort of gossip would be the misunderstanding of Plato's political principles to which his connection with Greek tyrants, and with the Dionysii in particular, would give rise, especially at Athens. Though there was a respectable body of "advanced" opinion that was beginning to look with un-Greek favor upon the exercise of absolute

[6] See pp. 143 f.
[7] Diog. Laert. II, 81.
[8] Diog. Laert. III, 9.
[9] Diog. Laert. X, 8.
[10] Diog. Laert. III, 34.

power, yet the typical democrat of the fourth century would look upon tyrants and tyranny with the same abhorrence as his ancestors of the Persian Wars. When Plato in the *Republic* allots to tyrants the supreme penalty in the life after death, and judges their misdeeds too great to be atoned for by any punishment, he is expressing not only his own conviction, but the common attitude of the liberty-loving Greek. Now of all Greek tyrants, the Dionysii were the most odious. The outbreak of feeling against the legation of Dionysius the Elder at the Olympic festival in 388 was a memorable indication of the detestation and fear with which he was regarded. Instigated by a fiery speech of the orator Lysias, who pictured the Greek world as about to be enslaved by the Persian king on the east and the Sicilian tyrant on the west, the assembled multitude actually laid hands on the tents of the legation; and when the poems of Dionysius were recited the people received them with jeers and hisses.[11] This event occurred some thirty years before the supposed date of the *Seventh Epistle,* but there is no reason to believe that the attitude of the Greeks toward the Dionysii underwent much change. The fear that caused the outburst in 388 might have diminished somewhat, but the power of Dionysius the Elder remained formidable to the very end of his reign. He erected new and larger fortifications about Syracuse, making it the largest fortified city in Greece. And the means whereby he had gained this position of power and retained it, the despoiling of temples, the destruction of the free Greek cities in Sicily, the heavy exactions imposed on the citizens of Syracuse, and the employment of mercenary troops to maintain his power, were certain to excite those feelings of repugnance that the Greeks always felt for tyrants, and excite them in this case to an unusual degree. The picture that Plato draws in the ninth book of the *Republic* of the tyrannical man was copied in all probability from the living reality which the character and career of Dionysius presented to the Greek world. The younger Dionysius might be feared less than his father was,

[11] Meyer, *Geschichte des Altertums,* V, 268 f.; Diod. XV, 7, 2.

but he would be loved and admired no more. Now Plato's connection with the Syracusan reigning dynasty was a continuous one from the year 388; for though he failed to gain the favor of the elder Dionysius on his first visit, yet he made friends with his brother-in-law, Dion, and this friendship was maintained during the twenty years that separated the first from the second journey to Syracuse. Plutarch [12] tells us that Dion defrayed the expenses of a choragic entertainment that Plato put on at Athens, adding that Plato permitted this because he thought it would gain Dion favor among the Athenians; and the event very likely tended to confirm whatever suspicions there may have already been of a personal interest attaching to Plato's friendship for Dion. It is true that while Dion was in banishment at Athens he seems to have been regarded with great honor and respect; but he was then an exile, himself a victim and a formidable opponent of the tyrant at Syracuse, and this favor could easily have been lost when he came into power at Syracuse and gave evidence in his conduct of traits hardly distinguishable from those that had made the Dionysii so odious.

In view of the Greek attitude toward tyrants and toward the Dionysii in particular, it is certain that Plato's long and notorious connection with Syracuse, when coupled with his known criticism of democracy, would be misinterpreted by Athenian public opinion. His view that a tyranny sometimes offers the best opportunity for introducing a good government would be hard for the Greek democrat to grasp. When the Athenian Stranger in the *Laws* (IV, 709e) introduces this doctrine, he has difficulty in getting Cleinias to understand it, and has to go over the point twice before it becomes plausible. In Plato's idiom, this signifies clearly that it is a point on which he had been, or was likely to be, misunderstood. It is not surprising, therefore, that Plato should seize the opportunity offered by the request for advice from Syracuse and utilize it for correcting some of the misrepresentations and replying to some of the criticisms to which he had been sub-

[12] *Dion* 17; *Arist.* 1.

jected. He may have already done something similar in his
letter to Dionysius (*Epistle III*) written three years before;
but that did not throw much light upon his political principles, and Plato probably felt the need of presenting a fuller
explanation of his relations with Syracuse.

There is also reason to think that Athenian public opinion
was especially sensitive and suspicious at this particular
time.[13] The date at which the *Seventh Epistle* seems to have
been written saw the appearance of another apologetic document, somewhat similar in character and purpose, the *Antidosis* of Isocrates. This must be more than a coincidence. Both
Plato and Isocrates were leaders of schools renowned all over
Greece for the training of statesmen. Both deplored the moral
laxness and political opportunism of their day. Both were
critical of democracy and sympathetic toward the ideal of
monarchy, at least as a temporary expedient; and what is
more important, both had intimate connections with powerful monarchs. The admiration of Isocrates for Philip of
Macedon was as well known as Plato's famous attachment to
Dion. In spite, therefore, of the difference in their philosophical views, they would be equally exposed to criticism
by the leaders of democratic opinion; and the fact that
Isocrates in 354 found it necessary to write the *Antidosis*
shows that a defense of Plato written in 353, such as the
Seventh Epistle professes to be, was not irrelevant to the
temper of the time.

There are also several interesting parallels between the
Antidosis and the *Seventh Epistle* that throw light on the
charges to which Plato is replying. The lengthy citations
Isocrates gives from his earlier speeches to show the precise
nature of his political views, his eagerness to prove that he
had recognized the full claims of Athens to leadership in
Greece, and had not refrained from offering advice upon
the conduct of her empire—all this, as we shall find, has its
counterpart in the *Seventh Epistle*. Again Isocrates thinks it
worth while to explain his relations with Nicocles, King of

[13] L. A. Post, *Thirteen Epistles of Plato* (Oxford, 1925), pp. 58 ff.

Salaminia, from whom he had accepted substantial gifts, and to whom in return he had given political advice. By way of defense he quotes a passage from his *Discourse to Nicocles,* prefacing it with these words:

I have chosen this passage, not because it is better written than my other speeches, but because it best shows the character of my relationships with private individuals and with kings. You will see here that I spoke to him like a free man, as becomes a citizen of Athens; and that, far from flattering his riches or his power, I had the interests of his subjects at heart, and wished to do my best to secure for them the mildest government possible. And from the fact that when speaking to a king I advocated the cause of the people, it is evident that if I had been advising the leaders of a democracy I would have counseled them to look after the interests of the multitude.[14]

The specific occasion for the writing of the *Antidosis* seems to have been the death of Timotheus, who was Isocrates' most famous pupil, and whose long and distinguished career as commander of the Athenian army and navy had been brought to a disgraceful close in 357 by his trial and condemnation for neglect of duty in the campaign against Samos. The state of public feeling against him is indicated by the fact that he was fined a hundred talents, the largest fine that had ever been imposed at Athens, according to Isocrates. Timotheus avoided payment of the fine by withdrawing from Athens to Chalcis, where he died about three years later. Subsequently the Athenians repented of their harshness and erected statues to his memory; but in 354 the feeling against him was still high, as is evident from the lengthy section of the *Antidosis* in which Isocrates recalls his great deeds as general, and from the care with which he avoids openly accusing the Athenians of injustice. The disgrace of Timotheus doubtless drew upon Isocrates the ill feeling of many parts of the Athenian public, who would link the teacher with the pupil, as Socrates a half century before had been associated with the treachery of

14 *Antid.* 69-70.

Alcibiades. It is interesting to note that the character of Timotheus, as painted by Isocrates, exhibited the same fault for which Plato (or Speusippus) reproved Dion in the *Fourth Epistle,* viz. a haughtiness of demeanor and lack of tact in his relations with his colleagues and with the leaders of the democracy.[15]

If Isocrates (who, after all, had considerable democratic leanings) thought it necessary to defend himself in this manner, we can readily understand how intransigent the patriotic and democratic sentiment in Athens was, and how charged with suspicions was the political atmosphere of these years. And Plato, the known aristocrat and relative of Critias, would be far more subject to such suspicions than Isocrates, though their political aims were in many respects similar.

Plato's defense against these suspicions, like that of Isocrates in the *Antidosis,* consists first of all in showing what his political principles really were and what were the precise objects he and Dion hoped to accomplish at Syracuse. It is clearly stated at the very beginning of the *Seventh Epistle* and repeated more than once that their purpose was to set the people of Syracuse free, and devise the best possible system of laws for them (324b, 327c, 335d, 336a, 351a). Plato's willingness to advise the friends of Dion who have just appealed to him is dependent upon whether or not they really share Dion's political views (324a); he is interested not in the triumph of Dion's party, but in the triumph of his ideas. He carefully distinguishes Dion's aims from those of an unscrupulous adventurer (351), and there is a ringing denunciation of the evils of absolute power (334d-336a). The desire to make clear to the Greek world his real political principles under-

---

[15] Post (*op. cit.,* 61) makes the interesting suggestion that Plato's passionate defense of Dion in the *Seventh Epistle* was in part called forth by Isocrates' praise of Timotheus' moderation in victory. This was in marked contrast to the civil strife and bloodshed that followed Dion's success at Syracuse, and Isocrates may have been making a covert attack upon the Academy. There are other attacks upon the Academy in the *Antidosis,* however, to which Plato makes no reply; therefore we cannot think the *Seventh Epistle* was written mainly to answer Isocrates.

lies the short autobiographical sketch that Plato inserts at the beginning of the letter, showing that it was from a long observation of Greek political life that he came to the conviction that philosophers should rule, or that rulers should become philosophers (326b). It is not hard to see in this autobiographical passage an almost apologetic reference to Plato's attitude toward the Thirty. His blood relationship to Critias and other members of the group would no doubt be remembered and would confirm any suspicions that might attach to him because of his later relations with the Dionysii. Plato admits that he was at first sympathetic with the aims of the Thirty and hopeful of good results from their accession to power; but "my attitude toward them," he says, "is not surprizing, because I was young" (324d). And he describes with emphasis his eventual disillusionment with this experiment in aristocratic despotism. Again his treatment of the restored democracy shows his care not to offend unduly the Athenian democracy of his day. "In general those who returned from exile acted with great restraint" (325b). The steady degeneration in Athenian public life had a more fundamental cause than the democracy, viz. the decay of morals and the decline of the authority of law, defects in Athenian life which the democratic leaders were as ready to acknowledge as Plato himself. It would be untrue to say that Plato falsifies his own attitude in order to placate Athenian opinion, for he emphatically states his position on the real point at issue between himself and the leaders of Athenian democracy, viz. the means whereby a reform of the existing evils could be brought about. Plato saw no hope except in a radical revolution, made possible by a union of scientific training and political authority; whereas they, of course, were bent upon preserving (and even extending) the mechanism of democratic government.

Beside these democratic critics of his connection with the tyrants at Syracuse, there seems to be another group of critics against whom Plato is defending himself. There were clearly some persons who felt that he had been too rigorous and severe in his treatment of the young Dionysius. It may seem strange that Plato should think it necessary to justify his treatment of Dionysius in a letter to the friends of Dion. But a little reflection will show that the situation is thoroughly plausible. First of all, Plato had in mind a larger public than the group of persons at Syracuse to whom this letter is addressed; and it is certain that among this larger public would be some who would say that most of the blame for the chaos at Syracuse should fall on Plato for having been too exacting in his demands on Dionysius, or for having prolonged the breach between Dionysius and Dion. Again, even among the party of Dion there may have been a philo-Dionysian group, as Hackforth suggests. The older antagonism between Dion and Dionysius would be overshadowed by the later rivalry between Dion and Heraclides; and now that Dion was dead, doubtless many of his followers would look with favor upon a return of Dionysius. Plato defends himself against these criticisms by showing, first, that Dionysius proved to be incapable of the moral and intellectual discipline required of the man who was to reform life and government in Sicily; and, secondly, that he did everything in his power to bring about a reconciliation between Dion and Dionysius, even at the cost of humiliation and actual physical danger to himself.

This is an altogether relevant and logical defense against real, not imaginary, criticisms. How real they are is shown by the fact that modern historians in dealing with these events have usually felt their force; and some, like Grote, have been inclined to support the charges against Plato. Meyer likewise accuses Plato of a lack of political realism and blames the disaster at Syracuse upon this idealistic venture. We cannot undertake to defend Plato against these later critics, but one may point out, as Ritter has aptly done,[16] that the downfall of Dionysius' power was due most of all to the weakness and inexperience of the young tyrant himself, and without Plato's and Dion's assistance at the beginning of his reign this downfall might have occurred sooner. And it should also be

[16] *Platon*, I, 158 ff.

pointed out that to accuse Plato of trying to make of Dionysius a philosopher-king after the model of the philosopher-guardians in the *Republic* is to misconceive Plato's program at Syracuse. Plato's demands upon Dionysius seem to have been less exacting, and more appropriate to the realities of the case, than the above accusation assumes. But the discussion of this matter belongs in another place.

Now that we have seen how appropriate is the defense in the *Seventh Epistle* to the circumstances in which Plato found himself after the death of Dion in 353, it is clear that no reasonable ground for condemning this letter can be found in the fact that it is an apology. The criticisms to which it replies were surely as rife in the later lifetime of Plato as they were after his death, and there is no reason why Plato should not have replied to these criticisms himself, especially since they touched so closely the reputation and prestige of the Academy, and involved so gross a misunderstanding of his political views. As to the criticism of his personal motives, that alone would hardly have drawn from Plato such a prolonged defense as this; but in defending himself against the more serious charges, Plato refers incidentally and occasionally to these personal accusations. "These were the motives I had in going to Syracuse, and not the ones which some people thought" (328c); "and so I went, from motives as rational and honorable as it is possible for a man to have" (329b). The scorn expressed for the Syracusan tables and the whole manner of life at the court of Dionysius may reflect Plato's indignation at the suspicion that he went to Sicily to enjoy the luxuries to be found there (326bc). But Plato does not waste much space upon such offspring of the jealousy and cynicism of his contemporaries. He realized that the central purpose of his political and moral teaching, and the ideals that guided him and Dion in Syracuse, were in serious danger of being completely misunderstood by his friends as well as his enemies; and the importance of the issue involved called forth from him an effort that resulted in one of the most impressive of all his written compositions.

That Plato should have attempted to make this public
defense of his political philosophy as part of an answer to
the request for advice from Syracuse seems natural enough.
But it must be admitted that structurally the *Seventh Epistle*
suffers by the attempt to combine these two purposes in one
composition. The transitions from *apologia* to advice and
back again are abrupt and awkward.[17] But there is no lack of
real unity in the letter. First of all, the two subjects are in-
timately related. What would be more relevant in a letter of
advice to Dion's followers than a sketch of Plato's political
views and an account of his relations with Dion? Only thus
would the remnants of Dion's party understand what the
underlying aims of Plato and Dion had been; only thus would
they be able to act in the spirit of their dead leader. We may
infer from the opening sentences of the *Seventh Epistle* that
Plato had some doubt of the sincerity and political idealism of
the professed friends of Dion. Since Callippus, Dion's assassin,
had formerly been one of Dion's most active and trusted sup-
porters, this doubt was quite justified. We must therefore look
upon the narrative and apologetic portions of this letter as a
kind of test of the sincerity and loyalty of Dion's professed followers, or better, as a necessary propaedeutic to the understanding of the advice Plato intends to give them.[18] Likewise
what could be more relevant to a public defense of Plato's
political views than the advice he now offers to the distressed
factions at Syracuse? The middle section (330c-337e), ostensibly devoted to advice, begins with a lengthy preface explain-

[17] It is possible that in writing the *Seventh Epistle* Plato made use of
previously existing materials. Both Howald and Post assume that there
was an apologia in preparation before 354, and that this was taken up by
Plato and incorporated in the letter to the friends of Dion. Similarly the
epistemological digression may be an insertion of a lecture on learning
that Plato had given in the Academy. But there is no stylistic or other
evidence to support such theories, and they do little justice to Plato's
literary powers.

[18] This has been well brought out by Egermann (*Briefe VII und VIII*,
pp. 35-40) and by G. Hell (*Untersuchungen und Beobachtungen zu den
Platonischen Briefen* [Berlin, 1933], pp. 49-60).

ing the conditions under which Plato thinks it profitable to press his political ideas upon the leaders in political life, a preface which is even more intelligible if we refer it to the existing state of Athenian public opinion and regard it as a defense of Plato's political inactivity in his native city. Then follow a few pages of actual advice; but here also, although the words are addressed to Syracuse, they are equally intended for Plato's critics at Athens. "This advice which I am giving you now is the same advice that I gave Dion and Dionysius," Plato says; and he adds, in effect: "This is a fair sample of my political views, and it will show any fair-minded man that I am not an exponent of despotism, but hold to the traditional ideals of the free city-state." [19]

Besides this relevance of the two purposes to each other, there is a more telling unity of feeling that pervades the whole composition. The emotions aroused by the tragic death of Dion and the conditions of the Greeks in Sicily are continually coming to the surface and interrupting the regular flow of the exposition. Expressions of personal grief are constantly mingled with indignation at Dion's murderers, as men who have deprived him of a beloved friend and frustrated his hopes for the regeneration of Sicily. Such a unity of feeling and of situation, sustained for so extended a composition, is more convincing evidence that it comes from the hand of Plato than would be the more superficial unity that any student of rhetoric could have produced. As a whole the *Seventh Epistle* produces as unified an impression upon the reader as does almost any of the later dialogues; and the very inadequacy of its form to the wealth of the material it contains is, if anything, a trait that suggests the hand of Plato in his old age.

The critical reader cannot fail to observe other minuter evidences that suggest the hand of Plato. The Platonic gift of imagery and some of the familiar images are here: in the description of the constitution as straying from the path of justice (330e); in the comparison of learners who get their

[19] See especially 331d, 332e, 334cd, and 335e-337e.

opinions at second hand to men whose bodies have been tanned by the sun (340d); in the analogy between the legislator and the physician prescribing for his patients (330cd); in the picture of evil as rooted in ignorance, and bearing a fruit of bitter taste to those who have cultivated it (336b), and of knowledge as flashing up in the soul from the contact between minds, like a flame when two sticks are rubbed together (341c, 344b). One should note also the complete appropriateness of the emotions expressed, and the absence of anything like exaggeration or conventionality; the naturalness with which the advice to Dion's followers is shunted from its main course into a lamentation on Dion's death and its tragic consequences (333ab); the convincing mixture of grief and indignation that pervades the whole passage; the subtle and apparently unpremeditated manner in which Athens is defended against the dishonor done her by the deed of Callippus ("I also am an Athenian," says Plato); the sincerity of the stocktaking to which Plato subjects himself when considering the first invitation to Syracuse (328bc). How simple but eloquent is the eulogy of Socrates (324e, 325b), recalling in its restraint the closing words of the *Phaedo!* We catch glimpses of a rich experience with mankind: the desires of a young man are unstable, and may turn overnight into their opposites (328b); the presence or lack of loyal friends is the true mark of a man's character (332c); the requests of tyrants have force behind them (329d). The moral earnestness of Plato's own character shines forth in the vivid description of the young man of noble nature, born to philosophy, who hears of its aims for the first time (340cd); in the condemnation of tyranny and the man who seeks absolute power (334d); in the observation that happiness comes only from a life of wisdom and justice (335d), and that to die when aiming at high ends is noble (334e). Especially Platonic are the scornful references to the mummeries of the political clubs (333e, 334b); the many references to the part chance plays in human affairs; and the mention of the gods and other expressions of religious emotion characteristic of Plato's old age. The sustained in-

terest and dramatic suspense of the closing narrative make it
in its way the equal of anything in the dialogues; and the
clarity and straightforwardness of the whole composition,
avoiding as it does all the artifices of rhetoric, show it to be
the work of a great thinker and stylist.

The fact that we have another letter (the *Eighth*) sup-
posedly written by Plato to Syracuse at about this time has
led some scholars to the conclusion that the *Seventh* was never
sent to Syracuse at all. Harward [20] contends that the request
for advice referred to in the opening lines is a dramatic arti-
fice used to furnish a pretext for the apology and heighten its
effectiveness. Wilamowitz [21] thought the *Seventh* and *Eighth*
were written at about the same time, the *Seventh* being
intended for the whole Greek public, and the *Eighth* being the real answer to the request for advice from Syracuse.
According to Howald [22] the letter was begun as an answer to
the call for advice, but it took some time to compose, and
before it was completed Plato had received a second appeal
from Syracuse. By this time he perhaps also realized that the
lengthy apology unfitted it for the original purpose, and so
laid it aside and wrote the *Eighth* in its stead. All these views
assume that the apologetic content of the *Seventh Epistle*
makes it an inappropriate answer to Dion's distressed followers. It has already been shown, however, that the lengthy
apology is exceedingly relevant to the advice Plato thinks
Dion's followers need. It serves the purpose of showing them
what Plato's principles really are, it removes the misunder-
standings current about his relations with Dion and Dionysius,
and it thus provides the larger context in which his precepts
can best be understood. Furthermore, even if the letter was
intended to serve primarily the purposes of defense, Plato
would want it read in Syracuse as well as in Athens. Harward
argues that the comments on Syracusan luxury would hardly
be appropriate in a letter intended to be read at Syracuse.

[20] *Platonic Epistles*, pp. 189-92.
[21] *Platon*, II, 302-4.
[22] E. Howald, *Die Briefe Platons* (Zürich, 1923), pp. 28-31.

But the reform of Syracusan life was a fundamental part of Plato's political program, and a genuine letter of advice could hardly have avoided it. Howald relies largely upon certain features of the text which he takes as evidence that the composition was not put into final shape. This interpretation of the text has been disputed.[23] In some cases more accurate construing removes the stumbling block; and of the other difficulties most, if not all, can be regarded either as manuscript errors or as peculiarities of Plato's later style. There is therefore every reason to believe that the *Seventh Epistle* was actually intended for, and sent to, the persons to whom it is addressed.

THE THEORY OF KNOWLEDGE IN EPISTLE VII

The lengthy digression on knowledge in the *Seventh Epistle* (342a-344d) has usually been looked upon with especial suspicion. Though historians have ordinarily made free use of the narrative portions of this letter, in spite of the once general doubt as to its genuineness, seldom until very recently has any exponent of Plato's philosophy taken account of this passage in the *Seventh Epistle*. And yet if the letter is genuine, it tells us a great deal about Plato's views on learning and throws some light on the later stages of his theory of knowledge. The doubt which this passage arouses has proved to be more difficult to silence than the objections raised against the rest of the letter; and no less an authority than Ritter, himself one of the chief agents in bringing about the more favorable opinion that is now current with regard to the *Epistles* as a whole, has consistently maintained that this passage in the *Seventh* is spurious, an interpolation by a later hand. It goes without saying that Ritter's judgment deserves the fullest respect. Yet there are important considera-

23 Egermann, *op. cit.,* pp. 35 ff.; Werner Jaeger, in *Deutsche Litteraturzeitung,* XLV (1924), 895.

tions that he seems to have omitted in arriving at his adverse judgment; and in view of the intrinsic importance of
the passage, most recent students who have become convinced of the authenticity of the rest of the *Seventh Epistle*
have not been satisfied to let it go without a more thorough
examination than Ritter seems to have made.[1]

The chief reasons for suspecting this passage are two: the
alleged irrelevance of a discussion of epistemology in a letter
of political advice, and the un-Platonic character of the
theory of knowledge expounded. Linguistically this passage
seems of a piece with the rest of the letter, if we make due allowance for the special demands of the subject matter; and it
has evident affinities with the language of the dialogues.[2]
Ritter's judgment that the style is labored and dull will
hardly find general acceptance, and even so could be accepted
without prejudice to the authenticity of the passage, when
we realize the relatively technical nature of the questions
involved. Most of the other objections that Ritter brings up
are of a subjective character, and they can be dealt with more
satisfactorily in connection with, and incidental to, the two
major objections above mentioned.

To evaluate the alleged irrelevance of the epistemological
passage, we must realize first of all that the *Seventh Epistle* is
not merely a letter of political advice; it is also, perhaps primarily, an apologetic document, a public defense of Plato's
political views and in particular of his relations with Syracuse.[3]
One of the criticisms that he must have had to meet was the
accusation that he had not been impartial in his treatment
of Dionysius. There must have been many persons in antiquity who, like Grote in modern times,[4] felt that Plato

---

[1] Ritter, *Platons Gesetze* (Leipzig, 1896), Appendix, pp. 371 ff.; Taylor,
in *Mind*, XXI (1912), 347-70; Apelt, *Platons Briefe*, pp. 135-39; Howald,
Die Briefe Platons, pp. 33-38; Wilamowitz, *Platon*, II, 292; Julius Stenzel,
Platon der Erzieher (Leipzig, 1928), pp. 302-24; Souilhé, *Lettres*, pp. xlviii-
lviii.

[2] Ritter, *Neue Untersuchungen*, p. 404.

[3] See pp. 46 ff.

[4] *History of Greece*, chap. 84.

was too rigorous in his treatment of Dionysius, and that with more patience something might have been accomplished. We have other evidence of such criticism in the *Third Epistle*, one of the purposes of which was to defend Plato against the charge of unfair treatment of Dionysius. That letter was evidently not sufficient to quiet the accusations, and Plato (if he was the writer of the *Third Epistle*) returns to the point more fully in the *Seventh*. His critics doubtless pointed with some justification to Plato's own admission that Dionysius was not unfitted for learning (cf. 338d); to the judgment of Archedemus and others that Dionysius was making great progress in philosophy (339ab); and to the fact that he had written a book on the "first and highest principles of nature" (344d), certainly a prima facie indication of his philosophical ability. Plato would then have to defend himself by showing that he was justified in abandoning all hope of doing anything at Syracuse through Dionysius. It will readily be seen that this was a delicate point; for Plato's judgment was in conflict with that of Archedemus and other philosophical friends of his who knew the tyrant, and in defending himself Plato had to address himself to them as well as to the general public. It was no easy matter to gain his point with the larger public for whom this letter was intended without losing the confidence of his Sicilian friends.

The situation was further complicated by the fact that Plato's own philosophy had been brought into disrepute by his relations with Dionysius, and especially by the book that Dionysius was said to have written. The fact that the gifted young ruler, with apparently such a good opportunity of learning from Plato, had consistently refrained from following him, would be no great recommendation for his teaching. If the book that he wrote was, as he claimed it was, a handbook of his own composition (341b), not an exposition of Plato's teaching, then it was not only an indication of Dionysius' ability, but also a judgment upon Plato's famous doctrines, since Dionysius had so soon mastered and gone beyond them. The more discriminating group who found in

Dionysius' book nothing but the commonplaces it probably contained would likewise, for a different reason, feel some contempt for the master who had, as they believed, "inspired" the book. So for one reason or another, Plato's connection with Dionysius, coupled with Dionysius' known interest in philosophy and his apparent neglect of Plato's wisdom, would tend to discredit Plato and cause his doctrine to be misunderstood.

These, so far as we can make them out, are the complicated aspects of the situation for which Plato is writing. When we keep these facts in mind we are much better able to comprehend the whole passage from 337e to 345c, including not only the epistemological digression strictly taken, but also the preceding four pages, which lead up to it. It becomes clear why Plato gives at such length the reasons that led him, contrary to his better judgment, to return to Syracuse and make further trial of Dionysius. He takes pains to give the judgment of Archedemus and others with regard to Dionysius; and he endeavors to explain how Dionysius could have acquired this reputation for ability in philosophy. Those who talked with the young tyrant seem to have thought that he had been fully instructed in the principles of Plato's philosophy (338d), and the visit of Archytas to the court at Syracuse (338c) would have confirmed them in their opinion. But he reminds his readers that he had already shown, in his narrative of his first visit, that Dionysius had refused to be instructed.[5] Above all we understand why he details at such length the test to which he subjected Dionysius immediately after his arrival. He saw at once that Dionysius' reputed philosophy consisted only of παρακούσματα, rags and tags of doctrine that a clever man might easily pick up from casual intercourse with philosophers. But the question still remained whether Dionysius had the character or the ability for any-

---

[5] It is this situation that makes intelligible the outburst of 339a: "I am justified in telling the truth about these relations and must put up with it if anyone, after hearing what happened, despises my philosophy and esteems the tyrant's intelligence."

thing more; and to test this Plato gives him in outline a picture of the philosophical task, its purpose, its difficulties, its requirements. If a young man has an aptitude for philosophy, this preliminary account will arouse his enthusiasm and his desire for more. If not, he will be satisfied with what he has heard, deluding himself into believing that he understands it all, or excusing himself from further labor on the ground that such questions are too deep for him. The outcome of this test of Dionysius is made emphatic: Dionysius was apparently satisfied, so that this one conversation constituted all the philosophical instruction he had from Plato (341b, 345ab).

At this point begins the passage that Ritter regards as an interpolation by a later hand.[6] The writer of the letter refers to the book Dionysius is said to have written, and defends Plato against the criticism and the disrepute that might arise from the existence of this book. The course of thought from this point to the beginning of the epistemological passage is not easy to follow, but the difficulty arises, I think, from the mixture of questions that are present in the writer's mind, and with a little attention and sympathy these questions can be disentangled and the thought of the writer shown to be clear and convincing.

The first question naturally is whether this book of Dionysius is to be taken as a version of Plato's philosophy. We are told later that this book dealt with the highest principles of nature (τὰ περὶ φύσεως ἄκρα καὶ πρῶτα, 344d). It is evident from what Plato has already said of his relations with Dionysius that the young man could not have learned Plato's views on these ultimate and abstruse questions from the single conversation they had on the subject. It follows that this book, whatever it may profess to be, cannot be taken as an exposition of Plato's views. But may it nevertheless be taken as evidence of the philosophical ability of the young

---

[6] Ritter proposes to omit the portion from πάντα μὲν οὖν (341a) to ἐγὼ φράζοιμ' ἄν (345c), possibly retaining εἰ μὲν οὖν . . . πώποτε ἔτι (345a) as support for the transition.

Dionysius? Though the writer of this letter quite evidently knows of the book only from hearsay, he has no hesitation in asserting that its author knows nothing of the matters in question. The reason is that anyone who knows anything about these ultimate principles knows also that they cannot be expounded in writing like other knowledge. "There is no writing of mine [i.e. Plato's] about these matters" (341c). The only way in which they can be learned is through long association between teacher and pupil. So convinced is the writer of this that he includes in his condemnation not only Dionysius, but also anyone else who has written a book on these matters (341b).

Thus Plato's position on these two points is perfectly clear and definite. But the reader is likely to be confused because the two questions are so closely related. There are two things that arouse the writer's indignation: the idea that a commonplace book like that of Dionysius should be accepted as a reliable version of Plato's doctrine, and the idea that questions of first principles can be expounded in writing like any other subject of knowledge. The book of Dionysius would therefore arouse Plato's double indignation. But we must remember that there are really two motives in the writer's mind, if we are not to misinterpret him. Thus Plato is not really indulging in "idle and foolish boasting," as Ritter thinks, when he says: "If these matters are to be expounded at all in books or lectures, they would best come from me. Certainly I am harmed not least of all if they are misrepresented" (341d). Here he has in mind chiefly his own doctrine, especially his teaching on first principles.[7] He is hardly laying claim to being the ablest philosopher of his time, but only to being the best interpreter of his own doctrine. Kant said something similar to Fichte, it will be remembered. On the other hand, when Plato says that no one who has ever written or ever will

[7] A similar explanation can be made of ὁμοίως γὰρ ἂν ἐσέβετο ἐμοί (344d). Plato might at first seem to be claiming that any attempt to expound first principles was a personal insult. But it is his own philosophy that is uppermost in his mind, as the following sentences show.

write "on these problems with which I am concerned (περὶ ὧν ἐγὼ σπουδάζω)" really knows anything about them, we misconceive the writer's motive entirely if we think this an expression of arrogant contempt for his rivals in philosophy. It is merely an emphatic assertion that no real student of these high matters will try to put them down in a book.

There is therefore no real clumsiness nor impropriety in this passage if we read it properly, and therefore no reason on these grounds for denying that Plato was its author. Furthermore, it would have taken a very clever forger to fit this passage so aptly into the context of the preceding pages; we would almost have to assume that the preceding passage, from 337e, had been "doctored" to prepare the way for this criticism of Dionysius' book. And lastly, as a matter of personal opinion, there seems something especially suggestive of genuineness in the mixture of motives displayed in this passage. A forger would have made the situation clearer and probably less real.

The chief difficulty in accepting this passage as genuinely Platonic arises from the statement that Plato has never written about "these matters" that were the subject of Dionysius' book. Dionysius wrote on the first principles of nature. If by the first principles we are to understand the Ideas, then clearly it would be erroneous to say that Plato has nowhere dealt with them in the dialogues, and the writer of this passage could certainly not be Plato. The Plato of the dialogues, however, deliberately and repeatedly withholds the ultimate doctrines which the development of his theory of Ideas requires. The ultimate principles here referred to are more ultimate even than the Ideas. We have various hints of what Plato had in mind here. The Idea of the Good in the *Republic* is put forward as the ultimate source of all being and of all knowledge, but Socrates steadfastly refuses to state more fully the nature of the Good. We know that Plato lectured on the Good in the Academy, but we have no writing on the subject. Again we know [8] that at least in his later years Plato conceived of the generation of the Ideas, symbolized by or

---

[8] Aristotle *Met.* 987b20 ff.

identified with ideal numbers, from the One and the In-
definite Dyad; and these speculations also, we know from
Aristotle, were part of the "unwritten doctrines." It is therefore quite certain that there were in Plato's philosophy principles more ultimate than anything we find in the writings he
left behind him. And consequently the statement in the passage we are examining creates no presumption against its
Platonic authorship. On the other hand, if we take it as
genuine, together with the pages that follow, we are in a
position to understand the significance of the fact that there
were unwritten doctrines in the circle of the Academy. We
learn that these doctrines remained unwritten, not because
they were regarded as a corporate possession which it was
disloyal and perhaps sacrilegious to divulge, but because of
the intrinsic difficulty of putting them into writing, and of
learning them in any other way than by the close association
between Plato and his pupils that prevailed in the Academy.
What these difficulties were, the writer of the *Seventh Epistle*
now proceeds to explain; and in order to make the matter
perfectly clear, he feels it necessary to go into some elementary principles involved in all learning.

So much then for the alleged irrelevance of this epistemological passage. It is clear that it bears a very close connection with the larger purpose of the *Seventh Epistle*. It is carefully prepared for and it develops naturally out of the defense
of Plato's dealings with Dionysius. Let us now turn to the
other question, the alleged un-Platonic character of the theory
of knowledge this passage contains. The reader who is familiar
only with the theory of Ideas contained in the dialogues of
Plato's early maturity may feel, upon reading this part of the
Seventh Epistle, that he is in unfamiliar surroundings. None
of the old landmarks are visible at first. The words "idea"
and "dialectic" occur nowhere. The distinction between
knowledge and opinion is apparently ignored, and instead we
find an unfamiliar contrast between the τί and the ποῖόν τι
(342b and *passim*). These terms—ποῖόν τι and τί—seem to be
used in a technical sense not found elsewhere in the Platonic

writings. The place of ἐπιστήμη in the scale of knowledge is not precisely determined. We might even say it is inconsistently represented, now as on a level with opinion, now as the ultimate and highest stage of mental apprehension (342c, 343e). But these are not insuperable difficulties. We must remember that this is a composition of Plato's last years, and that the dialogues written during Plato's later years present similar difficulties of interpretation. It would be far more suspicious if this passage merely reproduced the content and emphasis of the *Phaedo* and the *Republic*. Again, the writer of this letter is as much concerned with the difficulty of teaching and exposition as with the procedure of discovering truth. In fact it would perhaps be most appropriate to call this passage a digression not on epistemology, but on learning. As it was occasioned by the report that Dionysius had written a book on the ultimate questions of philosophy, its content is determined by the writer's preoccupation with the difficulty of imparting knowledge of any kind, especially knowledge of first principles, by formal expositions of the academic sort.

With these considerations in mind, let us examine the theory of learning put forward here. If we are to grasp the nature of any object there are three instruments that must be employed: names (ὀνόματα), definitions (λόγοι), and diagrams or images (εἴδωλα). Contrasted with these instruments of learning is the object itself, the "knowable" (γνωστόν) and "truly existing" (ἀληθῶς ὄν). And distinct from both the instruments of apprehension on the one hand, and the object of apprehension on the other, is the subjective apprehension itself, appearing in the various forms of reason (νοῦς), knowledge (ἐπιστήμη), and right opinion (ἀληθὴς δόξα).[9] There are presumably important differences between these three forms of ap-

[9] There is an interesting parallel to this passage in *Laws* X, 895d ff., written probably about this time. "Would you not admit," asks the Athenian Stranger, "that there are three things involved in knowing any object, viz. the being (οὐσία), the definition of the being (λόγος τῆς οὐσίας), and the name (ὄνομα)?" For example the name "soul," he says, belongs to a certain "being" whose definition is "the motion that moves itself."

prehension; but in this context Plato is not concerned with that side of the theory of knowledge. His interest is rather in pointing out how indispensable, and yet how defective, are the three instruments of knowledge first mentioned. And the criticism that Plato develops here of these instruments of learning, and of any system of instruction which makes no provision for correcting their defects, is clear and convincing. Everyone knows that the diagrams of circles and triangles that appear in our textbooks of geometry are, if taken literally, quite misleading. They are both too crude and too specific; they are neither perfectly accurate nor perfectly general. For this reason they must be supplemented by oral explanations which direct our thought from the sensible diagram to the reality which the diagram is supposed to illustrate. But words also have limitations. Plato mentions specifically the fact that their application is a matter of convention. We might use the term "straight line" to denote the reality "circle," and the word "circle" to denote the straight line, and the nature of the things themselves would be in no way affected. This is an obvious consideration, and I think, in spite of Professor Taylor's ingenious alternative interpretation,[10] that this is the main point of the passage. Every teacher knows that one of the greatest obstacles he has to overcome in presenting his thought is that the terms he employs have different connotations, and a fortiori different associations, for every one of his students; and it is the communication of thought from teacher to pupil that Plato has here in mind. But more than this, the arbitrariness with which a certain combination of visual or auditory symbols is used to denote this rather than that, or the ease with which it may be changed to denote that rather than this, exhibits in a most startling fashion the chasm between our words and things, and between our concepts and reality, which is the chief lesson of this passage and perhaps also of all the Platonic dialogues.

The incapacity of language, especially the ordinary language of common life, to attain the end which thought sets

10 *Mind,* XXI, 361.

before itself, due to its preoccupation with the sense-world
and its consequent vagueness on ultimate matters, is a theme
which occurs often in the dialogues. Socrates in the *Cratylus*
asserts that language is a form of art, having for its aim the
correct imaging of the nature of things; but like other crea-
tions of the artist it contains much that is accidental, and
much more that is purely conventional. Besides, it has been
constructed primarily by ignorant artists, interested in the
world of becoming, instead of by the dialectician, the real
master of words, who knows how to make them image true
being. Only when the dialectician stands beside the legislator,
and the ideal language becomes current among men, will it
be possible to affirm an inner or natural connection between
our words and the realities they symbolize.[11] Although some
of the simpler fallacies that arise from the uncritical use of
language are exposed in the *Euthydemus,* it is in the *Sophist*
and *Parmenides* that we find Plato laying bare the fundamental weaknesses of all formulations of thought in words.
The *Sophist* brings to light one of the most insidious ambigui-
ties in language, the ambiguity in the verb "is," which may
be either an assertion of identity, or a mere copula of predi-
cation. This ambiguity is the source of many of the paradoxes
in the second part of the *Parmenides,* and Plato was no doubt
even then fully aware of the double meaning of the verb
εἶναι, though it is not clearly formulated. Again, most of the
difficulties connected with the doctrine of Ideas as discussed
in the first part of the *Parmenides* arise from the vagueness of
language. What is meant by the "being" of ideas, and their
separateness? Clearly not spatial or temporal being, nor
spatial separateness; but language is inherently defective when
such logical meanings are to be expressed. With these dialogues in mind we can perhaps realize something of what

---

11 *Epistle VII* is therefore in full agreement with Plato's view in the
Cratylus in so far as we can determine what that view was, instead of
being, as Karsten maintains, the work of a bungling forger who errone-
ously substitutes for Plato's opinion the position of Hermogenes that
language is purely conventional.

Plato meant in the *Seventh Epistle* when he speaks of the weakness of language. Because of its vagueness on fundamental issues, it can only with great difficulty be made a medium for the expression of precise, or "ultimate" thoughts.[12]

We are now in a position to understand the contrast between the τί (the ἀληθῶς ὄν) and the ποῖόν τι. Clearly what the soul seeks to know is what is called the "fifth," viz. the object itself (the οὐσία of the parallel passage in the *Laws*) in its absolute and essential being. The ποῖόν τι is a quality, or set of qualities, that we regard as characterizing the object. The former is the real object of the soul's quest; the latter is the first, and sometimes the only, fruit of our inquiries, because of the defectiveness of the instruments of knowledge we have to employ. The region into which these instruments first take us is the region of sense perception and of practical life, the region of unavoidable vagueness and obscurity. The goal of thought, on the other hand, is the region of absolute clarity, the realm of precise meanings. When we try to express in ordinary language this system of precise meanings we quite often make ourselves ridiculous to the ordinary man, and a clever questioner may make it appear that we know nothing about the thing we are pretending to define. A physicist or mathematician who should attempt to explain in nontechnical language the general theory of relativity could easily be made to appear entirely ignorant, so far as common experience is concerned, of what time or space is. But as Plato says, it is not the mind or knowledge of the speaker that is being shown up, but rather the inadequacies of the medium in which he is trying to impart his knowledge. These embarrassments naturally do not arise in ordinary intercourse, be-

---

[12] It is good Platonic doctrine that sense perception is inadequate to the representation of ultimate realities; but does it make sense to say, as the author of this letter does, that this inadequacy is due to the weakness of language? The answer is that Plato has special reference to the defects of written expositions or τέχναι (cf. 341b). Since in such books it is customary to employ diagrams or figures to assist the reader, it is perfectly natural that Plato should mention the image in this connection.

cause we are not aiming at precision; we are contented with
rough approximations, and we use empirical concepts that
can be easily tested by sense perception. The same thing is
true of many of our sciences, especially the descriptive sciences, and even mathematics and physics as presented to elementary students. But when we come to advanced mathematical or logical or metaphysical questions, the weakness of
language is notorious. Then we are forced to invent a mathematical or logical symbolism to express refinements of thought
which are altogether useless for everyday life, or a technical
terminology which can be learned only by long and earnest
application.[13] Such a technical philosophical terminology
must actually have been in growth at this time in the Academy, to judge from the language of the later dialogues. It was
the inevitable response to the demand for intellectual precision inherent in the doctrine of Ideas.

The distinction between the $τί$ and the $ποῖόν$ $τι$ bears an
obvious resemblance to the familiar Platonic distinction between knowledge and opinion; and we should proceed at once
to identify the two doctrines, were it not for the somewhat unusual conjunction of $ἐπιστήμη$ with $νοῦς$ and $ἀληθὴς$ $δόξα$ among
the "four" which lead us to the $ποῖόν$ $τι$ as often as to the $τί$
(342e).[14] Karsten and other critics have made much of this
apparent identification of $ἐπιστήμη$ and $δόξα$, and also of the
inconsistency in the use of $ἐπιστήμη$, which is elsewhere (343e)
used to refer to the apprehension of the $τί$. But the classing of
$νοῦς$, $ἐπιστήμη$, and $ἀληθὴς$ $δόξα$ together does not mean that the
author of this letter denies all differences between them. In
fact the Plato of the Seventh Epistle is still aware of the important differences between these three forms of mental activity, and explains that they are classed together here as

13 A contemporary analogy is the dissatisfaction of logicians with the
verbal form of propositions. A mathematical friend of mine once remarked that Russell's Introduction to Mathematical Philosophy was as
accurate as any work could be which attempts to expound such matter
in words.

14 Cf. also 343b where each of "the four" is said to be $ἀσαφές$.

being all of them ἐν ψυχαῖς, and hence distinct both from the
name, definition, and image, which are sounds or bodily
shapes, and from the ultimate object of knowledge (342c);
and in the very next sentence the difference between them is
deliberately recalled in the assertion that of these three forms
of mental apprehension,[15] νοῦς is most nearly akin to the
absolute object, the other two being more distantly related
to it. Plato's terminology is by no means fixed, and it is
hazardous to infer identity of meaning merely because of
similarity of terms; nevertheless the parallel between νόησις,
the term used in the *Republic* (VI, 511d) to denote the highest activity of mind, and νοῦς, which is here said to be nearest
the absolute object, is suggestive.[16] Here, as elsewhere in the
Seventh Epistle, the freedom in the use of terms and in the
handling of familiar Platonic distinctions is one of the most
convincing evidences of the authenticity of this letter. A forger
would have stuck more closely to the letter of the Platonic
doctrine.

There is no denying, however, that the distinction between
opinion and knowledge, though certainly implied in this passage, is present in a form somewhat altered from that in which
it appears in the dialogues of Plato's early manhood. The
realm of opinion now includes much that would have been
put, by the younger Plato, in the realm of knowledge. Though
the Plato of this letter does not deny the possibility of real
knowledge, yet it is a distant and almost unattainable ideal.
And this change here evident in the *Seventh Epistle* is just
such a change as is observable in the Platonic dialogues themselves as one passes from the *Meno,* through the *Republic,* to
the *Theaetetus, Parmenides,* and to the dialogues of Plato's
last period. In the first enthusiastic employment of the

---

[15] Τούτων is taken as referring not to τὰ τέτταρα, but to ἐπιστήμη,
νοῦς, ἀληθής τε δόξα.

[16] Cf. also τὰ νενοημένα, 343a; φρόνησις καὶ νοῦς, 344b. The use of
νοῦς as designation of the highest and sovereign intelligence is especially
marked in the latest dialogues, e.g. *Phil.* 28c, 30d; *Tim.* 51e; *Laws* VIII,
836e, XII, 961e, 963a.

Socratic method of definition, when the contrast between opinion and knowledge corresponded to the simple opposition between the uncritical attitude of ordinary experience and the scientific search for clear and distinct concepts, the realm of knowledge seemed relatively accessible. But the *Phaedo* suggests that the use of concepts and principles is for the most part hypothetical. The *Republic* outlines for the dialectician the vast labor of constructing, from the isolated principles employed by the separate sciences, an all-embracing science based upon the Idea of the Good, which will be to the lower sciences as knowledge is to opinion. The *Theaetetus* tries in vain to define knowledge; every formula by which we try to grasp it, every illustration by which we try to symbolize it, and every proposition which we cite as an instance of it, turns out to be an illustration or instance of opinion rather than of knowledge. And in the *Parmenides* we find that the realm of Ideas, which was formerly thought to be the realm of knowledge, contains the same plurality, self-contradictoriness, and relativity which characterize the world of opinion. The connecting principles are still lacking; and these first principles, we are told in the *Timaeus* (53d), are known only to God, and to those whom God loves. By a parallel development, as the realm of real knowledge receded and became in time almost unattainable for man, the world of opinion took on more and more importance in Plato's eyes. The apprehension of absolute beauty and absolute good remains as before the goal of the soul's development; but it is an experience of which but few are capable, and we must make the most of the relative goods, which are after all the shadows of the ultimate good. Plato's preoccupation with the physical world in the *Timaeus,* and with the second-best state in the *Laws,* is a sufficient indication that right opinion has taken on for him some of the value which was formerly exclusively attributed to absolute knowledge.

Consequently we should expect, in a letter written during the last years of Plato's life, a less rigorous insistence upon the distinctions in terms of which he first conceived the intellectual world. The intermediate stage to which most science belongs will appear, when looked at from the standpoint of absolute knowledge, as belonging rather to the realm of sense experience than to that of knowledge. Every science begins, and many of them end, by being a classification or systematization of sense data; and frequently the concepts by which these data are arranged are but little less gross than the particulars themselves. Science, of course, means the interpretation of the sense-world in terms of "ideas" or concepts and laws; but there are all sorts of concepts, and the sciences differ enormously in the degree of precision and refinement which their concepts possess. Those sciences that seem clearest to the ordinary man, such as geology or descriptive biology, will rank lower, if judged by strictly logical standards, than a science like physics, the concepts of which have lost almost all significance for common experience. They are the sciences in which, as the passage before us says, we are not seeking exactness, but are satisfied with the images presented to sense perception. These are ἐπιστῆμαι, after all, but ἐπιστῆμαι not far removed from δόξα when compared with the precise knowledge of ultimate realities which Plato holds up as the object of the soul's desire.[17] As contrasted with this knowledge of the τί of things, the ordinary science of the textbooks and formal lectures belongs to the realm of pseudo clarity in which the ordinary man is most at home. It is indeed science, but it by no means reaches the ultimate principles involved, and therefore fails to attain the τί which is the end of all knowledge.

This passage makes no mention of the Ideas, which are supposed to be the distinctive feature of Plato's theory of knowledge; and this failure to mention the word has sometimes been used as ground for condemning the letter, or at least this passage, as spurious. But though the word εἴδη is not used, the doctrine is distinctly implied. An attentive

---

[17] Even the mathematical sciences, according to *Republic* VII, 533d, can be called science only in deference to common usage. They ought to be called by some other name indicating that they are clearer than opinion but less clear than science.

reader cannot fail to notice that the list of things which we attempt to know by means of name, definition, and image, is strongly suggestive of the objects to which the theory of Ideas is applied in the dialogues. Mathematical concepts and ethical and aesthetic notions lead the list, just as in the dialogues they are most frequently employed to illustrate the theory of Ideas. The "artificial body" of this letter recalls the bed and table in the tenth book of the *Republic* and the shuttle in the *Cratylus*. The reference here to fire, water, and "other such things," is paralleled by the discussion of the idea of fire in the *Phaedo* and by the query concerning such natural bodies in the *Parmenides* (130c). As examples of living beings we have the horse and the man of the *Parmenides,* the natural kinds to which, according to some interpreters, Plato in his old age restricted the doctrine of Ideas.[18] The discussion in the *Phaedrus* of the systematic knowledge of the various kinds of souls which the orator must possess throws light on the ἐν ψυχαῖς ἤθη of this passage; and, lastly, the actions and affections here mentioned are dealt with, partially at least, in the later dialectical dialogues, where the distinctions and interconnections between the logical categories are first attempted. The close similarity of this list of objects to the objects which in the dialogues are said to participate in or to copy the Ideas indicates that the doctrine of Ideas is distinctly, though implicitly, presupposed. The search for definitions was of course the aim of the Socratic dialectic; the definition is the formulation in words of the idea of the reality in question; and certainly there is nothing un-Platonic in designating the scientific aspect of the doctrine of Ideas in terms reminiscent of the Socratic doctrine of concepts. It is undoubtedly true that the Idea was for Plato something more than a definition. It was an οὐσία, or a τί; but the λόγος was the indispensable means of apprehending the οὐσία. Because the Idea was something more than a definition, this method of

18 This passage therefore would seem to throw light on the question of possible modifications introduced by Plato in his theory of Ideas. See W. D. Ross, *Plato's Theory of Ideas*, pp. 141, 165-75.

definition, though essential, is not capable, as ordinarily used, of reaching the absolute realities which the soul desires. The only way in which the defects of λόγοι can be eliminated is, here as in the dialogues, through dialectic. It is only by the constant comparison, or rubbing together (τρίβειν), of names, definitions, and images, testing each in turn by the others, and not for the purpose of victory in disputation but for the sole aim of reaching truth, that the defectiveness of the four factors of knowledge previously mentioned can be removed. If we keep in mind the origin of the Platonic doctrine of Ideas in the Socratic search for definitions, and its later preoccupation with the problem of the interconnections of the Ideas with one another, we shall not be tempted to question the genuineness of this letter on the ground that it ignores, or makes light of, Plato's fundamental doctrine.[19]

But dialectic at its best is only a preparation of the mind for an "illumination" (ἔκλαμψις). Without this experience all the preceding labor is in vain; for the knowledge of the τί— or, as it is now put, the knowledge of virtue and vice, of justice and all other forms of beauty—will not be attained. The meaning of this doctrine of illumination is not necessarily to be found in mystical insight. It was the problems of the teacher that were probably in the forefront of Plato's attention here. No thought is really transferable from one mind to another. Every acquisition of knowledge by a pupil comes as

[19] Karsten (*Commentatio Critica*, pp. 198 ff.) makes the strange objection to this passage that though the author is plainly referring to the Platonic dialectic, he pictures it in terms of the eristic which Plato regarded as a counterfeit of genuine dialectic. This objection is based, it seems, partly upon a mistranslation of 343cd which would make it appear that the dialectician is the one who is victorious in discussion about absolute reality, whereas the passage really says that the ordinary questioner can make the dialectician appear ridiculous before a popular audience; and partly upon the ground that the dialectician ought to be pictured as getting along somehow without words and definitions, since Plato everywhere condemns the eristic preoccupation with words rather than with realities! This is worth referring to because it is a sample of the kind of criticism that this passage has usually received.

a result of his own effort, and culminates in an insight whereby the preceding labor suddenly assumes significance, and he "sees the subject," as we say. And real knowledge is easily distinguished from "language behavior" or from παρακούσματα, by the fact that it feeds itself, to use Plato's own phrase. The Idea takes possession of the mind and develops into a world of unforeseen consequences. Every student is familiar with the difference between this method of apprehending a truth, and the mere taking hold of it from the outside, in such a way that he must constantly refer to his teacher for interpreting it in new situations. What Plato calls illumination is essential in all real learning; but it is especially important in the apprehension of ultimate realities. Here the real learner must be something of a mystic; his soul must possess more than quickness of grasp and tenacity of memory; it must be akin to the object, because of some divine quality which it possesses; and even then it can see this reality only after a long period of preparation. Such a vision of the absolute reality cannot be communicated in words like other knowledge. It must be acquired by the individual himself, and the task of the teacher is limited to finding well-constituted natures, and giving them the preliminary dialectical preparation for the vision.[20]

If we recall the Idea of the Good in the *Republic* we shall not be astonished at this transformation of what seemed a purely logical problem into the description of a moral or aesthetic experience. There is latent mysticism here, but no more than is found in the dialogues; and this mysticism does not involve here, any more than elsewhere in Plato, a repudiation of the rational method of seeking truth in terms of Ideas. Plato is here, as always, the uncompromising rationalist; but he never believed that the goal of knowledge is a set of logical

---

[20] The same image of friction leading to the bursting out of flame is used in the *Republic* (IV, 435a) where Socrates proposes, after having drawn an outline of justice in the state, to draw a similar sketch of justice in the individual soul, and then to "rub the two images together and make justice flash out like a flame."

formulas. The ultimate object of the soul's quest is the Good, whereby he meant not simply the subordination of knowledge to morality, or of science to human welfare, but the complete contentment of the whole man—reason, imagination, and emotion—with the ultimate scheme of things. Such an experience of complete satisfaction he recognized is the privilege of the few and the gift of the gods. The *Protagoras,* with its paradoxical thesis that virtue is knowledge but cannot be taught; the *Meno,* which says that virtue can be taught, not, however, as a set of precepts received from without, but as an awakening within the soul itself; the allegory of the cave, from whose obscurity the soul has to be converted before it can see the truth, the description in the *Phaedrus* and the *Symposium* of the soul's ecstatic vision of the realm of being—all these are expressions, from different points of view, and in different contexts, of this doctrine of illumination. To such illumination Plato would not dare refuse the name of knowledge, for the reasoned and impartial pursuit of truth through dialectic is the only way the soul can be prepared for it. And yet there is something in this experience that goes beyond logic and language. "To discover the Maker and Father of this whole is a hard task, and when one has found him he cannot tell of him to all." [21]

What now is the bearing of this whole matter upon the book of Dionysius or other written expositions? Any one who has had the illumination we have just described will not venture to put his thoughts upon these high matters into writing and expose them to the envy and criticism of men; and therefore—here follows a hard saying—wherever we find a written work, whether a treatise on laws or on any other subject, we can be sure, if the author himself is in earnest, that the book does not contain his deepest thoughts on the matters he is writing about. This is an unmistakable reference to Plato's own writings, particularly to the *Laws,* which was almost certainly in process of composition at this time. Does this betray the hand of the disciple trying to defend Plato by the

21 *Timaeus,* 28c.

easy method of claiming that his critics have not had access
to his real thought? Another interpretation at least lies near
at hand. We do not need to take this passage, as Karsten
perversely does, as prescribing that Plato's works on politics
are to be taken as jests. Plato is certainly in earnest in the
attempt to portray the just state and the just soul; but all
the while, in spite of the earnestness of these "lofty speculations upon the truths of nature," we can discern a certain
Platonic irony, which recognizes the difficulty of penetrating
to the real nature of justice, and the impossibility, having
once penetrated there, of expounding the truth in anything
but imperfect figures. There seems to be here a deliberate
warning against taking too literally the images of justice
which we find in Plato's political writings, against regarding
the *Republic,* for instance, as a set of detailed and unalter-
able specifications for the perfect state, to be imposed in its
entirety upon no matter what people in no matter what age.
The temptation has always been great to take the letter,
rather than the spirit, of Plato's teaching; and no doubt this
was the habit of many of Plato's students in the Academy,
who found it difficult not only to accept the details of their
master's images of political justice, but even more to reconcile
the details of the various images with each other. Aristotle's
elaborate criticisms of isolated provisions of the *Republic,*
unaccompanied by any conception of the *geistiges Band* without which these details are unimportant, show the kind of
misunderstanding to which Plato then, as now, was subject,
and against which he is in all likelihood protesting here.

But those who still persist in regarding this passage as something which Plato could never have written will have to
reckon with the *Phaedrus* (275d-278d), where almost the same
warning is clearly sounded against the too literal reading of
works on political justice, "whether written by Lysias or anyone else." The reason for this warning in the *Phaedrus* is the
same as the reason in this passage, viz. the inadequacy of
written exposition or set lectures to the communication of real
knowledge. The written word, says Socrates, is dumb and help-

less before its questioners. It is only the image of the intelli-
gent word written in the soul of him who has learned, the
counterfeit of the living writing which feeds itself and constitutes real knowledge. Such living knowledge can be produced
only by the trained husbandman, who will choose not the hot-
house method of written exposition, but the slower method of
dialectic. The only justification for writing at all is to guard
against the forgetfulness of old age, and to recall the details
of a previous dialectical inquiry.[22] The Socrates of the
Phaedrus then comes to the identical conclusion we have
here: in view of the difficulty of distinguishing between
dream and reality in connection with such matters as justice
and the good, no serious student of such matters is going to
expose his deepest thoughts to the misunderstanding and
jealousy of men. Therefore any political work, whether of
Lysias or anyone else, is bound to contain a great deal that is
"not serious." Plato could hardly refer to his own writings
more directly. Finally, the concluding sentences in the epistemological passage in the *Seventh Epistle* contain a clear
allusion to the "madness" which Socrates experienced when
delivering the *Phaedrus* myth: If any man has written his
ultimate thoughts on these matters, it is an indication of
madness—not, however, the divine mania of the philosopher,
but the raving of the demagogue.

EPISTLE VIII

The existence of two letters of advice from Plato to Dion's
followers in Syracuse is not in itself surprising and furnishes
no ground for suspecting either the Platonic authorship or
the *bona fides* of either letter.[1] A careful examination shows

---

[22] This justification of writing is mentioned in *Epistle
VII*, 344d, where the supposition that Dionysius wrote for the sake of remembering Plato's conversation is promptly rejected.

[1] See pp. 59 f.

that the situation at Syracuse presupposed by the *Eighth Epistle* is appreciably different from that implied in the *Seventh*.[2] The *Seventh* was written, as we have seen, shortly after the assassination of Dion by Callippus in 354, and the request for advice to which it was an answer was probably sent out by Dion's followers before they had fled from Syracuse to Leontini. The *Eighth* is clearly an answer to a second request, sent out after the expulsion of Callippus from the city by the joint efforts of Dion's party and Hipparinus, the half brother of Dionysius II. There is a reference to the assistance which Hipparinus has just rendered (356a) to Dion's followers and to Syracuse, which would seem to refer to his help in driving out Callippus. Hipparinus is said to be a man of "upright (ὅσιος) character" (356a); but Athenaeus tells us, on the authority of Theopompus, that Hipparinus turned out to be a drunken tyrant and was later assassinated,[3] so that this term would scarcely have been applied to him except at the beginning of his power. We can therefore safely ascribe this letter to the period immediately following the overthrow of Callippus, i.e. thirteen months after the death of Dion. There is a noticeable difference in tone between this letter and the preceding. Whereas the *Seventh* contains numerous references to the death of Dion, and repeated expressions of the writer's grief and disappointment, the *Eighth* makes only one incidental reference to Dion's death (357a), and the tone is considerably calmer, which would indicate that some time has elapsed since the composition of the earlier letter. Lastly, the political prospects seem to be decidedly more encouraging. Factional strife has been to some extent replaced by co-operation, and Dion's party in alliance with Hipparinus seems in a fair way to dominate the situation and bring about a reasonable settlement.

In style and diction this letter is of a piece with the *Seventh;* and what was said on that point in a previous chapter [4] ap-

2 Egermann, *Briefe VII und VIII*, pp. 17 f.

3 Athen. 436a; cf. also Aelian *V. H.* II, 41.

4 See pp. 10 ff.

plies equally here. But this letter has frequently been questioned because of certain historical inaccuracies it is said to contain. The first and most formidable arises from the reference to Dion's son, who is to be made one of the three co-ordinate kings (355e). This not only presupposes that this son is alive, but since it is further said that he and Hipparinus, the son of Dionysius I, may come to an agreement (357c), the presumption is that the writer of this letter believes him to be the leader (or one of the leaders) of Dion's party. Now according to the historical tradition there were only two sons of Dion. The first is said by Plutarch (*Dion* 55) and by Nepos (*Dion* 4 and 6) to have committed suicide shortly before Dion's assassination; and the second son was born shortly after the death of Dion (Plutarch, *Dion* 57), and must therefore have been an infant at the time this letter was written. Thus neither of these sons seems to fit the references in this letter. Post [5] indeed sees no difficulty in assuming that the son of Dion whom the writer of *Epistle VIII* has in mind is the infant son born after Dion's death. But apart from the strangeness of making a child of less than two years a king along with Dionysius II and his half brother Hipparinus, there is what seems to me the insuperable objection that this son and Hipparinus are spoken of as having in mind the plans that Plato proposes and as capable of agreeing upon them (357bc), which is language hardly appropriate if one of the persons concerned is a child of this age. Thus we seem to have an outright contradiction between the historical tradition and the statements of this letter.

To account for this contradiction we may assume, with Ritter,[6] that Plato had not heard of the death of Dion's son when he wrote this letter; but this assumption seems extremely unlikely in view of the positive statement that the two men have these plans in mind, which seems to imply, as do the

[5] *Thirteen Epistles,* p. 156, followed by Souilhé, *Lettres,* p. lxiv.

[6] *Neue Untersuchungen,* p. 406; R. S. Bluck, *Plato's Seventh and Eighth Letters* (Cambridge, 1947), pp. 165, 170. See also *Class. Quart.,* Harward, XXII (1928), 151 ff.; and Post's reply, XXIV, 113 ff.

other details of this letter, rather accurate information on the writer's part about the course of events. The assumption of Grote and Wilamowitz that there was still another son of Dion not mentioned by any of our authorities brings us into. conflict with the *Seventh Epistle,* which on two occasions (345c, 347d) refers to the son of Dion under circumstances that clearly imply there was only one son at the time of Plato's last visit. There remains the possibility that the story of the death of Dion's son, as we have it in Plutarch and Nepos, is false; and this last view is, all things considered, the most plausible.

In the first place, the setting of the story as given by these two authors is suspicious. Plutarch prefaces it with an account of a dreadful apparition seen by Dion—the vision of a tall woman dressed like one of the Furies, with a broom in her hand, sweeping the house clean—and relates the tragic event as the partial fulfillment of this ill omen. Nepos gives the story as an illustration of the fickleness of Fortuna, who having recently brought Dion to the summit of success now dashes him into the abyss of misfortune. These embellishments show that whatever core of truth there was in the story had been seized upon for edification by later editors of it. And the core itself is subject to doubt. We should note the way in which the alleged suicide of Dion's son advanced the schemes of Dion's political enemies. The conspirators against him spread abroad the rumor that Dion, being now childless (this in itself would be damaging to Dion's prestige with the people), was planning to send for Dionysius' son Apollocrates and make him his heir. It is easy to imagine that this story, or something like it, was a part of the plans of the conspirators (a suggestion originally put forward by Reinhold and since taken up by Hackforth and Egermann),[7] and since

[7] H. Reinhold, *De Platonis Epistulis Dissertatio* (Quedlinburg, 1886), pp. 9-18; R. Hackforth, *The Authorship of the Platonic Epistles* (Manchester, 1913), pp. 136-39; Egermann, *Briefe VII und VIII,* p. 51; see also Giorgio Pasquali, *Le Lettere di Platone* (Florence, 1938), pp. 23 ff., and for criticism of this hypothesis, Bluck, *ibid.,* pp. 165 ff.

the conspiracy was successful the story may have gained considerable currency among the public at Syracuse. Once it had received the moralistic embellishments with which it has been transmitted to us, its life would be assured. The fact that this story contradicts the statements of the *Eighth Epistle* could easily be overlooked by Plutarch and Timaeus (if he is the common source followed by Plutarch and Nepos),[8] since the discrepancy is not one that would be detected without a very careful reading of the letter. If furthermore this son died shortly afterwards, without accomplishing anything worthy of note, there would be no other remembered facts with which it conflicted. All things considered it seems wisest to place our reliance upon the *Eighth Epistle* rather than upon the questionable tradition that has come down to us through Nepos and Plutarch. This would be advisable even if we did not think the *Eighth Epistle* comes from Plato's own hand; for its style and diction show it to be a contemporary, or nearly contemporary, document, and it gives every evidence of having been written by someone very closely connected with the Platonic circle and very well informed about Sicilian events.

Dion's son is not given a name in the *Eighth Epistle,* but there can be no doubt that he was named Hipparinus, after his grandfather; although to avoid confusion with the other Hipparinus, the son of Dionysius I, he seems to have been sometimes called Aretaeus, after his mother Arete.[9] The opening sentence of the *Seventh Epistle* mentions a Hipparinus who is said to be the same age as Dion was when Plato first went to Sicily, viz. about twenty years old, and it is natural to conclude that this Hipparinus, though not called the son of Dion in *Epistle VII,* is the unnamed son of Dion in

8 I suspect that Theopompus played a part in giving this story currency, for one of the numerous digressions in his *Philippica* was a book on Marvels (θαυμάσια). Plutarch's account of the portents accompanying the start of Dion's expedition is explicitly drawn from Theopompus (*Dion* 24), and his story of the apparition that appeared to Dion (*Dion* 55) may come from the same source.

9 Plut. *Dion* 31.

Epistle VIII. If so, he was old enough to be a leader of Dion's party and to play the role that Plato designs for him as one of the three kings. This identification has indeed been disputed; [10] but the fact that Plato does not explicitly call him Dion's son in *Epistle VII* is no real objection, since the other Hipparinus had not then allied himself with Dion's party. Besides, there are difficulties in assuming that the reference is to the other Hipparinus, the son of Dionysius and Aristomache. For we learn from Diodorus (XIV, 44, 8) that the marriage of Dionysius and Aristomache took place in 398, whereas we must assume that this Hipparinus was born about 373 if he was twenty years old at the date of the *Seventh Epistle,* and this seems quite unlikely, to say the least. The identification of the Hipparinus of *Epistle VII* with the son of Dion in *Epistle VIII* seems therefore fairly certain,[11] and serves to confirm the reliability of the latter epistle.

Another historical inaccuracy that has been alleged in this letter is the role ascribed to the elder Hipparinus in the days of Dionysius I. According to this letter he was chosen along with Dionysius as στρατηγὸς αὐτοκράτωρ, general with absolute power (353ab); but Diodorus, who is our chief and almost our only authority for this period, makes no mention of Hipparinus in his account of the rise of Dionysius (XIII, 94). There was more to be said, however, than Diodorus gives us; for Aristotle (*Politics* 1306a1) says that Hipparinus was instrumental in putting Dionysius in power; and Plutarch (*Dion* 3) says that Hipparinus was joint ruler with Dionysius (Διονυσίῳ συνάρξαντος) when the latter was first made στρατηγὸς αὐτοκράτωρ. The further detail that Hipparinus was made elder and counselor (σύμβουλος καὶ πρεσβύτερος) to his younger colleague adds verisimilitude to the account in *Epistle VIII.*[12]

[10] Post, *Thirteen Epistles,* p. 157.

[11] For a fuller discussion of the identity of this Hipparinus see Egermann, *op. cit.,* pp. 48-51.

[12] Novotoný aptly calls attention to the references in Thucydides (II, 85, 1; III, 76; VIII, 39, 2; cf. Diod. XII, 79, 2) to the Spartan custom of appointing counselors (σύμβουλοι) to their commanders; and that these

Again there is some doubt of the accuracy of the statement that the ten generals immediately preceding Dionysius were stoned to death by the Syracusan populace (354d). Diodorus mentions the deposition of these generals after the fall of Acragas to the Carthaginians which they had failed to prevent, and he describes the heated meeting of the assembly in which they were violently denounced by Dionysius, who urged that the forms of law be dispensed with and that they be punished forthwith (XIII, 91-92); but he says nothing of their being stoned to death. There can be no doubt that this is the occasion to which the *Eighth Epistle* refers, and the disregard of legal process which Dionysius urged upon the assembly may actually have marked the deposition and punishment of these generals. But the judgment of Grote that the version of the action given by Diodorus is the more probable seems sound.[13] The writer of this letter has simply confused two similar events. At an angry meeting of the assembly at Acragas in the early days of the siege of the city, four of the city's generals were in fact put to death by stoning and without legal judgment in the manner Plato describes.[14] Since both these events occurred in 406, more than fifty years before this letter was written, Grote calls the writer's error "a fault of memory, both conceivable and pardonable."

The only other objection of this sort to the *Eighth Epistle* is the apparent divergence between the account of Lycurgus given in 354b and the parallel account in the *Laws* (III, 691e ff.). But in this letter Plato is simply following the time-honored Greek tradition that looked upon Lycurgus as the author of the entire Spartan constitution, whereas we have in the *Laws* a more careful historical statement of the successive steps by which the Spartan constitution assumed its fourth-century form. It would have been an irrelevant parade of accuracy to say that Lycurgus instituted only the Spartan

---

counsclors were also called elders (πρεσβύτεροι) is shown by Thuc. V, 65, 2.

[13] *History of Greece*, chap. 71 (Everyman's Libr. edn., X, 393n).
[14] Diod. XIII, 87.

gerusia, when Plato's main point is to illustrate the possibility of changing the government of Syracuse from an unstable tyranny to a stable constitutional kingship. And on the
central doctrine of the evils of absolute power and the necessity of making law sovereign in the state, the thought of the
Eighth Epistle is identical with that of the *Laws.*

I have treated elsewhere [15] at greater length the political
doctrines of this epistle, and shown their complete agreement
with the principles set forth in the *Laws.* Since we have found
that the objections to this letter on the ground of historical
inaccuracies either cannot be sustained or are easily explained
without prejudice to its authority, there is no further reason
for refusing to regard it as a genuine letter of Plato's, and at
the same time as a historical document of immense value, since
it contains the only contemporary evidence we have as to the
course of events in Syracuse immediately after the death of
Dion. And for the student of Plato it gives a firsthand picture
of what we are convinced, from the influence of the Academy
in Greek political life and from the temper and preoccupations of the author of the *Laws,* must often have happened: it
shows us the most eminent thinker in Greece bringing all the
resources of his knowledge and his eloquence to bear upon
the concrete problems of Greek political life.

EPISTLE III

This letter stands next to the *Seventh* and *Eighth* in importance as a source of information regarding Plato's relations
with Syracuse. If genuine, it must have been written sometime
shortly after Plato's return from his second journey to the
court of the younger Dionysius. There is a reference (315e) to
an assertion of Dionysius that Plato and Dion are attempting
to deprive him of his kingdom; and this indicates that the
letter was written sometime between Dion's declaration of hos-

15 See pp. 181 ff.

tility (*VII*, 350c), and the triumphant conclusion of his expedition. Like the *Seventh*, this letter is a defense of Plato and
is obviously intended for a larger audience than Dionysius, to
whom it is addressed. The defense presented in the letter is a
double one (316b). Plato, if he is the author, defends himself
first against Dionysius' charge that he had discouraged the
tyrant from liberalizing the government of Syracuse and resettling the Greek cities in Sicily—policies that were responsible for a great part of Dion's popular strength. Secondly, he is
answering the charge, brought by Philistus and others (315e),
that he was responsible for Dionysius' political acts. The
former charge is evidently a recent invention of Dionysius, or
so it is represented; for it seems to have just come to the ears
of Plato through some of the ambassadors at the court in
Syracuse (315c). The latter charge is of longer standing. It had
been first brought against Plato probably during his first visit
to the court of Dionysius the Younger. These two charges are
closely related, both of them concerned with Plato's official
position and political aims at Syracuse. The more recent
charge, which was the immediate occasion of the letter, naturally suggests the older accusations (315e), and it is natural
that Plato, or an apologist for Plato, should attempt to deal
with them both in the same letter. Let us see whether these
accusations are consistent with the historical circumstances as
we know them from other sources, and whether the defense
that is offered is one that Plato would be likely to make. The
Seventh Epistle is taken as an authentic document, and hence
as the most important single source to guide us in these inquiries.

When Dionysius II came to the throne in 367, the outlook
was very promising for those in Syracuse who hoped for a lib-
eralization of the government. The young tyrant celebrated
his accession to power by a three-year exemption from taxes
and by the release of many political prisoners. The recall of
Philistus, who had been banished by the elder Dionysius, was
another evidence of the intention of the new tyrant to govern
more liberally than his father had done. The invitation to

Plato and the enthusiastic reception given him on his arrival
would still further raise the hopes of the population for relief
from the tyranny. But this promising beginning was, as we
know, soon belied. Dion's banishment, and the more and
more repressive and arbitrary measures of Dionysius, showed
that some influence was at work with the tyrant to turn him
aside from his earlier more liberal views. Now Plato was, next
to Dion, the most influential person at court during the first
months of Dionysius' reign; and in spite of the estrangement
between Plato and Dionysius that began with the banishment
of Dion, they no doubt continued to be known as intimate
friends. Even on Plato's second visit, after the final collapse of
all his efforts to bring about a reconciliation between Dion
and Dionysius, and the consequent rupture of relations between the tyrant and himself, they were known to all the
world, he says, as ἑταῖροι (VII, 348a). In such a situation the
enemies of Plato, led by Philistus, would have abundant opportunity of throwing upon the philosopher a great part of
the blame for the unpopular measures of Dionysius. Though
they themselves were the real enemies of liberal government
they could, by picturing Dionysius as the obedient pupil of
Plato, throw upon Plato the odium of those measures that
might happen to be unpopular.

That this is actually what occurred in Syracuse there can be
little doubt. Plato himself refers to his unpopularity with the
mercenaries of Dionysius (VII, 350a). Probably they believed
he had recommended the reduction of their pay, against which
they had mutinied (VII, 348a). It is quite probable that other
unpopular measures adopted by Dionysius more directly affecting the people in Syracuse were attributed to Plato's influence. It must be remembered also that Plato was an Athenian,
and the memories of the great Athenian expedition against
Syracuse in the preceding century were still no doubt very
much alive.[1] It needs little imagination to see that Philistus

[1] This suspicion of Athens is clearly reflected in the Seventh Epistle.
Though Dion was slain by Athenians, Plato would have the Syracusans
also remember that an Athenian was Dion's truest friend (333d-334c).

and his party would exploit this distrust of Athens for the purpose of discrediting Plato and Plato's policies with the citizens of Syracuse.

So much for the earlier accusations to which the *Third Epistle* is an answer. As to Dionysius' personal grievance, that Plato had ever been partial to Dion and Dion's friends, there is little need to elaborate upon the evidence. It is a charge which upon the face of things is a natural one to bring. If more than one later historian has been inclined to criticize Plato for his unfair discrimination against Dionysius in favor of Dion, so Dionysius' friends and contemporaries would be even more disposed to find fault with Plato's attitude toward Dionysius. We find evidences of such criticisms in the *Seventh Epistle*,[2] and if Plato found it necessary or advisable to reply to such criticisms in 352, there would be nothing strange in the fact that he had essayed a shorter defense against the same charges in a letter written three or four years earlier. The specific complaint of Dionysius that occasions the letter, viz. that Plato had discouraged him from resettling the Greek cities and reforming his government—points that were cardinal in Dion's program—is only an aspect of the larger grievance that Dionysius had; and it would be a mistake to deal with it apart from the larger context of jealousy and misunderstanding that prevailed between Dionysius and Dion.

These are the charges against Plato presupposed by this letter, and it is clear that they fit very plausibly into the historical context, even where their existence is not supported by independent positive evidence. The writer's answer to these charges takes the natural course of giving a circumstantial account of Plato's relations with Dionysius, so as to show first of all the very modest part that Plato had taken in Dionysius' government, and secondly, the reason why he espoused Dion's cause so persistently in opposition to the wishes and the inter-

---

Again he advises the followers of Dion to summon to their aid all men interested in the restoration of Sicily, not distrusting Athens, "for Athens also has citizens pre-eminent in virtue" (336c).

[2] See pp. 54 f., 61 f.

ests of Dionysius. The writer insists that Plato's collaboration
with Dionysius in the affairs of government was limited to a
period at the very beginning of his association with Dionysius,
when he "thought he could do some good" (316a). He does
not specify what forms this collaboration took, except that,
beside certain other minor matters (ἄλλα τε βραχέα), Plato
worked on the composition of "preambles to the laws" (τὰ περὶ
τῶν νόμων προοίμια, 316a). What these preambles are is shown
by *Laws* IV, 719 ff., where Plato maintains that the wise legislator, in dealing with free citizens, will use persuasion as well
as command and preface his laws with exhortation and explanation. What are the laws for which Plato in 367 could
have been preparing such "preambles"? Possibly specific legislation which he hoped to see promulgated in Syracuse and
Sicily. Some of it may have been used, as Meyer thinks,[3] in the
constitutions of Phoebia and Tauromenium, two Sicilian cities
that Dionysius resettled in 358 and 357.[4] The information as
to Plato's political activities at Syracuse given in this passage
is of considerable interest and importance, if true; and there
is nothing in the historical context to lead us to suspect that it
is not true. In any event, the writer insists that Plato's respon-

[3] *Geschichte des Altertums,* V, 510.
[4] L. A. Post in *Transactions of the American Philological Association,*
LX (1929), pp. 5-24, has called attention to the fact that in *Laws* IV,
722cd, the whole of the preceding discussion is referred to as "preludes to
laws" (προοίμια νόμων); and he advances the theory that Plato in *Epistle
III* is referring to the composition of these early books of the *Laws.* In
support of this theory he shows that the contents of these books are particularly relevant to the needs of Dionysius and to the special difficulties
confronting Plato in Syracuse. But would the composition of these books
be cited by Plato as an instance of his political collaboration with Dionysius? Furthermore, the preambles referred to in *Epistle III* are said to have
been revised by Dionysius and his associates (316a). The writer of *Epistle
III* cannot then be referring to *Laws* I-IV in their present form. There is
nothing to preclude our supposing, however, that much of the material
included in the προοίμια composed at Syracuse was later used in the
Laws; and I agree with Post that these relations with Dionysius throw
considerable light on the special contents of these introductory books.

sibility for Dionysius' government was thus strictly limited. And after a short lapse of time, viz. after the banishment of Dion (which we are told in *Epistle VII*, 329c, occurred the fourth month after Plato's arrival), even this amount of collaboration was withdrawn, and Plato devoted all his efforts to reconciling Dion and Dionysius (316de).

Now we come to the second and more serious accusation against Plato: his siding with Dion rather than with Dionysius, and the unfairness of his treatment of Dionysius. It is evident that Plato's very refusal to have anything more to do with Dionysius' government until Dion was recalled would be taken as evidence of his partiality for Dion. Hence the writer endeavors to show that Plato was right in refusing any further part in the government (316b). There seem to be several lines of defense running through the indignant narrative of the following pages. First, the writer emphasizes the contrast between the characters of Dionysius and Dion—the former youthful, inexperienced in government, weak and vacillating, under pressure from all sides to live a life of luxury and excess; and Dion, of mature age, experienced in political affairs, and confirmed in his sobriety and moderation. It was the presence of Dion at court that made it seem possible to Plato in the first instance that a reform could be accomplished at Syracuse; and with him gone, and Dionysius surrounded by cabals of selfish politicians, what hope was there (316c-e, 317cd)? Again, the writer emphasizes the ties of friendship between Plato and Dion: would not any true friend have persistently endeavored to secure justice for Dion? It would have been a disgrace if Plato had been seduced by Dionysius' power or money to desert his friend in misfortune (316e, 318d). The estrangement that arose between Plato and Dionysius was the consequence of Dionysius' refusal to give Dion justice (318de); and this estrangement itself would be an insuperable barrier to any effective collaboration between them in political matters (316d, 318e). Lastly, on the specific charge that Plato had dissuaded Dionysius from reforming his government and resettling the Greek cities, the writer of *Epistle III* refutes Dionysius out of his own mouth, by reminding him of a memorable occasion on which he had asserted, in the presence of two witnesses whose names are given, that when Plato first came to Sicily he had urged the resettling of the Hellenic cities (319ab). The incident is the more telling as an answer to the charge against Plato in that Dionysius is said to have brought the question up himself in order to discredit Plato's political wisdom. Evidently on this occasion he is contemptuous of the value of this advice; but it is defended as the best thing that could have been done for Syracuse and all Sicily (319b,d). The writer's purpose in introducing this incident is clear enough: the fact that Dionysius had once cited this advice in order to discredit Plato affords a convincing answer to his later effort to discredit Plato by charging that he had advised the contrary. The point of the incident has sometimes been overlooked because of the fact that the writer, having established his contention, goes farther and adds the sequel to the remarks just quoted, since they throw an interesting light upon the character of Dionysius. Plato asked the tyrant if this was the whole of the advice he had given him. Dionysius replied, with considerable contempt and scorn, that Plato had also advised him to get an education before he undertook these projects. And that meant, he added, that he was to study geometry. This account tells us that Plato wanted to reply, probably to correct this inadequate statement of the training he thought Dionysius needed (cf. *Ep. VII*, 331de), but kept silent for fear he would not be allowed to depart from Syracuse. The remark is evidently cited in order to show the insolence of Dionysius' nature, and his scorn and contempt for Plato's principles. This "hybris" has brought its own retribution in the imminent collapse of Dionysius' power (319b). The writer then challenges Dionysius to deny the truth of the incident he has just narrated; and affirms that he could provide many more such proofs of the fact that Plato had constantly urged these political reforms, and that Dionysius had been unwilling to undertake them (319d).

In spite of the complexity of this apologia, it is intelligible and plausible enough when analyzed, and seems to fit very naturally into the situation that came about after the final rupture between Plato and Dionysius and the commencement of Dion's expedition.

Indeed, when we consider this situation, we can see why this letter of apology should have been written at just this time. It is clearly an open letter, and quite probably there was a political purpose behind it. We know that the real basis of Dion's prospects of expelling Dionysius from Syracuse lay in the popular indignation against Dionysius and the general confidence in Dion's liberal ideas. This popular support of Dion could not fail to be increased by a letter such as this, showing that Dionysius must bear all the blame for the mal-administration of his empire, and removing any doubts that might be felt with regard to Dion because of his known devo-tion to the principles of Plato. The exhibition of Plato's real fidelity to Dion through all these years, and the striking con-trast that is drawn between the abilities and characters of Dion and Dionysius, would be especially pertinent if this let-ter was written for the purpose of strengthening Dion's popu-larity at Syracuse. And the fact that it is presumably an open letter explains why the writer takes pains to narrate events which of course are well known to Dionysius. This narration would bring out clearly the faults of character which pre-vented him from securing Plato's confidence. To those with whom Plato's word carried any weight there could be no stronger inducement offered for espousing Dion's cause than this deliberate pronouncement that Dionysius was incapable of rescuing Syracuse from bondage and Sicily from the Cartha-ginians. There may have been many Greeks, both at Syracuse and elsewhere, who favored leaving Dionysius in possession of Syracuse, in the hope that he might some day realize the promise of the opening months of his reign, rather than take part in a revolution that would involve, even if ultimately successful, an intervening period of confusion and disorder. And a letter like this from Plato would be a powerful help to Dion's cause. Nor is there any inconsistency in assuming that

Plato would write such a letter after his refusal (*VII*, 350cd) to take an active part in Dion's expedition. If the *Fourth Epistle* is genuine, we know that Plato did follow with great eagerness the progress of Dion's adventure. In any case it hardly needs to be proved that once Dion had committed his life and his fortunes to the overthrow of Dionysius, Plato would not maintain the role of a disinterested bystander, but would do what he honorably could to assist the enterprise, both because of his long-standing friendship with Dion, and because of his interest in the welfare of Sicily.

In style and diction this letter closely resembles *Epistles VII* and *VIII*, as has been shown by Ritter,[5] who accepts it as genuine. But Adam, and later Pavlu and Hell,[6] have found this very resemblance suspicious; this letter contains so many similarities of phraseology with passages elsewhere in Plato—it is almost a mosaic of such reminiscences, says Hell [7]—as to suggest the hand of a very clever imitator rather than that of Plato himself. But this suggestion is not an assured inference, for it is at least possible that Plato in writing this letter should have "borrowed" from himself,[8] and it is quite probable that in writing another letter of defense in 352 he should have employed terms, phrases, and sequences of thought that he had already used in this earlier apologia. When looked at from this point of view, these similarities are much less startling in their implications.

In the narrative parts of this letter the writer introduces matter not mentioned in *Epistle VII*, and there is a marked freedom in the handling of details that are common to the two letters. The prooemia to the laws (316a) are not men-

---

[5] *Neue Untersuchungen*, pp. 410-15.

[6] Adam, *Archiv*, pp. 31 ff.; Josef Pavlu, *Mitteilungen des Vereins klassischer Philologie in Wien*, VIII (1931), 19-35; Hell, *Untersuchungen und Beobachtungen*, pp. 30-33.

[7] *Ibid.*, p. 32.

[8] A notorious case of such borrowing from himself is ἴττω Ζεύς in *Epistle VII*, 345a; cf. *Phaedo* 62a.

tioned in *Epistle VII* nor elsewhere in the *Epistles*.[9] That letters were written from Sicily to many of Plato's friends in 361 endeavoring to persuade Plato to return to Syracuse (317bc) is not specifically stated in *VII*, though it may be a fair inference from what is there said. The protests ascribed to Plato in the same passage in *III*, especially his distrust of the character of Dionysius, are not mentioned in *VII*. According to *III*, 317e, when Plato did return to Syracuse one of the first things he did was to demand the return of Dion from exile; this is not told in *VII*. There appears to be a discrepancy between *III*, 318a, and *VII*, 346-347; in *VII* Dionysius promises Plato that if he will stay the year out he will send all Dion's property to the Peloponnesus to be held in trust for him by Plato and his friends, and only after he has secured Plato's promise to remain does he change his promise to the form given here, viz. that one half of Dion's property is to be retained in Syracuse for Dion's son, the other half to be sent to Corinth. But the version in *III* could easily be only a condensed account of the lengthy negotiations that must have taken place; as the writer of this letter says, he has not space to recount all the promises that Dionysius made (318b). This freedom in the treatment of the same events seems as consistent with the hypothesis that both letters come from the hand of a man who has had a part in them, as with the theory that the writer of one of them is dependent entirely on matter he found in or inferred from the other.

Adam thinks the incident told in 319a is a confused combination of two incidents in *VII*, 349a and 349e. According to

---

[9] Adam indeed thinks that this detail in *III* is a construction based on the caution of *VII*, 344c, against taking seriously any man's writings on laws, and on the scorn Plato expresses in 341b ff. for the book Dionysius is reported to have written. But this book of Dionysius is said (344d) to have dealt not with laws, but with the first principles of nature; and furthermore Plato declares that there is no writing of his own on the subject dealt with by Dionysius. It is difficult to believe that the writer of *III* could have been such a bungler as he would have had to be on Adam's hypothesis.

III Dionysius accuses Plato, in the presence of Archedemus and Aristocritus, of favoritism toward Heraclides and the other persons opposed to Dionysius. This conversation, we are told, took place "in the garden," about twenty days before Plato's final departure. According to *VII*, 349e, this accusation is brought when Plato is at the home of Archedemus, not in the garden, where Plato was no longer living. What did take place in the garden is the dramatic incident told in *VII*, 348a-d, when Theodotes secures from Dionysius a promise to spare the life of Heraclides, and later appeals to Plato as a witness of this agreement. But why need we assume that the writer of *III* has either of these incidents in mind? Dionysius' reproach that Plato was on the side of Dion and Dion's friends probably was brought up more than once between them. And Plato apparently lived in the garden for some time (*VII*, 347a), so that there is no need to identify the conversation in 319a with the incident in 348a-d. Indeed the incidents described in the two letters seem to be different. In *VII* Theodotes is present, and on the next day Theodotes and Eurybius; in *III* the witnesses are Archedemus and Aristocritus. Since the conversation in *III* mentions Heraclides, it is quite probable that this scene took place after, perhaps very shortly after, Heraclides' treachery; and therefore would follow the dramatic incident in *VII*. If this is true, Plato's dismissal from the garden, his sojourn among the mercenaries, his appeal to Archytas at Tarentum, the sending of a τριακόντορος from Tarentum to Syracuse, and Plato's departure from Syracuse, all took place within the space of twenty days. This is certainly not impossible. The distance from Syracuse to Tarentum is about three hundred miles. With favorable wind and weather, ancient sailing vessels could travel four to six knots, and there are many recorded cases of speeds as high as six to eight knots.[10] At the slowest of the above speeds, and sailing only by day, computing a day's sail to be fifteen hours long,[11] a sailing vessel could reach Tarentum from Syracuse in about four

---

[10] A. Köster, *Das antike Seewesen* (Berlin, 1923), pp. 177 ff.

[11] *Ibid.*, p. 179.

days. By using rowers and traveling at night, one could no doubt cut this time in half, if there was need for speed, as there was in this case.

Thus the author of this letter cannot be properly charged either with slavish dependence upon *Epistle VII,* or with introducing material inconsistent with it. But there are other features mentioned by critics which cannot be so objectively disposed of. One is the parallel between the double defense presented here and the double defense that Socrates is described as making in the *Apology.* In both cases the defendant answers a recent charge by connecting it with another accusation of longer standing, and in both cases prefers to meet the older charge first. Add to this the fact that the colloquial ὦ τᾶν of 319a occurs nowhere else in Plato except in *Apology* 25c, and it is difficult not to infer the hand of an imitator. Yet it is certainly not impossible that Plato, having resolved to write a public letter of self-defense, should have remembered his earlier defense of Socrates and adopted a similar order of thought. Finally, the "silly" introduction, as Gomperz called it,[12] with its play on Plato's well-known use of the salutation εὖ πράττειν instead of the customary χαίρειν, hardly seems to be the kind of beginning that Plato would have chosen for a serious apologia against charges that touch his honor and his integrity as deeply as do those dealt with in this letter. Yet again it must be remembered that a reference to the salutation occurs not only in the doubtful *Epistle XIII,* but also in the generally accepted *Epistle VIII;* and such references may have become a kind of mannerism in Plato's correspondence.[13]

One thing is clear: if this letter is a rhetorical exercise, the writer has shown unusual skill in connecting it with the historical situation and bringing to the front the special nature of Plato's interest in the events in Sicily. We have examples of such rhetorical exercises in *Epistles I* and *II,* if the view to be advanced later is correct. These letters make but vague references to actual events, and they picture Plato's relations with

12 *Archiv für Geschichte der Philosophie,* XXV (1912), 472.
13 See pp. 106 f., and the note on this passage in the translation.

Dionysius in a fashion more or less inconsistent with the basic account given in *VII*. Most telling of all, their authors are concerned more with abstract and timeless questions, such as the relation of wisdom and power, or the friendlessness of the tyrant, than with the immediate issues that constitute the burden of the *Seventh* and *Eighth Epistles*, viz. the reform of Syracuse and the preservation of Greek civilization in the west. In contrast with *I* and *II*, *Epistle III* seems to arise out of the circumstances which it describes; its presentation of the relations between Plato, Dion, and Dionysius are consistent with what we know from other sources; and Plato's concern for the triumph of Dion's cause and for the future of Sicily and Syracuse is appropriately presented. These characteristics of the letter make it tempting to conclude that it is a document composed by Plato himself for the double purpose of clearing his reputation and strengthening Dion's cause among the people of Syracuse. But the numerous grounds for suspicion presented above, although much weaker upon reflection than they at first seem to be, prevent us from drawing such a conclusion with complete confidence.

EPISTLE XIII

Apart from the *Seventh*, this letter has aroused more controversy than any other in the collection. It is referred to three times by Plutarch,[1] but by no other ancient writer. It was the first to be suspected in modern times, and will probably be one of the last on which there is any unanimity of opinion among Platonic scholars. The large part it has occupied in the controversies concerning the *Epistles* is mainly due to the peculiar character of its content. It is the most intimate of the letters, and if genuine it throws light upon certain details of Plato's personal life that we get from no other source. Plato buying gifts for Dionysius and his wife

1 *Dion* 21; *De Vit. Pud.* 11; *De Cohib. Ira* 16.

and children, sending him books and a tutor, advising him about the management of his finances, reporting what "various persons" think of him at Athens, even acting as his private agent and sounding Dion on some unnamed project—all this gives us a peculiarly interesting picture of the private life of Plato. But the very intimacy of the picture causes it to have the most various effects upon different readers; and subjective factors have played and must unavoidably play a more decisive part here than with respect to most letters in the collection.

This letter, if genuine, was written not long after Plato's return from Syracuse after the banishment of Dion, probably about 366. There are references to purchases that Dionysius has commissioned Plato to make for him, and to an agreement that Plato is now carrying out in sending Helicon to Syracuse. The letter is so full of the minor matters of personal intercourse as to suggest that only a comparatively short time has elapsed since Plato left Syracuse. The references to the death of Plato's two nieces, which occurred evidently when Plato was in Syracuse, enables us to say that it is at most less than a year since Plato's return. The tone of the letter is quite friendly, and this has naturally aroused suspicion because of its contrast with the attitude of Plato toward Dionysius implied in *Epistles III* and *VII*. But it must be remembered that these were written years later, when the rupture between Dionysius and Dion was complete. There is every reason to suppose that for a time after Plato's return from Syracuse in 367 he endeavored to remain on good terms with the tyrant, as the best way of influencing him toward the recall of Dion and the philosophical reform of Syracuse. We know from the narrative of the *Seventh Epistle* (330b) that this was Plato's policy as long as he remained in Syracuse, and the same narrative tells us that Dionysius was most eager to gain Plato's affection; so that it is natural to suppose a friendly correspondence and interchange of gifts after Plato's return, the chief motives on Plato's part being to arouse Dionysius' interest in philosophy, and bring about a reconciliation with

Dion. This letter therefore fits quite naturally into the picture we get from the *Seventh Epistle*. It is true that when Plato is describing his motives for returning to the court of Dionysius he seems to deny any firsthand knowledge of Dionysius' attainments in philosophy (338-339), and this seems inconsistent with the existence of a correspondence between them. But we do not need to suppose that Dionysius' reply to this or any other letter that Plato wrote him gave any evidence of philosophical interests or attainments. It is probable also that as time passed and Plato saw no signs of arousing Dionysius' interest in philosophy or securing the recall of Dion, their relations became less intimate; and this would be the state of mind described in the *Seventh Epistle*. But there is no impossibility of reconciling the circumstances this letter presupposes with what we know from other sources of the course of events.

Again, this letter, if not written by Plato himself, was written by the boldest of forgers; for it abounds in specific references to persons and situations, and it is in such matters that a forger has to step most carefully. In spite of the care with which Ritter has examined the subject, no inaccuracy in any of these details has actually been established. It is possible, as Ritter contends, basing his contention upon an inference from Plutarch (*Dion* 19), that Helicon first went to Syracuse in 361; and if so the statement in the *Thirteenth Epistle* (360b) is inaccurate. But the inference from Plutarch is certainly not necessary, and I venture to think would not even have been suggested if the question of the authenticity of this letter had not been under consideration. The same can be said of other objections to the letter based on alleged inaccuracies of detail; and the striking way in which this letter both invites and withstands such examination certainly establishes a presumption in its favor.[2]

But there is a more general objection that will have to be met before the letter can be accepted. Many critics, Ritter in

2 Ritter, *Neue Untersuchungen*, pp. 327-64. Hackforth examines and replies to Ritter's objections in detail (*Authorship*, pp. 167-87).

particular, have felt that Plato's attitude toward Dionysius and Dion in this letter is an unworthy one, and inconsistent with his character as revealed to us in the dialogues. It is no answer to this objection to say that a man's conduct quite often fails to measure up to the standard of his own teaching; for, as Ritter aptly remarks, when that is the case the judgment of the man's contemporaries is likely to reflect this discrepancy, whereas we have abundant evidence of the reverence and esteem generally accorded Plato in antiquity.[3] But is the role ascribed to Plato in this letter an unworthy one, one that we would find difficulty in attributing to the man who wrote the dialogues? A careful examination will, I think, tend to minimize considerably the objections that Ritter brings against the picture. Those who find this picture unworthy of Plato do so on two main grounds; first, because they maintain that it represents Plato as a beggar and a sycophant, debasing himself like an Aristippus at the feet of the tyrant in order to gain his favor, and secondly, because he is apparently willing to connive with Dionysius in an act of injustice toward Dion, or at least makes no protest in Dion's behalf. Plato seeking to benefit by Dionysius' purse, and willing to sacrifice Dion's happiness to the tyrant's wishes—this is an ugly picture, certainly; but is it the picture the letter gives us?

With regard to the money matters about which there is much discussion in the letter, the situation presupposed seems to be this: Plato has been asked by Dionysius to make certain purchases, a statue of Apollo and other things; and we also hear of earlier commissions involving even more expensive objects. Again, in his capacity of guest-friend it seems that Plato has been authorized to make certain "payments to the city," e.g. the expenses of fitting out a chorus, or equipping a ship, which Dionysius, in pursuance of his father's policy, was glad to undertake in order to ingratiate himself with the Athenian people. Lastly, Plato has been at some expense on account of his journey to Syracuse, and it seems to

[3] See Eduard Zeller, *Plato and the Older Academy* (London, 1888), pp. 36-44, for the testimony in antiquity as to the character of Plato.

have been customary under such circumstances for the patron
to provide travel money, at least (cf. 350b, also *Ep. I* 309b).
Now for these expenditures Plato would naturally draw upon
Dionysius' agents at Athens, when possible. But the letter
implies that the tyrant's credit was none too good there, and
Plato not only has had difficulty in securing money for these
various purposes, but has even had to advance money for
some of them himself. A careful reading of the passages dealing with money matters clearly suggests that Plato has borne
more than his share of expenses that might justly be regarded
as the joint obligations of Dionysius and himself. "I thought
it best to tell Leptines that the expense of fitting out the
Leucadian ship, about sixteen minae, came from my funds"
(361b). How rich Plato was, we do not know. But though he
undoubtedly shared the view current in the Academy and the
Lyceum that the property of friends is at the disposal of all,
and though he was still willing to regard Dionysius as his
friend, yet he doubtless felt that his first obligations were to
his nieces' children and to his mother; and the frank description of his own personal affairs was probably intended not as
a list of future expenses that Dionysius would be expected to
bear (the usual interpretation), but rather as an explanation
of his own frankness in reminding Dionysius that he was in
Plato's debt. Upon the whole matter it seems fair to say that
if we had the full details before us, instead of the cryptic and
tactful references of this letter, and if we also knew more of
what the Greeks expected of friends in financial matters, we
should find nothing disturbing or undignified in Plato's attitude here.

One point seems quite plain. Nothing in these passages
would justify us in classing the Plato described here with a
man like Aristippus, who avowedly sought the favor of
Dionysius for the material returns it would bring. Yet this is
clearly the perverse coloring that Ritter puts upon it. "Even
Aristippus, who did not have to be urged to become a guest
nor pressed to stay longer, would have been a worthier friend

[than the Plato described in this letter]." [4] But the Plato of this letter really asks nothing for himself, and there is a noticeable absence of purely personal motives. Again the remarks that he proceeds to give Dionysius on the management of his finances show an independence of spirit quite incompatible with the assumption that their author was a "tyrant-flatterer." It is sound advice, fearlessly given, and most appropriate to the situation of the young man without self-discipline who had been suddenly raised to the control of the most considerable empire and fortune in all Greece; but it is not the advice that a Διονυσοκόλαξ would have given, for flatterers profit most when their patrons do not follow the rules Plato lays down. And it surely does not take much penetration to discover that when Plato tells what Andromedes the moneychanger, or Leptines and other persons at Athens, have said, it is for the purpose of bringing home more forcibly the advice he is giving, and at the same time justifying it on grounds that might make the strongest appeal to the tyrant. There is no necessity for interpreting this passage, nor the later "reports as to what various people think" (362c), as if Plato were endeavoring to curry favor by acting as a spy upon his companions and contemporaries.

Now we come to the attitude toward Dion that the Plato of this letter displays. Here again the issue is beclouded by our ignorance of the import of the short paragraph on which all the criticism hinges (362e). If Plutarch is correct in his interpretation of this passage, Plato has been commissioned to sound Dion on Dionysius' scheme of marrying Dion's wife, Arete, to one of the court favorites (*Dion* 21). This seems to Ritter to stamp Plato as a veritable tool of the tyrant. There is this, however, to be said. If we adopt Plutarch's interpretation (and this in itself is a big assumption), we ought in justice to take into account the whole of it; and Plutarch explains that there was a report to the effect that Dion and his wife were not happy together. This seems to me to alter the situa-

4 *Neue Untersuchungen*, p. 344.

tion, so far as Plato's loyalty to Dion is concerned. Ritter ignores this explanation given by Plutarch and indulges in sentimental pleading. "Dion loved his wife. . . . Plato knew well enough the feeling of Dion and his wife. And now he is supposed to have agreed to sound Dion on this proposition involving a vile wrong to him." [5] Of course those who think that even if Plutarch was right Plato should not have looked so lightly upon this severing of the marriage tie for political purposes will still find objections here; but they are occupying much less tenable ground. As Hackforth remarks, Plato did not look upon the institution of marriage from the standpoint of the Catholic Church.

But granting that this passage can be disposed of without discredit to Plato, there is a more general difficulty urged by Ritter. Having Dion's interests at heart as much as he did, could Plato conceivably have dismissed Dion *"mit ein Paar nichtssagenden Worten"*? But it must be remembered that when this letter was written we can readily assume, as was said above, that Plato still had some hope of winning Dionysius to the study of philosophy; and if this aim of Plato's efforts had been attained, Dion's restoration and the regeneration of Sicily would have come about also, or so he thought. Furthermore, it is hard to say what more Plato could have done at this time to further good relations between Dionysius and Dion. Plutarch's own account (*Dion* 21) indicates that Plato's advice on the subject of the marriage was accepted by Dionysius, at least for the time being, and thus the way was kept open for a reconciliation. And Plato smoothes matters still further by remarking on the moderateness of Dion's words and actions with respect to Dionysius (362e).

The most formidable objections to the authenticity of this letter can therefore, I think, be removed. But there remain certain points of detail that arouse suspicion. It is certainly suspicious that the letter begins with an attempt to prove its genuineness. On the other hand, a similar reference to the characteristically Platonic salutation $\epsilon\hat{\upsilon}$ $\pi\rho\acute{\alpha}\tau\tau\epsilon\iota\nu$ is found at the

[5] *Ibid.*, p. 341.

beginning of the *Third Epistle,* and the opening sentence of
the *Eighth* also hangs upon the import of the salutation. The
reference to the salutation in some form or other may have
become a sort of mannerism in Plato's correspondence. Again
it arouses suspicion that Dionysius should be cautioned to
preserve the letter, or at least an abstract of it. This may be
the trace of the forger's hand, trying to make plausible the
fact that the letter has been preserved. But if so it would
seem a rather gratuitous piece of ingenuity, as Plato's prestige
in his own lifetime would be sufficient to account for the
fact; while if the letter is genuine, Plato might well want
Dionysius to preserve it, since it is a letter of advice and a
statement of certain financial obligations that he wants
Dionysius to keep in mind, as well as certain suggestions regarding gifts to their mutual friends. These details Plato
would certainly want Dionysius to keep in mind, either by
preserving the letter, or by taking an abstract of it. As confirming the importance Plato attached to these matters of
advice, it is interesting to note that Aristocritus is to be told
to remind Dionysius to pay heed to the contents of Plato's
letters (363d).

The style and diction of the letter, while not above suspicion, are not demonstrably un-Platonic. Most of the suspicious traits cited by Ritter are of minor importance, and
it is doubtful if he would regard them as sufficient by themselves to prove the letter spurious.[6]

In conclusion a word needs to be said about the position
this letter occupies in the collection. Wilamowitz argued [7]
that *Epistle XIII* was regarded as spurious in antiquity because it entered the collection after the doubtful *Epistle XII.*
But we do not surely know that the ἀντιλέγεται accompanied
Epistle XII when it was first admitted to the collection; it
may well have been added by a later editor, and this pos-

---

6 These stylistic difficulties are treated in Hackforth, *Authorship,* pp.
166-97.

7 In *Hermes,* XXXIII (1898), 496.

sibility renders Wilamowitz' inference precarious. And in any case how can we be sure that an ancient editor would have insisted on putting a letter believed to be genuine in front of one believed doubtful? Although the position of *Epistle XIII* does not throw much direct light on the question of authenticity, yet it clearly indicates that this letter entered the collection at a fairly late date. If the usual theory regarding the composition of *Epistle XII* is accepted, then *Epistle XIII* cannot have entered the collection prior to the first century B.C. It must be admitted that this tends to raise a doubt as to its authenticity. There are some considerations, however, that when duly weighed may somewhat lessen the difficulty of accepting it. It is probable that the original collection of letters had a dogmatic, not a biographical, purpose: some editor put together those letters of Plato that throw light on his political and ethical principles. If this is true, then we can understand why the *Thirteenth,* even if known to the original editor, was not included in the collection; for its interest is wholly biographical and historical. But because of its biographical interest it would be admitted to the collection of letters as soon as the purpose of the original compilation was lost sight of. Even a later editor who knew and sympathized with the purpose of the original editor might be inclined to add this letter to the collection, as a document worth preserving and hard to assign to any other place in the Platonic corpus. Even if the original editor intended to include all extant Platonic letters and not merely those of political interest, there are reasons why the *Thirteenth,* even though genuine, might have been unknown to him. For it is not a public letter, nor such a letter as Plato would have preserved in duplicate; an abstract would have sufficed. It could only have been acquired by the editor of Plato's manuscripts from Dionysius himself or from the person into whose hands Dionysius' possessions had fallen. Considering the checkered career that Dionysius led during the later part of his life, it is hardly likely that this letter remained in his possession; and it could easily have had a long and adventur-

ous history before finally coming into the Platonic canon.
The case is quite otherwise with the other letters in the collection addressed to Dionysius. The *Third,* if genuine, is obviously a public document as well as a private letter, and
would naturally be known to the compiler of the collection;
and though the *First* and *Second* are private letters, yet if
they are spurious they could easily have been in circulation
long before the *Thirteenth* came to light. These considerations, hypothetical as they admittedly are, may serve to prevent a too hasty rejection of the *Thirteenth Epistle* because
of its late admission to the collection. They may even provide
a sort of confirmation of its claims to genuineness, since, if it
is what it professes to be, its fortunes must have been quite
different from those of the other letters.

EPISTLE II

This letter professes to be a reply to an inquiry from Dionysius through Archedemus (who, we learn from *Epistle VII,*
339a, was one of the men Plato esteemed most highly in
Sicily) as to how the relations between himself and Plato
could be improved. Dionysius has also had difficulties with
certain problems in philosophy, and has instructed Archedemus to get help on them from Plato. The letter therefore
has two chief divisions: the first makes suggestions as to the
improvement of their personal relations, the second deals with
the philosophical difficulties Dionysius has asked about. The
two parts are, however, closely related in thought, for it is
made clear that the best way of improving relations between
Plato and Dionysius is for Dionysius to accept and publicly
endorse Plato's philosophy. We get the impression that the
two men are on friendly, though not cordial, terms. Dionysius
is interested in philosophy, and particularly in the teachings
of Plato. This is apparently not the first occasion on which
there has been an exchange of letters. Plato has previously

sent Polyxenus, a pupil of Bryson (314c; cf. *XIII*, 360c) to Dionysius, and has made certain requests of the tyrant that have
been granted. Plato evidently believes in Dionysius' philosophical ability, and is hopeful of securing his allegiance to
the Platonic doctrine. His main concern is lest the general
public have an erroneous conception of the real relations between them, owing to a false interpretation of what has happened in Sicily.

It is difficult to determine the date at which this letter, if
genuine, could have been written. It is impossible to believe
that it was written after Plato's return from his third journey
to Syracuse, as Meyer [1] and Harward [2] contend. The letter pictures the relations between Plato and Dionysius as on the
whole friendly. But the third visit had ended in a definite
rupture between Plato and Dionysius, and was followed very
shortly by the preparations of Dion for an expedition against
Syracuse; and it is inconceivable that no reference should be
made to these events, even if we could imagine Plato writing
in this friendly fashion to Dionysius after the treatment he
had just received at Syracuse. This letter, moreover, pictures
Plato as still having some hope of Dionysius' interest in philosophy, whereas *VII*, 345d, tells us definitely that he had
come to realize the true nature of Dionysius' pretended interest in philosophy. Lastly, the writer's stout denial that his (i.e.
Plato's) associates had spoken evil of Dionysius at the Olympic
games could hardly apply to 360, when Dion vowed he would
punish Dionysius and called upon his friends to help him.

On the other hand, it seems equally difficult to believe that
the letter was written between the second and third journeys.
For the account in *VII*, 338-339, of Plato's decision to return
to Syracuse does not mention any such correspondence on
philosophical questions. This omission is highly significant,
since the question Plato debates is whether there was any
chance of arousing Dionysius to an interest in philosophy.
Plato himself evidently feels in the *Seventh Epistle* that there

[1] *Geschichte des Altertums*, V, 504, 509.
[2] *Class. Rev.*, XL (1926), 186; *Platonic Epistles*, p. 167.

is not much hope. He mentions the many rumors that have come from Sicily to the effect that Dionysius was enthusiastic about philosophy; he refers specifically to the letters of Archytas and others in Tarentum, and to the statements of Archedemus and other Sicilian friends confirming these rumors and praising the tyrant's aptitude and progress in the subject. If Plato had had any other source of information about Dionysius' interest in philosophy, such as a personal inquiry through Archedemus relating to specific difficulties, he certainly would have mentioned it, since the passage plainly indicates he was eager to find every justification for having undertaken his second journey. The plain implication of *VII* is that Plato knew nothing about Dionysius' progress in philosophy except what others had told him; and if we take *VII* as authentic, this seems to preclude any such exchange of philosophical correspondence as *II* represents.

Besides the difficulty of finding a satisfactory date for it, there are other features of this letter that arouse suspicion. It nowhere mentions the banishment of Dion, or the project that Dion was interested in at Syracuse and that had been frustrated temporarily by the suspicions of Dionysius. It was this that constituted the main obstacle to a free and friendly intercourse between Plato and the tyrant. Even if we make allowance for the intimacy permissible in a personal letter, it seems hardly possible that Plato should have been, as he shows himself to be here, chiefly interested in his own personal standing with the tyrant, and desirous primarily of securing public recognition for himself and his philosophy. Again, in this letter Dionysius is described as seeking a pretext for sending Plato away so that he could consult other philosophers, whereas in *VII*, 329-330, the tyrant is pictured as desiring to retain Plato against his will, and as eager to gain his respect and favor. That this difference is not due merely to the fact that Plato in the one case is writing to Dionysius and in the other to the friends of Dion is shown by comparing this letter with the *Third*, where the picture of their mutual relations is equally irreconcilable with that given in the *Second*. There is no mention of those larger issues that form the burden of Plato's *Seventh Epistle*. Instead Plato is represented as desiring a personal triumph over his philosophical rivals, and as interested in the reputation he will have with future generations.

The philosophical content of this letter is also very questionable. The suggestion of a secret Platonic doctrine to be carefully guarded lest it fall into the hands of ignorant men is unlike anything found in the dialogues, and unlike the point of view of the *Seventh Epistle*. There are verbal similarities between the two letters, it is true; and it may at first seem that the author of the *Second* is merely expressing what we found to be good Platonic doctrine, viz. the difficulty of insight into first principles, and the inadequacy of language to express such insight. Thus the writer, in the spirit of *VII*, says that "one must hear these doctrines expounded again and again, perhaps for many years, and even then their gold is with the utmost difficulty separated and refined." The writer represents Plato himself as still occupied with inquiry into the nature of this first principle, and as referring ironically to Dionysius' own former claim to have solved the problem. All this is in the spirit of *VII*. But the writer of *II* injects into his composition the wholly un-Platonic idea of a secret teaching that must only be imparted by word of mouth to responsible hearers. This first principle must not be written down, or if so, only in enigmatic terms. Archedemus is to explain it to Dionysius, and help with any difficulties that may arise, after conferring with Plato. This is a line of thought quite different from the thought of the *Seventh Epistle*. It is one thing to say that long study and familiar converse are necessary for apprehending the ultimate principles of nature, and quite another thing to insist that the exposition of these principles be confined to personal intercourse through trusted intermediaries. It is one thing to distrust language because it is an inadequate instrument for the transmission of philosophical doctrines, and quite another thing to distrust written words because "when a thing is written down it is bound to get abroad sooner or later" (314c). In the *Republic* (VI, 506e) Plato explains the nature of the first principle by means of an analogy; but the writer of this letter would have us believe that Plato thought it was not safe to speak of these ultimate principles *except* in enigmas. There is no hint in *VII* of an esoteric Platonism to be guarded as a private possession; but this seems to be the chief point in *II*. There are difficulties in understanding what Plato means in *VII* when he speaks of the "first principles of nature," but it is not because he has deliberately tried to keep the reader from understanding his doctrine. His main concern there is to point out under what circumstances and to what persons the doctrine can fruitfully be imparted. This apparent similarity but real divergence between the thought of the *Seventh* and that of the *Second Epistle* suggests that the writer of the latter tried to give his composition the necessary Platonic coloring, but failed through a misunderstanding of Plato's doctrine.

Nor is the writer of this letter consistent in his attitude toward these doctrines. Plato is supposed to be warning Dionysius against writing on these matters, just after he himself has written, though enigmatically. Again, Plato has disguised his doctrine in riddles so that no accidental reader can understand; even so, the letter must be burned, to prevent the uninitiated from getting hold of the doctrine. Why should Plato write anything at all on the matter, since Archedemus was entrusted with the responsibility of explaining it in conversation to Dionysius? And is it likely that this alleged secret doctrine would be revealed to Dionysius, when it is not even certain that he does not altogether despise the Platonic philosophy? These are internal contradictions that suggest the hand of a forger, and a not very clever forger, at that.

If the *Second Epistle* is a forgery, its writer would have been tempted to borrow from the *Seventh;* and if he was none too well versed in Plato's teachings, especially if he looked at them from the point of view of a third-century sectarian, we can understand why he would borrow unintelligently. All this must be kept in mind in interpreting the difficult passage in

314c. On its face it seems to be an expanded version of *VII*, 341c. In the latter passage Plato says, "There is no writing of mine about these matters [i.e. the first principles of nature], nor will there ever be one." In the *Second Epistle* we read: "I have never written on these subjects. There is no writing of Plato's, nor will there ever be; those that are now called so come from an idealized and youthful Socrates." Burnet, believing in the genuineness of this letter, welcomed this passage as confirmation of his theory of the Platonic Socrates.[3] But the passage is notoriously obscure, and no meaning that we can assign to it seems compatible with what we know of Plato's writings. (*a*) Does it mean that the doctrines of the dialogues, at least of those written before this letter is supposed to have been written, are all Socratic, not Platonic? It seems absurd to think that Plato would disavow, for example, the central doctrine of the *Republic,* when he describes it in *VII* as the result of many years of observation of Greek political life; and the *Republic* was certainly written before the *Second Epistle.* A further difficulty is that the language suggests that Plato never had any intention of writing anything but a Socratic dialogue. But the letter was written, if genuine, sometime between 366 and 358, and it was certainly not long after, if it was not indeed during this time, that Plato was at work on the *Sophist, Timaeus,* and *Laws;* so that he must have soon abandoned the firm resolution ascribed to him in this letter. (*b*) There is a less sweeping interpretation of the above passage, as follows: "There is no writing of Plato's [on first principles]; those [on that subject] that are called Plato's are the work of Socrates." [4] But this interpretation is equally impossible. For there seems to be no Socratic dialogue of Plato that deals with these first principles. The only Platonic dialogue that could qualify at all as an account of first principles is the *Timaeus,* but in the *Timaeus* it is not Socrates who gives the exposition. The difficulty of finding any meaning for this passage indicates

---

[3] John Burnet, *Greek Philosophy,* Part I (London, 1914), p. 212.
[4] Taking περὶ τούτων as implied in the two following clauses.

that it is another example of the unintelligent way in which the writer has borrowed from the *Seventh Epistle*.

There are other indications of the dependence of this letter upon the *Seventh*. The mention of Archedemus as the messenger of Dionysius may well have been suggested by *VII*, 339a. We know nothing of Archedemus except what is told us in the *Epistles*. Similarly the "dishonor" inflicted upon Plato by Dionysius seems to come from *VII*, 335c. Dionysius' claim to have discovered the nature of the first principle recalls *VII*, 341b and 345a. The inept reference to immortality (311c) may be another imitation of 335ab, where, however, the emotional tone of the passage makes the reference a natural one, and where, moreover, there is no attempt at proof, but only a reminder of the "sacred word." Hackforth [5] also sees in the enigma (312d) an unintelligent reproduction of the doctrine of the three instruments of knowledge in *VII*, 341 ff.

A great deal of ingenuity has been expended in the attempt to interpret the riddle in 312e relating to the three principles. Paradoxically enough, those who think the letter is from the hand of Plato, such as Raeder, Andreae, and Apelt, have least doubt as to their ability to decipher it and therefore to circumvent Plato's attempt at disguising his doctrine. Still more paradoxically they find the answer to the riddle in the *Timaeus*, ignoring the fact that if this letter is authentic, Plato in writing the *Timaeus* has violated his own reiterated prohibition against committing these secrets to writing. Probably if we are to fix upon a meaning at all for this enigma (and undoubtedly the writer of the letter, whoever he was, meant to suggest something like Platonic doctrine), our most plausible recourse is to the *Timaeus*. Whether we are to identify the three principles respectively with the demiurge, the world-soul, and the "source of evil," [6] or with the demi-

---

[5] See this discussion in *Authorship,* pp. 47 ff.

[6] Hans Raeder, "Über die Echtheit der Platonischen Briefe," *Rheinisches Museum,* N. F. LXI (1906), 537.

urge, the world-soul, and the human soul,[7] seems to me a problem incapable of solution, least of all on the supposition that the letter is genuine. On the alternative supposition I think it fairly certain that the writer had vaguely in mind one of these or some other threefold classification found in the *Timaeus*. But in spite of the labor of exposition that has been given to this passage by the Christian Fathers, the Neoplatonists,[8] and the modern commentators above mentioned, it is a subject which it seems hardly worth while to pursue further.

Thus the picture of Plato's philosophy and of his relations with Dionysius which this letter gives us is altogether different from, and even discrepant with, that given in the *Seventh;* and this fact, coupled with the difficulty of finding a satisfactory date for it, justifies us in condemning it as spurious. It is not difficult to understand how it may have come into existence. We know that it was customary in the schools of rhetoric of the third century and later to construct letters and speeches appropriate to historical personages and events, and certainly Plato's relations with Dionysius would become a well-worked theme. We have already noted certain indications that the writer of this letter borrowed from the *Seventh;* [9] and the letter as a whole looks like a rhetorical exercise upon the theme of the relation between wise man and king, a theme doubtless chosen because of its affinity (or supposed affinity) to Plato's doctrine of the rule of philosophy. But there is nothing really characteristic of Plato's political teaching in the writer's theme. "It is a law of nature that wisdom and great power go together; they exert a mutual attraction and are forever seeking to be united." This is a rhetorical commonplace, none too true at best, and bearing only a specious

---

[7] W. Andreae, "Die philosophischen Probleme in den Platonischen Briefen," *Philologus,* N. F. XXXII (1922), 75 ff.

[8] Proclus, *Plat. Theol.* IV.

[9] See also other evidence presented by Pavlu (*Mitteilungen,* VIII, 1-19) of borrowings not only from *Epistle VII* but also from the dialogues.

resemblance to Plato's doctrine that the rule of philosophers is the only salvation for the ills of Greek cities. For the writer of this letter, the association of wise men and kings is one of the recurring facts of history; for Plato the union of philosophy and supreme power in the same person is an event to be devoutly prayed for but scarcely to be expected. The significance of this doctrine for Plato was that it would remedy the crying evils of Greek political life. But instead of any reference to these evils, the writer of this letter gives us a schoolboy exercise in finding historical parallels, with edifying references to posthumous fame and immortality. The reference to the opinion of future generations suggests that the writer was one of that future generation, more interested in the personalities of Plato and Dionysius than in the great issues that concerned Plato.

The literary history of the letter provides no ground for questioning this condemnation. It is not referred to by either Cicero or Plutarch, though the latter refers to *Epistle XIII*, nor is it quoted by any other extant writer prior to the canon of Thrasyllus. We know from the testimony of Diogenes Laertius that the *Epistles* included in that canon were identical with those of our present collection, so that this letter must have found a place there. After this time it was referred to by Galen, Aristides, Athenaeus, Stobaeus, Clement of Alexandria, Eusebius, and Origen. The letter makes relatively little attempt to avoid hiatus.[10] This fact, however, cannot be used to prove its spuriousness. Raeder in fact argues that the avoidance of hiatus is a confirmation of his belief that the letter was written by Plato, for if genuine the date at which it was written is probably earlier than the date of those dialogues that show an absence of hiatus. The only striking feature in the vocabulary of the letter is the use of the word αἰνιγμός (312d) instead of αἴνιγμα, the form usually employed by Plato. The only other case where αἰνιγμός occurs in the Platonic writings is *Timaeus*, 72b, where it occurs in the same

10 Raeder, *Rheinisches Museum*, pp. 440 ff.

construction as here, viz. δι' αἰνιγμῶν. This fact may have some significance in view of the supposition above mentioned that the writer of the letter was basing his "enigma" upon the doctrines of the *Timaeus*.

PLATO AND GREEK POLITICS

For all the space devoted to political questions in the dialogues, Plato's personal connection with the politics of the fourth century has been somewhat of a mystery. We cannot doubt that political questions occupied a large place in Plato's thinking; but the dialogues contain no clear reference to contemporary political issues, nor any indications that Plato ever attempted to put his political philosophy to the test of practice. For a man so imbued as Plato seems to have been with the Greek tradition of the small city-state and with the duty of the citizen to take part in the work of government, this seeming abstention from political life is surprising. We may be tempted to infer, from the tone of Book VI of the *Republic,* that Plato despaired of his native city and therefore held himself aloof from all political activity there.[1] On the other hand, the voluminous and detailed prescriptions of the *Laws* suggest that Plato had spent many years in preparing for a position of political responsibility, and that he still hoped, even at the close of his life, for a chance to serve his native city.

Again there is no difficulty in formulating in the abstract (it has often been done) the system of political principles that Plato thought essential to the well-being of man in society. But the dialogues do not make clear the relation of these principles to the age in which they were put forth. Our

1 Even so, it is surely going too far to say, as Burnet does, that Plato "had given up all interest in the politics of his native land before the age of thirty" (John Burnet, *Platonism* [Berkeley, 1928], p. 92).

natural assumption is that Plato is writing for his own time. But, the *Laws* and *Politicus* apart, the political dialogues seem, curiously enough, to concern themselves with the problems and personages of a former generation—with Protagoras, Thrasymachus, Callicles, Pericles, Themistocles, and other thinkers and statesmen of the Periclean Age and the decade or two immediately following. There is no mention made of the political leaders and problems of the fourth century. We are tempted to assume that Plato is employing the personages and doctrines of the bygone age as an indirect way of attacking the political issues of his own day. The fundamentals of the political problem change very little from generation to generation, and for a man interested in getting back to first principles the thought of the Periclean Age could easily serve as an instructive approach to the political issues of the fourth century. And it is probably true, as Field has pointed out,[2] that Plato and the other thinkers of the fourth century did not draw the sharp dividing line we are accustomed to make between their own age and the preceding century. For them, their own age, down to the Macedonian Wars, was part of a single period that began with the Peloponnesian War or earlier. The contrast they drew was between this age and the age of the Persian Wars. Hence in portraying the policies and theories of the last half of the fifth century, Plato would not be as conscious, as we too often are, of the diversity between the period he was portraying and the period in which he wrote. Beside this, there are numerous details in the political dialogues which can more naturally be referred to the fourth century than to the Periclean Age. The criticism of the power of the orators in the *Gorgias;* the condemnation of athleticism and litigiousness, and the denunciation of ruthless warfare between Greeks, in the *Republic;* the emphasis upon the need of a special soldier class, in the same work—these are examples of doctrines which, though not exactly out of place in the mouth of a fifth-century speaker,

[2] G. C. Field, *Plato and His Contemporaries* (London, 1930), p. 106.

certainly seem more appropriate to the fourth century, since the conditions they presuppose were much more prominent in that century than in the preceding one.

But the problem is complicated by another factor, viz. the role ascribed to Socrates in the dialogues. Since the doctrines of the *Gorgias,* the *Meno,* and the *Republic* are expounded through the dramatic person of Socrates there may be some doubt how far we are justified in calling these doctrines Platonic. It has been maintained by competent scholars that in these dialogues Plato is merely giving a historical and dramatic portrayal of the intellectual disputes of the fifth century. If this is so, the political doctrines of the *Republic* and of the dialogues that preceded it are primarily the views of Socrates, and refer primarily to fifth-century problems; they are not the views that Plato himself developed through reflection on the conditions of his own times. Thus the "Socratic problem" causes difficulty in interpreting Plato's political ideas even more than it does in interpreting the Platonic metaphysics or theory of knowledge. For in the nature of the case, political ideas thrust their roots much more deeply into external circumstances than do logical or metaphysical doctrines; and to understand them historically it is much more necessary to see the soil in which they grew. There is much in the Platonic teaching on politics that is timeless, because based on universal elements in man's political experience; but even this timeless heritage can be better appreciated and understood if we can ascertain how much of it was intended to apply to the problems of the author's own generation. Aside from this, there is the biographical interest that insists on knowing whether we are to look upon Plato as chiefly a great dramatic artist, so far as these earlier dialogues are concerned, or as a profound original thinker, alike in the *Republic* and the *Laws* hunting desperately for a way of remedying the evils of his time.

Fortunately the *Epistles* throw considerable light upon almost all these questions. Plato appears in them primarily as a political thinker and reformer. Eight of the thirteen letters relate to the famous venture into active politics at Syracuse, when the death of the elder Dionysius and the accession to power of his son Dionysius under the tutelage of the gifted and high-minded Dion seemed to offer a dramatic opportunity for political reform. The other letters also, except the *Twelfth,* are of political importance, either as testifying directly to Plato's political views and aims, or as exhibiting the opinion of some early imitator as to the nature of those views and aims.

First of all, with regard to the Socratic problem, the *Seventh Epistle* contains a statement that seems decisive as to whether the political doctrines of the *Republic* (and by implication the other political dialogues) are genuinely Platonic. The priceless bit of autobiography at the beginning of the *Seventh Epistle* tells us that Plato, as we should have expected, originally intended to enter political life, but that he was discouraged, first by the excesses of the Thirty, later by the treatment of Socrates at the hands of the restored democracy, and finally by the conviction that he could do nothing worth while in the existing state of Athenian politics.

The more I reflected upon what was happening, upon what kind of men were active in politics, and upon the state of our laws and customs, and the older I grew, the more I realized how difficult it is to manage a city's affairs rightly. . . . And the corruption of our written laws and our customs was proceeding at such amazing speed that whereas at first I had been full of zeal for public life, when I noted these changes and saw how unstable everything was, I became in the end quite dizzy. . . . At last I came to the conclusion that all existing states are badly governed and the condition of their laws practically incurable, without some miraculous remedy and the assistance of fortune; and I was forced to say, in praise of true philosophy, that from her height alone was it possible to discern what the nature of justice is, either in the state or in the individual, and that the ills of the human race would never end until either those who are sincerely and truly lovers of wisdom come into political power, or the rulers of our cities, by the grace of God, learn true philosophy (325c-326b).

This seems decisive evidence that the fundamental doctrine of the *Republic* was the result of Plato's own reflections upon the political scene, not merely a conviction he had inherited from Socrates. This is the more evident because Socrates is mentioned in the passage just preceding the section quoted, and is praised as being "the wisest and justest man of that time." If Plato felt that he merely came to appreciate, at long last, the truth of Socrates' teaching, it seems inconceivable that he should not have said so.

Furthermore, it leaves no doubt in our minds that this doctrine was the result of reflection upon the political life of the fifteen or twenty years after the death of Socrates. It thus confirms our natural and instinctive feeling that the indignation and satire of the *Republic* were called forth by the evils present to Plato's observation, not by the memory of the practices of the preceding century. The Great Beast of Book VI of the *Republic* is the Athenian demos of the early fourth century; its "trainers" are the demagogues and orators to whom the political leadership of the age was mainly entrusted; and the imperfect forms of constitutions and the causes of revolutions are drawn from life, from the states that were significant powers in the fourth century. It has often been pointed out that the picture of tyranny and the tyrant seems to be inspired by the career of Dionysius the Elder. Plato explicitly says that the timocratic polity he describes is best exemplified by Sparta and Crete; and it is equally certain that his descriptions of oligarchy and democracy are based upon real though unnamed fourth-century examples.

Again, the *Epistles* give us welcome information as to Plato's personal relation to Greek politics. The autobiographical passage above referred to shows us some of the reasons for his political inactivity at Athens. Later, in another impressive passage of the *Seventh Epistle* (330d-331d), he gives the conditions under which he thinks it worth while to offer political advice. This is clearly a bit of apology, an answer to the critics who accused him of inconsistency or lack of patriotism in not entering political life at Athens. But Athens was not the only place where a patriotic Greek could do something for Hellenic civilization. The venture into Syracusan politics would alone be sufficient evidence that Plato's political interests were not merely academic; and the letters to Hermeias, to Perdiccas, to Laodamas, show that his influence extended into many Greek communities. And finally, the *Epistles* show us something of the form Plato's principles took when they were put to the test of action. The *Seventh* and *Eighth Epistles* reveal Plato attempting to reform the government of the greatest city in Greece, first in the hope of converting the tyranny into a "rule of philosophy," and later in order to bring peace to a faction-ridden city. There may be some who feel that the meaning of the "rule of the philosophers" is sufficiently clear from the *Republic* and the *Politicus;* but those who are not so easily satisfied that they understand what Plato meant by this famous doctrine will welcome the information contained in these two long and intimate letters.

Faction and Disorder in Fourth-century Greece

The fourth century was suffering from political evils which many of the more thoughtful men of the time regarded as incurable, and the sight of which only too often induced a feeling of pessimism and despair. As we look back upon Greek history, we are apt to regard most of these ills as the direct or indirect consequences of the Peloponnesian War; and indeed many of them unquestionably are so. The fourth century labored under a material handicap that it never succeeded in overcoming, so far as we can see. Considering that for thirty years industry and trade had been diverted from their normal channels into the making of war, considering that accumulated resources in city treasuries had been exhausted, and olive orchards and other capital equipment had been destroyed, we do not wonder that fourth-century politics was dominated by the economic problem. The war had brought about other social changes that aggravated the political distress. A full generation had grown up whose chief activity had been warfare; unfitted for peaceful labors, still less inclined toward them, many of these men became professional soldiers, men without a city, willing to hire themselves for any adventure; and the existence of this class of mercenaries made it only too easy for partisans in politics to appeal to the sword. In addition to these economic and social changes, the struggle for supremacy among the Greek cities continued throughout the first half of the fourth century, until all of them were reduced to a position of jealous and vindictive impotence. As a result of these internecine struggles, the Greeks were no longer able to hold the Persian at bay; he reappeared on the Mediterranean early in the fourth century, and in 387 dictated a humiliating peace to the contending cities. And on the west the rising power of the Carthaginians and of the Italian tribes in southern Italy threatened the destruction of Hellenic civilization in Sicily and Italy.

One of the most sinister features of this somber state of affairs was the prevalence of factional strife within the Greek cities. Political societies are always suffering in some measure from this chronic ailment; but the peculiar intensity and ruthlessness of the factional animosities in the city-states of the fourth century has seldom been equaled. Thucydides draws a memorable picture of the ruthlessness and vindictiveness of the struggles between oligarchic and democratic factions that became common all over Greece during the Peloponnesian War;[3] and, as this war lasted almost thirty years, these habits must have been well ingrained in the Greek nature when it ended. At Argos in 370 the people fell upon the oligarchs and slew fifteen hundred of them. Twenty-five years later Isocrates says of the Argives that "when their enemies cease from harrying them, they themselves put to death the most eminent and wealthy of their citizens; and they have more pleasure in doing this than other people have in

3 Thuc. III, 82.

slaying their foes." [4] From the same writer we get an equally depressing picture of the state of things in other cities of the Peloponnesus. "They feel such distrust and hatred of one another that they fear their fellow citizens more than the enemy; . . . those who own property had rather throw their possessions into the sea than lend aid to the needy, while those who are in poorer circumstances would less gladly find a treasure than seize the possessions of the rich; having ceased sacrificing victims at the altars they slaughter one another there instead; and more people are in exile now from a single city than before from the whole of the Peloponnesus." [5] Xenophon tells a gruesome tale of the slaughter of the oligarchs by the democrats at Corinth on the occasion of a feast, some of them even being put to death in the temples to which they had fled for refuge.[6] Athens, to her credit, was relatively free during the fourth century from these bloodier manifestations of party spirit; but the clash of interest between oligarch and democrat was present, and its economic manifestations were sometimes as unprincipled as the bloody scenes at Argos or Corinth. The practice of political ruthlessness grew by the very exercise of it. This condition of affairs made any healthy political life impossible and threatened the continuance of the city-state. It is in the forefront of Plato's mind in all his political writings. "Our present states are not really polities at all; they are merely aggregations of men dwelling in cities who are subjects and servants of a part of their own group." [7] Whether monarchies or oligarchies or democracies, "they can only be called στασιωτεῖαι, not πολιτεῖαι"; [8] and aggravated as it was by long precedent, and defended in some quarters of advanced thought, this disease in the body politic might well seem incurable.

[4] *To Philip*, 52.
[5] Isocrates *Archidamus* 67.
[6] *Hell*. IV, iv, 2-4.
[7] *Laws* IV, 712e.
[8] *Laws* VIII, 832c; cf. IV, 715b and *Rep*. IV, 423a.

But for Plato this factional strife was but one manifestation of a more fundamental malady pervading Greek life. The foundations of all social order are moral; they are laid in men's unconscious and unquestioning feelings of the rights of others and of what is and is not done in the relation of fellow citizen to fellow citizen. In the fable Plato puts in the mouth of Protagoras, it is said that Zeus sent αἰδώς and δίκη "to be the orderers of cities, and bonds of friendship drawing men together." [9] Both these terms—αἰδώς, respect, or reverence, and δίκη, the sense of what is just—imply the feeling of an order imposing itself upon the individual desires; and for Plato it was this sense of a binding order that brings self-control to the citizen and peace to the state. When this feeling for a higher order of obligation loosens its hold upon men, the conditions of all political stability are gone. In the breakup of the older customs and practices that continued without interruption during the period of Plato's life, he saw a steady moral degeneration. In the passage from the *Seventh Epistle* quoted above (p. 121) describing his growing appreciation of the difficulties of political reform, Plato lays most stress upon the breakdown of the old standards of conduct, and the moral uncertainty that seemed to reign both in theory and in practice, rendering any stable order impossible. It is wise to make generous allowances in accepting any man's estimate of the morals of his own age; yet there is undoubtedly much to justify Plato's judgment that his own epoch was one of moral decline, as compared with the period of the Persian Wars. Public corruption seems to have increased. Ruthlessness and cruelty in warfare—from which the Greeks, as compared with Oriental peoples, were in general happily free—became more and more pronounced in the later fifth and the fourth centuries. Assassination is a common incident in the disputes of the period. The despoiling of temples and the violation of the rights of sanctuary are heard of oftener. More significant than perhaps anything else was a notable decline in public spirit, an increase of self-interested

[9] *Prot.* 322c.

individualism. The able men of the century, even when ostensibly serving the state, played for their own fortunes; and the wholehearted devotion to the polis was becoming only a tradition. The citizen seems to have been much more inclined to demand largess of the public treasury than to recognize any obligation to serve the state. Demosthenes tried in vain to stir the Athenians of his day to acts of heroic patriotism by recalling the glorious deeds of the fifth century. The Greek city-state was losing that moral hold upon the affections of its members which was essential to its existence; and Plato was quite right in looking upon this as the passing of the old order. It was the beginning of something which he could only regard as the negation of the conditions of a good life.

The root of the disorder, then, as Plato saw it, was the decline of the binding sense of a law over and above individual desires. Law had become the tool of the politician, the instrument by which a party may retain itself in power, the expression of the interests of the strong man, the few strong men, or of the demos, rather than the guardian of the common good and the rightful sovereign over all special interests and private desires.[10] This state of affairs had been partly brought about by the commerce and travel of the fifth century that had broadened the horizon of the Greeks and brought them into contact with other civilizations and other laws. It had been stimulated by wars waged in disregard of Hellenic law. When one is fighting for one's very existence, as were the Athenians and their allies in the last years of the fifth century, one easily renounces the hard-won gains of centuries of civilization and relapses to the more primitive law of the strong arm. And this retrogression had received powerful support from some sections of advanced thought. The Sophists of the fifth century had seriously defended the doctrine of might as the source of right, and had regarded it as "natural" (this word already infected with all the ambiguity that has clung to it in the history of thought) that those in power should use their power to further their own

10 *Ep. VII*, 325d, 326a, 337cd; cf. *Laws* IV, 715a-d.

ends. They found nothing but "conventions" in the human formulas of justice and right that an earlier generation had looked upon as a part of the very order of nature. Thus both oligarch and democrat could justify their struggle for power by the principle that justice is the interest of the stronger. And a man could work for purely private ends, in disregard of polis and Hellas, and justify himself by the plea that he was acting in accordance with the law of nature.

Seen against this background of fourth-century conditions, Plato's political philosophy appears primarily as an effort to combat the factions and moral uncertainty that were draining the life out of the Greek city-state, by restoring to its proper position the authority of law. It is only the recognition of the authority of law that can restore order and measure to the conduct of the citizen and unity to the city. This is the burden of his earnest advice to the citizens of Syracuse in the *Seventh* and *Eighth Epistles*. "The god of wise men is the law" (*VIII*, 354e). Lycurgus arrested the degeneration of his native city by making law "the lord and king of men, not men tyrants over the laws" (*VIII*, 354bc), as did the people of Syracuse, when they stoned their generals, "without any legal judgment . . . in order not to be subject to any master, not even justice and the law" (*VIII*, 354de). Here Plato is not an innovator, but is merely restating in earnest terms the presupposition that underlay all Greek thought on man and nature, the fundamental article of Greek political faith. That there is order in nature, and a similar order in human relations, which it is the duty of the wise man or the priest to apprehend and declare to his fellow men; and that these deliverances of eternal law are the source of all authority and right—these were the principles that had guided the Greek people since at least the days of Homer. And Plato's greatest indignation and scorn is reserved for the specious wise men of the fifth century and later who refused to acknowledge the existence or the authority of this rightful sovereign.

But for a thinker of the caliber of Plato, the solution to the problem was not to be found in merely reaffirming what had been generally questioned. The remedy for his time was not merely a return to the practices of the fathers. He was not one to ignore the acute criticism the Enlightenment had focused upon the nature of law and legislation. His stature as a thinker is shown by the fact that he had thought through the claims of the Sophist doctrine of nature and had found a point of support on the other side. He recognized both the conventional character of human legislation and the reality of a divine order, a genuine "law of nature," that must serve as the pattern for human laws and political institutions. The *Republic*, written in Plato's early maturity, and the *Laws*, product of his old age, are both attempts to find a theoretically satisfactory principle, a conception of political justice that could commend itself to the critical intellect as a reasonable formula of the rights and obligations of citizens. The *Republic* gives us a statement in general terms; the *Laws* attempts to specify the details of legislation required to embody the principle; but both of them are constructive attempts to get beyond the palaver about "convention" to a permanently satisfying basis of political order.

In both these great works it is significant that the desire for "community" is the dominant feature of Plato's thought. He puts forward, most clearly in the *Republic*, an impressive and historically influential conception of the common good—not as the welfare of the greatest number, "the people," not merely as the maintenance of the basic conditions of security and peace required alike by all members of the state, but as a unitary and comprehensive good in which all members of the state participate when fulfilling their proper functions in the common life. This means for Plato an organic state, a common life resting upon a differentiation of functions and a corresponding distinction of classes; a differentiation that is the essence of justice, since it exacts of each his appropriate contribution to the common life, and makes of all a single political whole. The dominant idea in Plato's doctrine of justice is not equality, nor merit, but unity. The principles that create and maintain this unity in the city are the essence of justice; they constitute the law, the "right law" (as a modern jurist would say) which has legitimate sovereignty over desires and furnishes a standard of action for every reasonable man. Here again Plato is no innovator. No doubt the importance of unity in the state, and of the law that is the basis for this unity, had been especially impressed upon him by the turbulence and faction of his own day; but the ideal itself had been present from the very beginning of the city-state. It was the desire for a greater and more effective unity in the citizen body that had inspired most of the reforms in Athenian constitutional history; this desire for unity underlay the continuous movement toward democracy that had begun with Solon, and it had come nearest to a successful realization in the early days of the Periclean democracy.[11]

The Ideal of the Strong Man

The political controversies of the fourth century centered about democracy. The preceding century had been a century of experimentation in democracy under the leadership of Athens; but the end of the century saw Athens impoverished and helpless, her leadership discredited, and the victory of Sparta and her allies seemed to confirm the verdict of Alcibiades that democracy was "an admitted folly." But just as democracy persisted at Athens and elsewhere, in spite of the supremacy of the Spartan arms, so the controversy as to the value of democracy continued into the fourth century. Against democracy were arrayed most of the foremost writers of the period: Xenophon, Aristotle, Isocrates on occasion, and Plato. The bitterly satirical delineation of democracy and the democratic man in the *Republic* shows the disillusionment of a highly sensitive mind. Plato had lived under a democracy, and he knew its weaknesses. His most impressionable years were spent under the shadow of the Peloponnesian War, when the Athenian democracy was working under the

11 See J. L. Myres, *Political Ideas of the Greeks* (New York, 1927), Lect. II.

severest strain it had ever experienced. The war was already
four years old when Plato was born, and he was a man of
twenty-three when it ended. He must have received unforgettable impressions of the weakness of the democratic assembly—its subservience to the eloquent demagogue, its vacillation
on points of fundamental policy, its unwillingness to assume
responsibility for its own decisions, its thirst for vengeance
when things went wrong, and its growing disregard of principle and of "Hellenic law" as the war dragged on. It is
significant that in Thucydides the doctrine of the sanctity of
might, and of expediency as the highest law, seems to come
oftenest from the lips of the Athenians and their representa-
tives. In spite of the studied impartiality of Thucydides' narrative, we get an overwhelming impression of the disillusion-
ing effect produced by the acts of the Athenian democracy
upon his deeply thoughtful mind. Plato's was a mind of a
similar mold, and we probably cannot overestimate the
effect of the events of these early years in determining Plato's
feeling toward democracy.

But there was a better side to Greek democracy that we
must not overlook, an aspect of things too easily forgotten by
a modern reader in the chorus of denunciation that comes
from the greatest writers of this period. We can easily find
much to praise if we look more soberly at the functioning of
Athenian democracy, even in the fourth century. The Athens
of Plato's manhood and old age was not a city of anarchy and
futility; indeed it had some notable achievements to its credit.
Athens was remarkably free from the bitterer forms of factional strife during the long period from the restoration of
the democracy in 403 to the time of Philip, and the manner
in which the democratic party laid aside its grievances at the
restoration in the interests of the city's harmony testifies to no
small degree of political sagacity and public spirit in the
demos. This seems to have made an impression on Plato, for
he refers to it in an early passage of the *Seventh Epistle*
(325b). And when we consider the temptations to an abuse of
political power for economic ends that were inherent in the

power of the assembly and the courts, we are rather surprised that we do not hear of more actual cases of deliberate spoliation of the rich for the benefit of the poor. Again the way in which Athens gradually repaired her economic structure and regained her foreign trade and even a large part of her former empire during the first three decades after the Peloponnesian War shows that her public policy was directed with a great deal of consistency and skill. Again we must not forget that the Athenian constitution of the fourth century had devices for preventing hasty and tyrannical action on the part of the demos, in both its legislative and judicial capacities.[12] These devices often failed to work; but we must remember that we hear mainly of the exceptional cases in which these provisions were overridden. They must have operated as effective checks a great part of the time, and the necessity that was felt of giving a pretense of legality to an actual evasion probably shows that these constitutional provisions had considerable hold upon the mind of the Athenian citizen.

These saving features must be borne in mind if we would understand why Plato, in spite of his satire on democracy in the *Republic,* gives considerable recognition to the democratic principle in the constitution of the *Laws.* The *Laws* outlines a constitution which is a union or mixture of monarchy and democracy, thus embodying both the principle of authority and the principle of liberty.[13] And we shall see later that in the advice to Dion's party in Syracuse Plato proposes a constitution that has a noticeable share of democratic features. In the *Laws* the mixture of monarchy and democracy is especially evident in the mode of election prescribed for the members of the council and for the Guardians of the Laws. Practically universal suffrage, a board of scrutiny to pass on the qualifications of candidates, and finally the typical democratic device of the lot to effect the final decision—this is the complicated procedure prescribed for the choice of the governing bodies. The democratic principle by no means has

[12] P. Vinogradoff, *Historical Jurisprudence* (Oxford, 1922), II, 133-52.
[13] III, 693de; VI, 756e. See my *Plato's Cretan City,* chap. X.

free play; it can never operate to put manifestly incapable
men in public office; but it has a definite and unmistakable
sphere within which to operate. The causes and the precise
significance of this apparent change in Plato's attitude are a
matter of dispute. Was it merely a realistic concession to an
irresistible demand of the times? Or is it evidence of a more
favorable estimate of democracy? Or is democracy brought in
only to counteract the tendency of monarchy toward absolutism? However bitter his criticism of democracy in the
Republic, Plato never makes light of the principle of liberty.
It is the false and illusory liberty of the democratic man that
is the butt of his satire.[14] True liberty is attainable only under
order and law; and democracy represents the principle of
liberty in so far as it resists the tendency of monarchy to
override the law. But the demos, it is clear, can never fulfill
this function unless it is in some sense the source of political
wisdom, and this is sometimes admitted in the *Laws.* "For
the many are not so far wrong in their judgment of who are
bad and who are good as they are removed from the nature
of virtue in themselves. Even bad men have a divine instinct
which guesses rightly, and very many who are completely de-
praved form correct notions and judgments of the differences
between the good and the bad." [15] It would seem, then, that
Plato's attitude toward democracy changed to this extent, that
he came to value somewhat more highly the political intelligence of the demos. But his judgment of pure democracy as a
form of government seems to have remained unchanged. His
belief in its futility, its inconsistency, its incapacity to pursue
any distant or long-time end, is as pronounced in the *Laws* as
in the *Republic;* and the position assigned to democracy in
the *Politicus* is a clear statement of what seems to have been
his mature attitude: democracy is midway in the scale of excellence, because from its very nature it is incapable of doing
any very great harm or any very great good.

Most fourth-century thinkers who were aware of the evils

14 *Rep.* VIII, 557b-e.
15 XII, 950b. Jowett's trans.

of democracy and desired to find a form of government that
would rescue the Greek cities from their internal factions and
mutual jealousies looked to monarchy as the salvation of
Greece. This was the century of kings and strong men. Evagoras, a soldier of fortune, established himself in Cyprus,
where he maintained for many years a Greek kingdom that
was a thorn in the side of the Persian power. Dionysius, the
clerk, became tyrant of Syracuse and united the Greek cities
in Sicily and Italy into an empire that held back the invading
Carthaginians. Both of these men, though tyrants, were admired for the services they had rendered in uniting Greeks
against the barbarians. In the North, Jason of Pherae consolidated the cities of Thessaly into an imposing, though
short-lived, kingdom. Still farther north was the kingdom of
Macedonia, from which eventually came the power that finally
put an end to the independence of the Greek cities. The terms
tyrant and tyranny had formerly indicated all that was most
repugnant to the liberty-loving Greek; but throughout the
fourth century these words were losing something of their
unsavoriness, at least in advanced circles. In his *Hiero* Xenophon begins with the usual Greek conception of the tyrant,
as an outlaw on the throne, the most miserable and hated of
men; but cleverly converts the dialogue into a picture of what
an enlightened and public-spirited monarch might do for his
city, and incidentally for himself, by working for the welfare
of his subjects.[16] Even the once despised and hated Oriental
monarchy became attractive. Xenophon drew an enthusiastic
picture of Cyrus the Great, the model of a good king, and con-
fessed that he had found in monarchy of this sort the solution
of the problem of governing men.[17] We hear of a dialogue by
Antisthenes on the same theme and with the same hero.[18]
Plato, both in the *Laws* and in the *Seventh Epistle,* writes in
praise of Cyrus and Darius.[19] How much political experience

16 Cf. Isocrates, *To Nicocles,* and *Evagoras.*
17 *Cyropaedia* I, i.
18 Diog. Laert. VI, 16.
19 *Laws* III, 694ab, 695cd; *Ep. VII,* 332ab.

and political disillusionment had come since the days of
Herodotus! The ideal of a strong man would have undeniable
attractions for a century tired of factional strife and eager for
some authority strong enough to impose obedience upon the
warring factions. It would also appeal to those who, like Isocrates, saw the threat to Greek liberties from the rising power
of Persia on the east and Carthage on the west, and hoped
that a strong leader could unite the Greeks in a crusade
against the barbarians.[20] In short, an absolutism, more or less
enlightened, seemed to many of the foremost thinkers of the
fourth century the best remedy for the faction and political
selfishness of the age.

Thus it is that Plato, in his earlier political writings, regarded absolute monarchy as the best form of government.
The ideal government of the *Republic* is a personal rule of
one or more philosophically trained guardians. A more realistic and perhaps maturer attitude is evident in the *Laws,*
which looks upon absolute government with distinct distrust.
That this point has not been emphasized more by commentators on Plato's political theory is due partly to the relatively
greater attention always given to the *Republic,* and the neglect of the *Laws.* It is time, however, that we regarded the
doctrine of the *Laws* as also Platonic, indeed (if experience and
maturity count for anything), as the ripest expression of Plato's
political principles. And the *Laws* affirms in no doubtful tones
the importance of the principle of liberty, in the sense above
explained. Plato knew that the Cyrus whom Xenophon pictured as a paragon of virtue, a living embodiment of law,
existed chiefly in Xenophon's idealizing imagination. The
temptations of supreme power are more than any man can
withstand;[21] and long experience of this fact has led mankind rightly to regard the rule of one man with suspicion.[22]
Absolute monarchy must fall into the ignorance that selfishness brings; and Plato's judgment is based upon the history of

[20] See his *To Philip* and his letters to Archidamus and Dionysius.
[21] *Laws* IX, 875ab.
[22] *Politicus,* 301c-e.

what were in his opinion some of the most promising ventures
in Greek government, the ancient states of Argos and Messene.
Sparta was saved only because its monarchy was not absolute,
being carefully limited by its having two kings instead of
one, and by the power of the ephors.[23] The history of Persia,
that Asiatic Sparta, furnished abundant confirmation of this
opinion. The *Laws* and *Politicus* both insist that the really
important distinction between governments is not that between monarchies, oligarchies, and democracies (an obvious
classification that is at least as old as Herodotus) but between
governments that have a body of fundamental law which
rulers as well as subjects respect and observe, and those in
which the ruler, whoever he may be, is regarded as above the
law. An absolute monarchy, admitting no higher law than the
will of the monarch, may be suitable for the age of Kronos, but
is distinctly not an ideal for the government of men in the
conditions of the present age. Plato, then, was not in favor of
entrusting the welfare of Athens or of any other Greek city
to the hands of an absolute monarch, staking everything on
the chance that he will turn out to be the divine shepherd of
the *Politicus;* and he seems even to have believed that the
rule of the divine shepherd would sit better with its human
subjects if it had a constitution and a supreme court.

But Plato always seems to have recognized the advantage,
if not the necessity, of having a strong government in an age
when drastic reforms in a people's life must be made. When a
people's moral and political habits have to be fundamentally
changed, the personal and unfettered rule of a strong man,
provided that he is also enlightened and benevolent, is
well nigh a necessity. The ideal state of the *Republic* can be
brought into being, Socrates says, if fortune should provide a
young and able tyrant who is at the same time interested
in philosophy.[24] Such a tyrant could set his people an example
of virtue (as does Cyrus in Xenophon's romance). He would
have the force to suppress recalcitrant elements and impose

[23] *Laws* III, 683d-692a.
[24] *Rep.* VI, 502ab; *Laws* IV, 709e-710d.

upon his people a system of training that would bear fruit in distant generations. Plato sometimes speaks as if the power of an absolute ruler were the only way in which a regime of justice could be established, and he seems ever to have been ready to avail himself of the power of enlightened tyrants. But it is one thing to recognize the need of a strong ruler at a time of drastic reform, and quite another thing to look upon the reign of a despot or a group of despots as the form of government permanently best for a people. Much of the tendency to regard Plato as an Oriental theocrat in Greek guise is due, beyond a doubt, to the confusion of these two positions. It is the *Seventh Epistle* that shows us how Plato could make use of absolute power on occasion, and also how bitterly he denounced it as a permanent principle of government:

> Do not subject Sicily nor any other state to the despotism of men, but to the rule of laws; this at least is my doctrine. For despotic power benefits neither rulers nor subjects, but is an altogether deadly experience for themselves, their children, and their children's children; and no one grasps at the prizes it offers except petty and illiberal souls who know nothing of the divine and human goods that are now and for all time good and just (334cd).

Plato's Political Inactivity at Athens

Believing as he did that the first step toward health in Athenian politics was a drastic reorganization of the political institutions and a revival of the ancestral morality of his people, it is not surprising that Plato came to the conclusion that he could accomplish nothing by direct participation in political life at Athens. There was first of all the futility of a democratic constitution, incapable even under favorable conditions of accomplishing anything very admirable or far reaching. And however moderate and public spirited it might be on occasion, the Athenian democracy was in no temper during Plato's lifetime to consider limitations of its powers. Certainly many of the thoughtful democrats of Plato's time sincerely deplored as he did the moral uncertainty and the loss of civic unity, but their remedy was an extension of the democratic principle, rather than an abandonment of it. And the demos had powerful means at its disposal for preventing changes that it disliked. Possibly there would have been real personal danger involved in attempting to do directly what Plato thought ought to be done. "Whoever attempts to go to the rescue of justice . . . will be like a man that has fallen among wild beasts, destined to perish before he can be of any great service to his country or his friends, and do no good to himself or anyone else." [25] These are passionate words, but there was more than a grain of truth in them. Much later, in the *Seventh Epistle,* he gives a public explanation of the conditions under which it is profitable for a man to give political advice:

> When one is advising a sick man who is living in a way injurious to his health, must one not first of all tell him to change his way of life and give him further counsel only if he is willing to obey? If he is not, I think any manly and self-respecting physician would break off counseling such a man, whereas anyone who would put up with him is without spirit or skill. So too with respect to a city; whether it be governed by one man or many, if its constitution is properly ordered and rightly directed, it would be sensible to give advice to its citizens concerning what would be to the city's advantage. But if it is a people who have wandered completely away from right government and resolutely refuse to come back upon its track and instruct their counselor to leave the constitution strictly alone, threatening him with death if he changes it, and order him instead to serve their interests and desires and show them how they can henceforth satisfy them in the quickest and easiest way—any man, I think, who would accept such a role as adviser is without spirit, and he who refuses is the true man (330de).

And somewhat earlier Plato, or some member of the Academy, in a letter to Perdiccas, gave a similar defense of Plato's political inactivity at Athens:

25 *Rep.* VI, 496d.

If anyone hears this and says, "Plato apparently claims to know what is good for a democracy, but though he is at liberty to speak in the assembly and give it his best advice, he has never yet stood up and said a word," you can answer by saying, "Plato was born late in the life of his native city, and he found the demos advanced in years and habituated by former advisers to many practices incompatible with the advice he would give. Nothing would be sweeter to him than to give advice to the demos as to a father, if he did not think he would be risking danger in vain and accomplish nothing" (*Ep. V,* 322ab).

But it is hard to believe that Plato completely despaired of ever having an opportunity of taking a direct part in political life at Athens. He no doubt hoped for some crisis to occur that would lead the democracy of itself to seek a change of constitution and entrust the making of its laws to him or some other wise man or group of men. Similar crises in the past had been the occasion of the great reforms in Athenian government brought about by Solon and Cleisthenes, and probably Ephialtes. No doubt the revision of the laws after the restoration in 403 was accomplished in somewhat the same way, though it involved less drastic changes.[26] Some such procedure as this is what Plato recommends to the distraught citizens of Syracuse in 353. They are to select a group of wise men (chosen from other cities in Greece, including Athens) to draw up laws for the common good; and this is the way in which the constitution of the *Laws* is to be instituted, the first group of thirty-seven nomophylakes to be selected from the mother city of the new colony. The Athenian Stranger of the *Laws* is not only ready, but eager, to help in making laws for this new colony; and his literary creator would have been only too glad, we may well believe, if his fellow citizens had asked him, to help rebuild the laws of Athens.

Some have seen in Plato's abstention from practical politics an unwilling admission by Plato himself of his unfitness for

[26] On this method of legislative reorganization and its use by Greek cities of the fourth century, see Vinogradoff, *Historical Jurisprudence,* II, 135.

public life, an unconscious recognition that his own talents
were those of the speculative thinker, the poet and mystic,
rather than those of a molder of constitutions and a maker
of men. And the disastrous outcome of his intervention in
Sicilian affairs is usually taken as a clear confirmation of this
alleged distrust of his political powers. There is an element
of truth in this view, but it has probably been pushed too far.
It is indeed very doubtful whether Plato's actual participation
in Athenian politics would have been beneficial to the Athens
of his day. Whether he would have been able to realize any
of his principles working through the machinery of the existing democracy is highly questionable; and the attempt to do
so, accompanied by the deep moral earnestness that Plato put
into his political principles, would perhaps have given rise
to new factional divisions. But this does not imply that Plato
did not possess statesmanlike powers to a high degree. His
insight into the spirit and purpose of the city-state, the wealth
of his knowledge of Greek political institutions and their history, his unusual ability (attested in various fashions) to en-
list the co-operation of others for high ends, above all, his
intense love of Athens and his loyalty to Greek civilization—
all these are qualities that under more favorable circumstances
might have made him a leader of his people and a builder of
political institutions. It has become the tradition to draw an
unfavorable contrast between Plato's "idealism" and Aristotle's sense of political realities. But this seems to be a mere
convention. Whoever carefully studies Plato's political writings, especially those of his later years, with their amazing
knowledge of Greek political life, cannot fail to see that Plato
is doing (and doing equally well) just what Aristotle is doing
in the *Politics*. He is attempting to discover the forces at work
in political life, and attempting to express his political ideals
in a form that can take account of these forces and utilize
them. The sense of political realities is not lacking in Plato;
and we cannot doubt that this sense of reality, coupled with
his high idealism and his unrivaled capacity for influencing
men for noble ends, would have been a powerful and benefi-

cent force if it had found conditions suitable for its exercise.

If Plato did not put himself at the service of the democratic party at Athens, neither did he take part in the oligarchical intrigues against the democracy. There was an oligarchic party at Athens that no doubt for some time after the restoration of the democracy cherished the hope of an overthrow of the government, and Plato was related by blood to some of the prominent members of this party. We hear of the hetaeriae or political clubs of an oligarchic cast, throughout the fourth century. They were distrusted by the democracy as centers of conspiracy, and justly so, for they had played a decisive part in the overthrow of the democracy in 403. But Plato, on the rare occasions when he mentions these organizations, speaks of them with contempt.[27] Dion seems to have joined one at Athens, and Plato evidently thought it no great stroke of policy, and its consequences were in fact disastrous for Dion. Plato had no faith in the capacity or the good intentions of the oligarchic party at Athens. He was disillusioned decisively by the brief rule of the Thirty, from which, as he tells us in the *Seventh Epistle,* he had hoped for great things. And the principle of oligarchy never receives much favor in the dialogues; in the *Laws* it is taken as representing the principle of faction and political selfishness par excellence.[28] Even if he had been sympathetic with the oligarchic principle and had had any confidence in the oligarchical party at Athens, he would still have been averse to the violent methods that invariably accompanied the oligarchical *coups d'état* of the fourth century. It is by no means clear that he would advocate ruthlessness in the accomplishing of political ends, as Ritter suggests.[29] He says in the *Politicus,* it is true, that a real legislator will not scruple to use the knife to cure political

[27] *Theaet.* 173d; *Rep.* II, 365d. In *Laws* IX, 856b, the influence of ἑταιρίαι is regarded as the greatest threat to the sovereignty of the laws.

[28] IV, 710e. Aristotle tells us that it was customary for the oligarchical die-hards to swear: "I will be an enemy of the demos and do it whatever harm I can" (*Politics* 1310a9).

[29] *Platon,* II, 653.

ills (293); but the significant qualification is introduced that
what alone justifies such ruthless procedure is the possession
of science by those who rule, and the same dialogue makes it
clear that those who can lay claim to possessing such royal
science are few, if any. The brutality and bloodshed that occurred in Syracuse as a result of the attempt of Dion to establish himself in power caused Plato real distress, as the
Seventh Epistle plainly shows; and he defends Dion (and
himself) by reiterating that these were due to unforeseen and
incalculable factors that frustrated the peaceable realization
of their plan (327d). He would naturally have been even more
averse to summary methods at Athens. "Let [the wise man]
not use violence upon his fatherland to bring about a change
of constitution. If what he thinks is best can only be accomplished by the exile and slaughter of men, let him keep his
peace and pray for the welfare of himself and his city." [30]

The Political Purpose of the Academy

But the oligarchical clubs may have impressed one lesson,
at least, upon Plato; viz. the importance of having like-minded
followers if one is to accomplish any political end. "I saw it
was impossible to do anything without friends and loyal followers; and to find such men ready to hand would be a piece
of sheer good luck, since our city was no longer guided by the
customs and practices of our fathers, while to train up new
ones was anything but easy" (*VII*, 325d). But to this difficult
task of training a band of followers, companions in virtue
and sharers of his political and moral principles, Plato addressed himself as the best way of serving his native city. The
important thing was to create a body of sentiment at Athens
favorable to the political reforms that Plato regarded as necessary and a group of men competent to legislate wisely, if the
opportunity offered, for a peaceful reform of the constitution.
It is a clear inference from the passage in the *Seventh Epistle*
just quoted that the Academy was founded to accomplish,

[30] *Ep. VII*, 331d.

among other things, this definitely political purpose: it was
intended to serve as a training school for statesmen and
public-spirited citizens. To say this is not to imply that the
studies pursued in the Academy were narrowly political; when
we understand Plato's doctrine that only philosophy should
rule we easily see that his future statesmen had to take all
knowledge for their province. But political in purpose the
Academy certainly was. All other similar associations prior to
the founding of the Academy seem to have been more or less
political in character. The Sophists established no schools, but
the training they professed to give their groups of students
was the knowledge necessary for the citizen and the public
man. Isocrates' school of rhetoric had avowedly the aim of
training statesmen. And the Pythagorean brotherhoods with
which Plato seems to have become personally acquainted only
a short time before, and which may have been the inspiration
for the founding of the Academy, were groups of learned
politicians.

And political in its influence the Academy certainly became.
It was known in the fourth century as a place where the governing of men was studied scientifically; and we hear of many
of its members who took an active part in the political life
of Greek states. There is a famous passage in Plutarch that
tells us the names of some of these influential members of the
Academy.[31] Phormio, he says, gave laws to the city of Elis.
Aristonymus was sent out from the Academy to draw up a
constitution for the Arcadians, probably for the new federal
city of Megalopolis, founded shortly after 371. Menedemus
was sent to the Pyrrhaeans, Eudoxus to the Cnidians, and Aristotle to the Stagirites. Euphraeus, of Oreus, a member of the
Academy, resided for several years at the court of Perdiccas
III, King of Macedon, and was very influential there.[32]
Hermeias, tyrant of Atarneus, maintained the most intimate
relations with Aristotle and Xenocrates, and at an earlier date
with Erastus and Coriscus, two members of the Academy from

[31] *Adv. Colot.* XXXII.
[32] Athen. 506ef.

Scepsis, near Atarneus.[33] Alexander is said to have asked political advice of Xenocrates. Delius of Ephesus, a pupil of
Plato's, was an influential adviser to Philip and Alexander in
their wars against Persia; and another of Philip's agents was
Pytho, also a pupil of Plato.[34] The *Epistles* give many indications of the influence and the prestige the Academy enjoyed
with the rulers of Greek states. The *Fifth* is supposed to be
the letter Plato, or some member of the Academy, wrote introducing Euphraeus to King Perdiccas. The *Sixth* is a similar
document written to Hermeias commending Erastus and
Coriscus to his protection and advising him to enter into a
friendly alliance with them. The *Eleventh* purports to be an
answer to a letter from a certain Laodamas who had requested
Plato to come or send his pupil, Socrates, to help in drawing
up laws for a colony he was about to establish, or had just
established, probably in Thessaly. There must have been
many more such cases which we do not hear of, but the evidence we do have indicates how widespread was the actual
political influence of the Academy.

These particulars show that there were two chief ways in
which the direct influence of Plato and the Academy was
exerted upon the political life of the fourth century: first,
when a colony was to be founded, and a code of laws was to
be drawn up for it; and secondly, more rarely, when some
despotic ruler, who had conceived the ambition of ruling
more wisely and justly, called to his side the philosopher, and
thus brought about that juncture of wisdom and power from
which great things might come. Of all the cases in which the
Academy participated directly in Greek politics the most celebrated was the attempt of Plato, in conjunction with Dion
and the younger Dionysius, to bring about a constitutional
government at Syracuse. Since it is this attempt and its consequences with which most of the letters in our collection are
concerned, it deserves to be studied in some detail.

[33] See pp. 211, n. 1 and 212, n. 3.
[34] Plut. *Adv. Colot.* XXXII.

DION AND THE REFORM OF SICILY

Of all the strong individuals of the early fourth century who pursued personal fortune at the expense of their native cities and in disregard of Hellenic traditions, Dionysius the Elder, of Syracuse, was, on the whole, the most successful; and his career is an exceedingly significant episode in the history of the last century of the free city-state. Syracuse was the most important Greek city in the west, and perhaps the largest and richest of all Greek cities. Dionysius came into power during the Carthaginian invasion of the island at the end of the fifth century when the Syracusan assembly, as a war measure, conferred upon him the office of *strategos autocrator,* general with unlimited powers. For thirty-eight years thereafter, until his death in 367, he maintained his position as virtual tyrant of the wealthiest city of the Greek world and ruler of an empire that at its widest included nearly all of Sicily and a large portion of southern Italy. He was an unscrupulous and unprincipled adventurer, but he had also some of the qualities of a great general and an astute statesman. As a military leader he inaugurated a new era in the art of warfare, discarding the traditional practices of the fifth century and anticipating the tactics of Philip and Alexander. He met and for a while successfully stemmed the rising tide of Carthaginian invasion. In politics and diplomacy he was extraordinarily astute, never at a loss for a way out of difficult situations; and no sentimental patriotic scruples prevented him from playing up the Carthaginian menace in order to maintain himself in power, or using the barbarian tribes of Italy and Sicily as mercenaries or as allies to subdue a recalcitrant Greek city. Endowed with immense energy, he found time in the intervals of warfare and diplomacy to write tragedies, and regularly competed for the prize at Athens, on one occasion successfully. His power and prestige in the Greek world were so great that he was alternately looked on as the savior of Greek civilization in Sicily, and as the hated tyrant who threatened to destroy the liberties of all Greece.

The office which he held at Syracuse seems never to have been anything but *strategos autocrator;* to this office he seems to have been elected annually by the assembly. Along with the assembly he probably retained most of the other institutions of democratic government that Syracuse had enjoyed in the fifth century; but he saw to it that they should so function as to carry out his will. He had an effective instrument for maintaining his power in the vast body of mercenaries, to a great extent Italian and Gaulish, with which he surrounded himself and garrisoned the rocky islet of Ortygia, just off the mainland at the entrance of the Great Harbor of Syracuse. Though nominally a constitutionally elected *strategos,* he was in reality a tyrant, and as such he was regarded in all Greece. The Syracusans themselves would have no doubts on the matter when they looked upon the fortifications of Epipolae and the walls of his great castle at Euryalus. His power over the other Greek cities in Sicily was equally absolute. His policy seems to have been to centralize all power at Syracuse, thereby destroying the autonomy and local initiative of the free Greek cities. Some of these ancient communities, such as Naxos, the oldest Greek settlement in Sicily, were completely destroyed; while others, such as Catana, were emptied of their Greek population and new settlers from Italy and from the non-Hellenic tribes of Sicily were brought in to take their place. A similar fate befell the Greek cities of southern Italy. The name of Dionysius thus became to all Greeks the symbol of unscrupulous, arbitrary, unbridled power, a threat not only to all the ancient institutions of the free city-state, but also to Greek culture in its struggle against the native population; and yet the man's undoubted ability, his services in saving Sicily from the Carthaginians, and the splendor of his empire, aroused not only wonder but even respect and admiration.

Plato's relations with Syracuse began about the year 388 when, on a visit to the Pythagorean philosophers in southern

Italy, he received an invitation to come to the court of Dionysius (*VII*, 324a). At this time the power of the tyrant was approaching its height. He had succeeded in driving back the Carthaginians within the boundaries of their ancient sphere of influence, the northwest corner of the island, and he held the rest of Sicily firmly under his control. He had also stretched his hand across the Straits of Messina and subdued Rhegium, laying the foundation of his Italian empire that was eventually to extend over all the Greek cities in Italy. Plato no doubt was eager to make the acquaintance of the tyrant, and as Dionysius himself had some literary and philosophical pretensions, it was natural that he should invite the distinguished philosopher to come to Syracuse. But the chief cause of the invitation, we are told by Plutarch, was Dion, the brother-in-law of Dionysius, then about twenty years old, who had become attracted to Plato's philosophy from afar, and who now was eager to see the philosopher and talk with him. This Dion, like Dionysius, was a person of unusual strength of character. Plato testifies in the *Seventh Epistle* (327a) to his unusual mental powers and his moral earnestness and sincerity. His father, Hipparinus, had been for a time associated with Dionysius in the government of Syracuse. From this fact, and from Dion's own temper and conduct, we may infer that he was connected by blood with the aristocracy, and thus was by inheritance unsympathetic with the principles of democracy. At the same time a certain moral austerity in his disposition made him dissatisfied with the luxury and license of Sicilian life and with the political absolutism of Dionysius' rule which, with its shameless disregard for the law and constitution, was the political counterpart of the prevailing moral laxness. The political and ethical teachings of Plato therefore found in him a receptive hearer, and thus there began a deep friendship between Plato and Dion which was to last until the death of Dion, more than thirty years later.

In view of the influence this meeting between Plato and Dion was to have upon the next thirty or forty years of Sicil-

ian history, let us see more exactly what the political principles were that Dion is said to have got from Plato.[1] When
Plato went to Syracuse in 388, we are told, he had already
arrived at the conviction that philosophers should rule, or
rulers become philosophers, if the steady degeneration in
Greek political life was to be stopped. This is easily recognized as the central doctrine of the *Republic*. When therefore he met Dion, and communicated to him his opinions
about what was best for mankind (τὰ δοκοῦντα ἐμοὶ βέλτιστα
ἀνθρώποις, 327a), we may be quite sure that the rule of the
philosophers was central in the doctrines he taught Dion. But
this does not help us much, for the phrase is at best a vague
one, and we desire to know what specifically the rule of philosophy would mean for Syracuse and Sicily in the fourth
century. It would be clearly illegitimate, I believe, to conclude that Plato would recommend for Syracuse all the specific doctrines of the *Republic*, such as the community of
women and property for the guardians. If Plato's conversations with Dion descended to the needs of Syracuse in the
fourth century, as must certainly have been the case, what
specific proposals of reform did he suggest to Dion?

One of the first things that struck Plato's attention and
aroused his profound disapproval when he arrived in Syracuse was the great luxury and license to be found there. He
was already familiar by hearsay with these features of western
life, as we know from references to them in the dialogues.
"Syracusan tables" had become proverbial in Greece. But the

[1] To do this we have to depend principally upon the *Seventh* and
Eighth Epistles, which were written some thirty-five years after this first
visit to Syracuse and with special reference to the situation there after
the death of Dion; and the information they give us regarding these
early conversations between Plato and Dion is necessarily bound up with
the later issues that were in the forefront of Plato's attention. On the
other hand, one of the purposes of the *Seventh Epistle*, as we have seen,
is to make clear to the world the principles that had guided Plato
throughout in his relations with Syracuse; and there is accordingly more
reference to these early opinions of the reforms necessary at Syracuse than
would otherwise be the case.

actual contact with this luxurious civilization seems to have
surprised as well as shocked him. It struck him as a life of
gluttony and sensuality; and the profound disapprobation it
aroused is recorded in the *Seventh Epistle:*

> No man under heaven who has cultivated such practices
> from his youth could possibly grow up to be wise—so
> miraculous a temper is against nature—or become temper-
> ate, or indeed acquire any other part of virtue. Nor could
> any city enjoy tranquillity, no matter how good its laws,
> when its men think they must spend their all on excesses,
> and be easygoing about everything except the feasts and the
> drinking bouts and the pleasures of love that they pursue
> with professional zeal. These cities are always changing into
> tyrannies, or oligarchies, or democracies, while the rulers
> in them will not even hear mention of a just and equitable
> constitution (326cd).

From the striking impression this feature of Sicilian life made
upon Plato and the space that is given to the matter in this
account of his early relations with Syracuse, it is certain that
one of the lessons he taught Dion was the necessity of bringing about a change in these habits, if any political reform was
to endure. Elsewhere he declares that the Syracusans must
return to the Dorian customs of their ancestors if they are
ever to establish a stable political order (*VII*, 336cd); they
must adopt laws which enforce the traditional scale of values
—soul first, body second, wealth third (*VIII*, 355bc). We know
also that as a consequence of Plato's teaching, Dion himself
adopted a simple and austere manner of life, contrasting
sharply with the customs of the tyranny (*VII*, 327b).

It also seems that Plato impressed upon Dion the necessity
of replacing the tyranny by a constitutional regime. We are
told that Dion got from Plato, on his first visit, the conviction
that the people of Syracuse "ought to be free and live under
the best of laws" (324b). What was meant by being free is clear
enough from the second half of this sentence, and is confirmed
by other passages. "Do not subject Sicily nor any other state
to the despotism of men, but to the rule of laws" (334cd). It
was recognized from the first by the champions of the tyranny

that the goal of Plato's and Dion's efforts in 367, after the death of the elder Dionysius, was the destruction of the tyranny and the restoration of liberty to Syracuse.[2] Several other passages in the *Epistles* testify to the importance of this aim in the program of Dion and Plato in 367 and later (*III, 315d; VII, 336a; VIII, 354a,c, 355e*). The question might still be raised whether this was their aim in 388. But again the *Epistles* leave no room for doubt; the most striking of all the passages in which Plato asserts the sovereignty of law and pictures the wretchedness of personal despotism is followed by the explicit assertion that this is the doctrine that Plato had taught on three distinct occasions at Syracuse, first to Dion, second to the young Dionysius, and lastly to Dion's party after the assassination of their leader (334cd). Plutarch tells us that the elder Dionysius, on the occasion of Plato's first visit to Sicily, was displeased because Plato refused to show any admiration for his position (*Dion* 5). Whether apocryphal or not, the story Plutarch recites in this connection accords well with the attitude of Plato toward tyranny as expressed in the dialogues. There can be little doubt that Plato disapproved of the tyranny of Dionysius, and the sovereignty of law must have been a part of his teaching in 388, as the passages cited above say it was. This is an important point, for it throws considerable light upon the meaning of the famous Platonic doctrine of the rule of philosophy. The evidence of the *Epistles* shows that the rule of philosophy and the sovereignty of law were not incompatible doctrines for Plato in 388.[3]

The sovereignty of law is the most fundamental of all the political doctrines of the *Epistles;* it underlies all the advice that Plato gives to the friends of Dion. The important thing is to establish good laws and to make them sovereign in the state, ruling over both king and subjects (*VIII, 355b-e*). This

---

[2] Cf. Nepos *Dion* 3: "tyrannidis facere finem, libertatemque reddere Syracusanis."

[3] On the relation between the rule of philosophy and the rule of law see my *Plato's Cretan City*, chap. XII.

doctrine is enforced, as in the *Laws*, with historical illustrations of the value of a constitutional government and of the chaos that ensues when personal absolutism or democratic anarchy takes its place. The success of Lycurgus and the stability of the Spartan constitution are said to be due to the fact that Lycurgus made law the king of men, instead of men tyrants over the law (*VIII*, 354c). In this same passage the laws are personified and represented as uniting with the citizens in praise of the lawful monarch; and Plato draws lessons from Sicilian history to show the evils of arbitrary authority, on the one hand, and of unbridled freedom, on the other, just as in the *Laws* he had illustrated the same doctrine by lessons drawn from Persian and Athenian history.[4] In one of the most earnest passages in the *Seventh Epistle* (337de), Plato tries to impress upon the warring factions at Syracuse that the only way in which the evils of civil war can be brought to an end is for the victorious party to renounce political reprisals and set the example of voluntary subjection to laws devised by an impartial board of legislators for the common good of all parties.

Another matter that Plato must have impressed upon Dion was the need for protecting Greek civilization in Sicily and Italy against the advance of the barbarians. The decisive defeat of the Carthaginians at Himera in 480 had been followed by a long period of peace and prosperity for the Greek cities in Sicily; but at the end of the fifth century the Carthaginians had again become aggressive. It is true that Dionysius had done good service, during the early part of his reign, in staying their advance. In the year 385, about the time of this visit of Plato's, the Greeks were in possession of all of Sicily except the northwest corner, the traditional seat of Carthaginian power. But the later wars of Dionysius were less successful, and for several years before his death in 367 he was paying tribute to Carthage (*Epistle VII*, 333a). Thus when the Syracusan letters were written, the Carthaginians were a serious and ever-growing menace to the Greek cities in Sicily. These

4 *Laws* III, 694-695, 698-701.

cities were in no position to meet this danger, partly because the wars with Carthage had destroyed or weakened many of them, including the great city of Acragas, once the second Greek city in Sicily; and partly because of the policy of Dionysius himself. As we have seen, it was his purpose to weaken these cities and force them into dependence upon Syracuse.

Dionysius' reign was therefore of doubtful value to the cause of Greek civilization in Sicily. In spite of the imposing empire he created, he did not break the power of Carthage in the island, and at his death he left the Greek cities less capable than they had been forty years before of resisting the Carthaginian power. More than this, he had done much to create a new danger in the north. By employing Italian mercenaries to fight against Greek troops, by settling these barbarians in Sicily, and by allying himself with the Lucanians against Rhegium and the confederated Greek cities in southern Italy, he had opened the way for an attack upon the Greek cities by the barbarians of the north. Dionysius was not a devout philhellene. Any benefits he conferred upon the Greeks in Sicily and southern Italy were incidental to the accomplishment of his private ends, and it is highly doubtful whether in the long run these benefits outweighed the injuries he inflicted upon them in pursuance of the same policies.[5]

Plato realized very keenly the threat to Greek civilization in Sicily (*VIII*, 353e). To resettle the Greek cities that had been destroyed, to strengthen the Hellenic strain of those that had been settled with aliens, and unite them all against the barbarians of the west—these were cardinal points in Dion and Plato's later policy (*III*, 315d; *VII*, 332e, 336a, 336d; *VIII*, 357ab). Here again there may be some room for doubt whether or not this part of their program was formulated as early as 388. At that time, as we have said, the power of Dionysius in the island was at its greatest extent, and the

[5] This anti-Hellenic tendency of Dionysius' policy is well brought out by Renata von Scheliha, *Dion: die Platonische Staatsgründung in Sizilien* (Leipzig, 1928), pp. 5-12.

Carthaginians retained only a somewhat precarious hold upon the northwest corner. Yet it must have been clearly evident even then that Dionysius was no wholehearted champion of Greek civilization, and that his conquests (as well as his numerous concessions to the Carthaginians) were dictated primarily by personal ambition. In fact it was decidedly to his interest to keep alive the menace of Carthaginian dominion, since it was partly this menace that kept him in power. Any one solicitous for the welfare of the Greek cities in Sicily and shrewd enough to discern the real motives of Dionysius may well have trembled to think that their fate hung upon the caprice of such a despot. It is hardly to be questioned, then, that Plato in 388 looked upon the policies of Dionysius as detrimental to the interests of Greek civilization in Sicily, and his power as but a feeble and untrustworthy bulwark against the Carthaginians.

The policy which he and Dion favored, and which the younger Dionysius also seems to have adopted for a time, was to restore these ancient cities and make them independent but loyal allies of Syracuse. Some of them had been left desolate by the Carthaginians. These were to be resettled by their former inhabitants, and no doubt also by groups of colonists from Syracuse and other Greek cities with a surplus of population. As for the cities formerly Greek but now inhabited by barbarians, they were to be cleared of the barbarians and their former inhabitants reinstated.[6] In all these cities, laws and constitutions were to be set up that would achieve an ordered freedom for their inhabitants and at the same time unite them against the barbarians (*III*, 315d; *VII*, 332e, 336a,d; *VIII*, 353e, 357ab). All that we know of Plato's devotion to the ideal of the autonomous city-state forbids us to

---

[6] An interesting exception to this policy was announced by Dion when he was engaged in his struggle with Dionysius; he seems to have offered to allow the Italians whom the elder Dionysius had settled in Sicily to remain on condition that they unite with him to overthrow the tyranny at Syracuse (*VIII*, 357a). So Grote interprets this passage in *History of Greece*, chap. 83 *ad fin.*

think that he contemplated anything like the sovereignty of Syracuse over the other cities, and any federation that he may have had in mind must have been of the loosest sort. In the *Republic* (V, 469, 471) it is only the similarity of Greek customs that is to unite Hellenic states against the barbarians. The praise given in the *Laws* (III, 684 ff.) to the ancient Dorian alliance of Sparta, Argos, and Messene indicates clearly the sort of union he had in mind. The member cities of the projected Sicilian league would have similar constitutions, and each would give the other guarantees to come to its aid if the stability of its constitution should ever be endangered. The strength of the bond ultimately would be similarity of ideals. If that could be secured, there would be no temptation toward mutual aggression, nor any fear that all would not unite when one of their number was threatened by barbarians. This is Plato's solution to the problem presented by the particularism of Greek political life: a friendly alliance between autonomous city-states, based upon mutual guarantees to preserve their common political institutions and customs. It is worth noting that Plato here turns his back on the policy of the later Athenian empire, involving the sovereignty of one city over others, and advocates instead a union of free city-states on the order of the Spartan League.[7]

These are the three chief points in Plato's and Dion's program of reform for Syracuse and Sicily, so far as we can judge from the *Seventh Epistle*. And this would seem to be excellent authority, since one purpose of the letter was to make clear to the followers of Dion and to the entire world the precise nature of Dion's policies at Syracuse, and since, furthermore, Plato at the very beginning (324a) asserts with some vigor

---

[7] The confederation of southern Italian cities in the fourth century under the leadership of Tarentum is another example of what Plato had in mind. Since this league was established about the time of Plato's visit to Archytas in 388, it is tempting to see here the influence of Plato. Cf. Scheliha, *op. cit.*, pp. 111-12. In *Epistle VII*, 351b, it is indignantly denied that Dion had in mind anything like the arbitrary rule of one city over its weaker neighbors.

that he ought to know what these policies were, since he had
taught them to Dion. The substance of the program of reform is summed up in the declaration that if Dion had been
allowed to carry out his plans he would first of all have
"cleansed his native city of her servitude and put on her the
garment of freedom," and secondly, he would have instituted
laws to make the daily lives of the citizens orderly and
virtuous; and then, with this accomplished, he would have
made every effort to resettle the whole of Sicily and free it
from the barbarians (VII, 336ab; cf. also 336d; VIII, 357a).
Ἀρετή, ἐλευθερία, κατοικισμός, ἰσονομία: whatever else the rule of
philosophy may have meant for Plato, these were the cardinal
elements of the doctrine as applied to Syracuse in the fourth
century.

THE EXPERIMENT WITH DIONYSIUS II

Plato was less happy in his relations with the elder Dionysius than with Dion; otherwise the rule of philosophy might
have been instituted then and there. The man who had
gained his power by flouting Greek law and tradition was
not the one to accept Plato's doctrine of the sovereignty of
law; and though Plato must have appreciated the force of
Dionysius' character, he could scarcely approve of the arbitrary and unprincipled exercise of power that characterized
his reign. Plutarch tells us that Plato's evident disapproval of
the position of Dionysius, when the tyrant himself would have
liked to be regarded as the most fortunate man in Greece, so
exasperated him that he contrived to have Plato on his home-
ward journey sold as a slave at Aegina. That Plato was really
put up in the slave market at Aegina in 388 and ransomed
by Anniceris of Cyrene seems to be well attested. The
Aeginetans at the time were systematically preying upon
Athenian commerce, and the vessel on which Plato was returning may well have been captured and its famous passen-

ger put up for sale. But the story that Dionysius was an accomplice to the act, as well as other interesting bits of gossip
regarding the quarrel between Plato and Dionysius, are probably the inventions of a later age. Plato is strangely silent
about his relations with Dionysius; but we can safely infer
that he and Dionysius would have little in common, and no
doubt they parted on the coolest of terms.

But Dion's devotion to Plato's principles lasted; and his
appreciation of their importance must have increased in the
following years as he saw the growing weakness of the empire
of Dionysius and the double threat to Greek civilization in
Sicily presented by the increasing strength of Carthage and
by the very despotism of Dionysius. At the same time he retained the favor of Dionysius, and remained until the end of
his reign his loyal and trusted adviser, though disliked, so
Plutarch tells us, by many of the court party on account of
the austerity of his manners. These must have conveyed to
them very clearly his disapproval of the existing order of
things. Whether or not Dion attempted to use his influence
with Dionysius to modify the rigors of the tyranny and reform the manners of the court we do not know; but Plato
tells us that Dion never ceased to hope for a reform of Sicilian
life, especially since in the course of time he observed that
there were others at court beginning to have opinions similar
to his own (*VII*, 327bc). The opportunity that Dion dreamed
of seemed to have arrived when, in 367, the elder Dionysius
died and his son Dionysius succeeded him in the tyranny. The
younger Dionysius was a young man of considerable native
ability, and was at first quite amenable to suggestions from
Dion, who remained in power as his chief adviser, and who
began to urge upon him the program of reform he had at
heart. Dionysius himself, it seems, was not at first averse to a
reform of his government, involving the surrender of a large
part of his powers. It is said that he celebrated his accession
to power by a three-year remission of taxes, and by the release
of many political prisoners. He desired to be popular with
his subjects, and the prospect of being known as an enlight-

ened ruler attracted him. Probably because he himself had felt the oppressive measures of his father, he was inclined to sympathize with the popular demands for freedom; and he made public declarations of his liberal intentions. But he was altogether without experience in public affairs, for his father had consistently excluded him from the government. He had even been left without the rudiments of the education which his station required. Moreover, the position in which he found himself was such that even a more experienced man would have had difficulty in carrying through any of these reforms successfully. He was surrounded by astute courtiers and powerful influences bent on retaining the tyranny; and the luxury of his court tempted him constantly to indolence and self-indulgence, where enterprise and resolution were most required. Worst of all, his own character seems to have been fatally weak; but he was vain and obstinate, as are those who suspect their own weakness. Incapable himself of adhering consistently to a course of conduct that did not promise personal advantage, he suspected the motives of others; and in his inexperience he was constantly suspecting the wrong persons.

Nevertheless Dion thought the situation was full of hope, and wrote Plato that the opportunity had arrived for realizing their ideal of uniting philosophy with political power, and earnestly begged him to come to Syracuse and co-operate with him in this ambitious venture (*VII*, 327c-328b). The *Seventh Epistle* shows clearly that Plato was not enthusiastic over the enterprise (328 ff.). He knew that Dion's character could be depended on; but the young Dionysius was a doubtful factor. No doubt Plato's experience at Syracuse twenty years before had given him a clear idea of the obstacles the young tyrant would encounter in carrying out these reforms, even supposing him to be sincerely and consistently committed to them; and he knew also that the purposes of a young man are variable and inconstant. But in spite of these unpromising features of the situation, Plato made up his mind to go; since, as Dion pointed out to him, this was the situation he had so

frequently described as favorable to the introduction of an
ideal government, viz. a young tyrant, willing to listen to and
able to enforce the principles of philosophy. To refuse to put
his hand to this task under circumstances so closely resembling
those he had long hoped for would be to confess that he was
nothing but a theorist, unwilling to engage himself in action.
It is significant that Plato dislikes to think of himself as a
mere "academic" influence upon Greek politics. Besides this,
there was real danger to Dion in the situation as it existed at
Syracuse, and friendship demanded that Plato do what he
could to further the interests and protect the life of his friend.

What then did Plato hope to accomplish at Syracuse in
367? We have already seen what he considered to be the chief
reforms necessary in Sicilian life: the substitution of lawful
government for the tyranny at Syracuse, the curbing of the
luxury and license of Sicilian life, and the re-establishment
of the Greek cities in Sicily. These reforms certainly continued to be the chief end of Dion's and Plato's efforts, as the
above-quoted passages from the *Epistles* show. The accession
of the young Dionysius, and the ascendency that Dion had
gained over him, afforded the opportunity of bringing about
these reforms in an easy and expeditious way. So much is
certain; and we know that it was in thorough accord with
the practice of the Academy to utilize such opportunities as
this to influence Greek politics. Did Plato and Dion hope for
more than this? Did they, as is often supposed, entertain "the
somewhat fantastic notion of remodeling the city's constitution upon the ideal lines of Plato's Utopia?" [1] Did they hope
to make of Dionysius a philosopher-king after the model of
the *Republic*? This is very questionable. It is true that Dion's
urgent request for Plato to come to Syracuse referred to the
prospect of "uniting in the same persons philosophy and political power" (τοὺς αὐτοὺς φιλοσόφους τε καὶ πόλεων ἄρχοντας,
328a). And later in the *Seventh Epistle,* Plato refers with indignation and sorrow to the lost opportunity which the great
power of Dionysius had afforded of bringing about a real union

[1] C. E. Robinson, *History of Greece* (London, 1929), p. 285.

of philosophy and political power (φιλοσοφία τε καὶ δύναμις ὄντως ἐν ταὐτῷ, 335c). But precisely what is the significance of the τοὺς αὐτούς of Dion's letter and the ἐν ταὐτῷ of Plato's lament? There seems no compelling reason for taking these phrases to mean that a regime identical with that described in the *Republic* is to be established; they may mean no more than that Dionysius is to be induced to use his political power for the carrying out of the reforms that Dion and Plato suggested. Talented as Dionysius was, he very clearly lacked some of the qualities enumerated in the *Republic* as characteristic of the true philosopher (VI, 485 ff.); and he was besides too old to undergo the prolonged and difficult training prescribed there for those who are to be invested with supreme power. Add to this Plato's avowed reluctance to go to Syracuse at all, and we must conclude that his aims were much more modest than have sometimes been ascribed to him. The most emphatic part of Plato's advice in the *Seventh Epistle* is his condemnation of unlimited power: "Do not subject Sicily nor any other state to the despotism of men, but to the rule of laws; this at least is my doctrine" (334c); and six lines later he asserts that this is the doctrine he preached to Dion (i.e. in 388) and later to Dionysius (in 367 and 361). It is clear that the rule of philosophy, as Plato tried to introduce it in Syracuse under Dionysius, meant the rule of laws by which Dionysius as well as his people would be bound; it meant the establishment of a constitutional government, instead of the irresponsible rule of a single man.

What sort of constitution Plato and Dion had in mind for the Syracuse of those days is not told us in this letter. Probably it would have been a "mixed" constitution, including monarchical, aristocratic, and even democratic elements, such as is portrayed in the sketch of a constitution given in the *Eighth Epistle* after the death of Dion. This proposal in the *Eighth Epistle* is presented as coming from the mouth of Dion, and dramatically emphasizes Plato's belief that these are the measures Dion would advocate if he were alive to speak to his followers. In any case it is what Plato believed

Dion was working for when he was alive. It may be that a monarchy with less limited powers would have been Plato's and Dion's goal in the days before the fall of Dionysius and the rise of bitter factional strife; but it seems beyond question that the subordination of the monarch himself to the authority of the laws was a necessary part of any constitution they had in mind. If Plato favored the limitation of the sovereign's powers in the case of his own trusted pupil Dion, he would certainly regard it as indispensable to any government headed by Dionysius.

There is an obscure passage in the *Seventh Epistle* which has been taken as evidence that Plato contemplated a somewhat drastic economic reform at Syracuse in 367. After advising the followers of Dion to lay aside partisanship, adopt the Doric virtues, and work wholeheartedly for the restoration of lawful government at Syracuse, Plato remarks (337d):

> These proposals are akin (ἀδελφά) to those that Dion and I tried to accomplish for the benefit of Syracuse, but second best (δεύτερα); the best (πρῶτα) were those that we earlier tried to effect with the aid of Dionysius himself [goods to be common to all] (πᾶσιν κοινὰ ἀγαθά).

It is tempting to give the πρῶτα and δεύτερα of the text the sense they bear in the famous passage in the *Laws* (V, 739bc). There Plato contrasts the ideal community, in which there would be no distinction between mine and thine, with the scheme laid down in the *Laws,* which recognizes, but limits, the right of the citizens to own property. One of the chief sources of faction in the fourth century was the jealousy between the rich and the poor; and in a luxurious city like Syracuse, whose richer classes seem to have set a high-water mark for luxurious living, this source of faction would be particularly in evidence. In the *Republic* Plato had attempted to eliminate this evil in the state by the abolition of private property and the institution of a thoroughgoing communism for at least the ruling class. In the *Laws* he proposed to reach a similar end, on a more general scale, by limiting the wealth that any man might acquire and by forbidding the alienation of the ancestral lot; so that there would never be any penniless class in the community, nor any persons more than five times as rich as the poorest. But this, he says, is merely a second-best arrangement. Now if we interpret the above passage of the *Seventh Epistle* in the light of this passage from the *Laws*, it would seem that Plato originally contemplated something like the communism of the *Republic,* as a measure that would introduce a genuine sense of common interests among the citizens at Syracuse. And on general grounds, knowing the value Plato placed upon the unity of the state and his recognition of the divisive influence of property, it is quite likely that he should have seriously thought of a drastic measure like this for Syracuse, where the function of wealth in breeding factional animosities would constitute an especially grave danger.

Nevertheless I do not think this interpretation of the matter justified. The concluding phrase of the passage ($\pi\hat{a}\sigma\iota\nu$ $\kappa o\iota\nu\grave{a}$ $\dot{a}\gamma a\theta\acute{a}$) proves nothing, since it could be a marginal gloss that has crept into the text, a notation added by some early scribe, perhaps inspired by the considerations we have advanced above. In fact the phrase is most easily interpreted as such an intrusion, since its grammatical status in the sentence is a most anomalous one. And the utter irrelevance of the $\pi\hat{a}\sigma\iota\nu$ $\kappa o\iota\nu\grave{a}$ $\dot{a}\gamma a\theta\acute{a}$ to what has gone before or comes later in the *Seventh Epistle* makes it even more suspect. Nowhere else, in either the *Seventh* or the *Eighth Epistle,* do we find any suggestion of an economic reform of this sort. The proposals of these letters, when they are specific at all, are concerned with the means of establishing a regime of law, and the division of authority among the various elements in the government. The *Seventh Epistle* contains a ringing denunciation of Sicilian luxury, and the *Eighth* exhorts the Syracusans to value wealth less than soul and body; but there are no references to the desirability of a community of goods. If then this phrase is a part of the original text, it is a singularly isolated expression of a very important part of Plato's original program of reform.

The πρῶτα and δεύτερα can be easily explained if we forget the *Laws* for the moment and consider the immediate context. The three preceding pages have been concerned with advising the remnants of Dion's party (1) that the sovereignty of law is all important, and (2) that it can be established only by bringing in arbitrators and legislators from the rest of Greece.[2] Now obviously it would have been far better if Plato and Dion had been able to carry out their original intention of reforming the laws of Syracuse with the aid and example of Dionysius. To legislate before factional animosities have been aroused is a more hopeful undertaking than to have to reconcile factions made hostile by several years of bitter and cruel retaliation. Again, it may be presumed that the legislation of Plato and Dion would have been based upon a deeper understanding of the principles of right and good than that which would be set up by even such a venerable and disinterested body as Plato describes. There are evident reasons, then, why these proposals that Plato makes to the remnants of Dion's party should be deemed inferior to the original plans of Plato and Dion; yet they are inspired by the same spirit that animated Dion and Plato from the first, viz. the desire to institute a reign of law, and that is why they can be called ἀδελφά.

It is probably not correct, therefore, to ascribe to Plato and Dion in 367 the intention of establishing a philosophical Utopia at Syracuse. What we know specifically of their undertaking seems to indicate that they had a much more modest aim, the establishment of a constitutional government of a "mixed type" presumably, and along with that the restoration of the ancient Greek cities in Sicily. Even for such relatively modest ends, however, it was necessary to make of Dionysius a philosopher, that is, to give him the strength of character and conviction that would enable him to push these reforms through in the face of the inevitable opposition they would encounter at court. Here we have, I think, the real reason for the insistence of Dion and Plato that Dionysius

2 See pp. 181 ff.

should go through a course of philosophical training. As we have seen, Plato and Dion felt that the prospect of bringing about civil and political order in Syracuse was dependent upon a moral change in the citizens and a return to the simpler and more austere Doric customs of their ancestors (336cd). Now it is important to note that Plato and Dion did not rely, for effecting this transformation of Sicilian habits, merely upon the processes of legislation; for the power of a legislator in such matters, even when supported by the absolute power that Dionysius was supposed to possess, is distinctly limited. Plato and Dion would make use of more subtle and effective forces; they sought to make temperance and self-control and obedience to law fashionable, by making the head of the state an example of these virtues. In such matters the influence of the court is tremendous; and if simpler and more austere habits of life came to prevail at court and among the aristocracy, they would tend to filter down into the mass of the population. Dion, we are told, after Plato's first visit in 387, had himself been setting an example of the Doric virtues (327bc). Naturally, since he was not the head of the state, his influence was not sufficient to set the tone of court life in opposition to the example set by Dionysius the Elder; yet Dion did have the satisfaction of seeing that his principles were taking hold upon some individuals at court, including even his own nephews and other members of the royal household (327c, 328a).[3] And he seems to have had some hope that the young Dionysius could be made one of this number (327c), a not altogether unfounded hope, as we can infer from the influence that Dion seems to have had at court during the opening months of the young Dionysius' reign. The strategy

3 Among these nephews were Hipparinus and Nysaeus, the sons of Dionysius I by Dion's sister Aristomache. The former is probably the Hipparinus referred to in *VIII*, 356a, as an ally of Dion's partisans. Dion had two other sisters, who married Leptines and Thearides, the brothers of Dionysius I, and whose children would doubtless be members of the household. See Novotný's note on τοὺς ἀδελφιδοῦς (328a), *Platonis Epistulae*.

of Plato and Dion seems therefore to have been to reform
Syracusan habits by first effecting a reform at court, and this
is one of the chief things they hoped to accomplish in their
education of Dionysius.[4]

That this is the real purpose of the efforts made by Plato
and Dion to convert the young Dionysius into a "philosopher"
is also shown by a significant passage in the fourth book of the
Laws. Post [5] has pointed out to how great an extent the contents of the early books of the *Laws* seem to be determined by
Plato's interests in Dionysius and the needs of Syracuse.
Whether or not Plato was writing *for* Dionysius when he
composed these books, as Post is inclined to maintain, he was
certainly writing *from* his experience with Dionysius and
Syracuse. It is laid down in the *Laws* (IV, 709e-711c) that the
transition to a good government is easier from a tyranny than
from any other form of government. The reason for this is
that a virtuous tyrant, without much trouble, and in no very
long time, can effect a change in the manners of a state, merely
by setting the example of virtue to his subjects, and award-
ing praise and reproof in accordance with the principles of
his own conduct. Plato and Dion need not have had in mind
making Dionysius a model ruler, after the picture given in
the *Republic* of the fully trained guardians. There would
have been no basis for this hope, so far as we can see. But
there was a prospect of strengthening Dionysius' character so
that he could serve as a moral support for the projects of reform which Plato's political philosophy demanded.

We would give much to have more information as to the
details of this education of Dionysius. Besides a few passages
in the *Epistles,* our only information on this point comes
from Plutarch, *Dion* 9-14. Though Plutarch is doubtless following a "good authority" here, viz. Timaeus, as Ritter sur-

[4] Cf. 336ab, where the same view of the influence of the court upon
popular opinion is expressed with reference to what might have happened if Dion had succeeded in holding power after the expulsion of
Dionysius.

[5] *Trans. Am. Philol. Assoc.,* LX, 13 ff.

mizes,[6] we may well ask whether any account of this instruction, other than what Plato has himself given us, deserves any
but the most cautious hearing. From the very nature of the
case this instruction could not have been known, except indirectly, to those who were not parties to Plato's and Dion's
conversations with Dionysius. And the prevalence of factions
at the court interested in discrediting and making ridiculous
the regimen to which Dionysius was subjected, together with
the natural tendency of later writers—including perhaps
Timaeus—to interpret Plato's course of instruction at Syracuse in terms of the course of study laid down for the guardians in the *Republic,* should make us pause before accepting
anything on this point in Plutarch that we do not find in the
Epistles.

The only passage in the *Epistles* (*VII,* 331d-333a) that describes at any length the education of Dionysius deals entirely with the moral and political advice that Plato and Dion
gave the young tyrant. They urged upon him the importance
of self-control and temperance if he wished to have loyal
friends and followers to support him in power. These were
traits of character in which Dionysius seems to have been
notoriously lacking. Plutarch tells us that he once went on a
drunken debauch that lasted without intermission for ninety
days, and that during this time no person was allowed to talk
to him about affairs of state.[7] Plato and Dion pointed out that
the chief weakness of his father's power was his lack of trusted
subordinates. This, they say, was what forced him to centralize
the government in Syracuse; and even then he maintained
himself in authority only with the utmost vigilance and effort.
They pointed by way of contrast to the authority exercised
by Cyrus over an area more than seven times as great as all
Sicily; and this they ascribed to his ability to attract the un-
selfish devotion of others. And the possession or lack of trusty
friends they affirmed was the best indication of a man's character. Consequently they urged Dionysius to discipline him-

---

6 *Platon,* I, 124.

7 *Dion* 7; an obvious exaggeration, but it shows the reputation he had.

self, and to induce his kinsmen and associates to become his
friends and companions in virtue:

> Above all [he must] become a friend to himself, for in this
> respect he was incredibly deficient. We did not say it thus
> openly, for that would not have been safe, but made veiled
> references to his weakness, striving by our words to show
> him that everyone must do this who would save himself and
> the people over whom he rules, whereas any other course
> will accomplish his ruin and theirs. Let him take the path
> we pointed out and perfect himself in wisdom and self-
> control; then if he should resettle the deserted cities of
> Sicily, and bind them together with such laws and constitu-
> tions as would make them friendly to himself and to one
> another and a mutual help against the barbarians, he would
> have an empire not twice but actually many times as power-
> ful as his father's had been; he would be ready to inflict
> upon the Carthaginians a far heavier defeat than they had
> suffered in the days of Gelon, instead of paying tribute to
> these barbarians as he was doing at present under the agree-
> ment his father had made (332d-333a).

This doctrine that only the ruler who distinguishes himself
in virtue can enjoy the loyal support of his people seems to
have been rather widely held in the fourth century. Xenophon's *Cyropaedia* is a romantic exposition of the theme.[8]
We find many other echoes of the doctrine in the *Epistles*.
The importance of loyal friends as a support to political
power is emphasized frequently (*VI*, 322d; *VII*, 325cd, 332bc),
and virtue is said to be the only basis of durable friendship
(*VII*, 333e; *X*, 358c).[9] The members of the Academy seem to
have set great store by the possession of these solid qualities of
character, and this was doubtless one of the grounds on which
their claim to political competence was based. The writer of
Epistle IV, certainly some member of the Academy, urges
Dion to endeavor even to eclipse Lycurgus and Cyrus in virtue
and statesmanship (ἤθει καὶ πολιτείᾳ, 320d). All of this helps to

8 See esp. VII, v, 74-86; VIII, vi, 12, vii, 13.

9 Cf. also Aristotle's conception of friendship, *Nic. Eth.*, Books VIII
and IX.

explain why Plato and Dion felt so strongly that Dionysius' power could only be firmly grounded if he acquired the qualities of character that could command respect and loyalty. And this, it should be noted, is the point in that instruction which Plato takes pains to emphasize when he is describing, fifteen years later, the ill success of this venture.[10]

In addition to these more purely moral injunctions, Dionysius seems also to have been subjected to a course of intellectual training. We have very few hints as to the particular studies that he was expected to pursue in order to make himself into the wise and temperate ruler that the situation required. We learn, however, from one passage (*Epistle III*, 319bc) that he later reproached Plato for having made him study geometry when he would rather have been carrying out the political reforms in which Dion and Plato had interested him. That geometry should have been a part of his course of study is not surprising in view of the important part played by mathematics in the education of the guardians of the *Republic*. Plutarch gives us a memorable picture of the taste for reasoning and philosophy that spread throughout the court after Plato's arrival and records the tradition that the very palace

[10] Plutarch's version (*Dion* 10) of this part of Plato and Dion's instruction can be profitably compared with the account just quoted from the *Seventh Epistle*. It is a subject which would be likely to undergo expansion at Plutarch's hands, as indeed it seems to have done. To the fundamental doctrine that the virtue and self-control of the sovereign is the best support of his power, Plutarch adds several elements which show the influence of the thought of the intervening centuries. Thus Dionysius is advised "to live after the likeness of the divine and glorious model of being, out of obedience to whose control the general confusion is changed into the beautiful order of the universe"—a bit of Stoic rhetoric that does scant justice to the realistic implications that seem to have been uppermost in Plato's and Dion's minds. Again Dionysius is told that when he has learned justice and moderation the people will obey him as a father, a phrase far more Stoic than Platonic in character. If Plutarch has embellished Plato's teaching elsewhere as he has clearly done here, it is evident that we must accept with caution any further statements he makes with regard to the instruction given by Plato to Dionysius.

floor was covered with sand so that the students in mathematics could work their problems there (*Dion* 13). Plutarch
also records that the enemies of Plato and Dion warned Dionysius that this instruction was a clever ruse to induce him
to pursue the ineffable Good (τὸ σιωπώμενον ἀγαθόν) and seek
happiness in mathematics, while Dion seized the power for
himself and his sister's children (*Dion* 14). But the inquiry
into the Good was for Plato the content of the last stage of
philosophical education, and it is hardly likely that he was
able to advance so far with the young man's education in the
four months or less during which Dionysius was amenable to
his instruction. If Dionysius' education had been totally neglected by his father, as Plutarch affirms (and Plato himself
seems to say, 332d), these months must have been devoted to
far more elementary studies than the doctrine of the Good.
As confirmation of this conclusion we need only recall the
famous "prince's test" to which Plato subjected Dionysius
upon his return in 361, to determine whether or not Dionysius had any genuine knowledge of these ultimate problems
or any interest in them.[11] Plato there tells us that he expounded these matters to Dionysius in a single interview, and
that the subject was not later brought up between them
(345a); and this clearly implies that Plato had not previously
gone so far into philosophical problems with Dionysius, and did
so on this occasion only to satisfy his friends in Sicily and Italy
who felt that Dionysius had some philosophical ability and
attainments. We need not therefore attach much importance
to the passage in Plutarch; for this again is a case where later
generations would be inclined to add embellishments to the
plain tale. Plato's "secret" doctrine of the Good was one of
the most celebrated features of the philosophical tradition.

Another passage in the *Third Epistle* tells us that during
these early months at Syracuse Plato was busy composing
preambles to laws (316a). He was thus evidently making preparations for carrying out the projects of reform he and Dion
had so much at heart: the resettling of the Greek cities and

11 See p. 64.

the establishment of a constitutional government at Syracuse. But beside serving as parts of possible codes of laws, these preambles probably also formed part of the instruction that Plato gave Dionysius. In the *Laws* the officer in charge of education is advised to make the study of laws an important part of the training of the young (VII, 811d). We are told also that these preambles had been drawn up by Plato in collaboration with Dionysius, and that Dionysius had edited them after Plato's departure (*Ep. III, 316a*). This certainly suggests that Plato made use of them as a means of instructing Dionysius in the principles of politics and legislation.

Such was the instruction, so far as we can determine it, which Plato and Dion attempted to give Dionysius, in order to assure the accomplishment of the reforms they had so much at heart. At first everything seems to have gone well with their plans. Plutarch tells us that Plato on his arrival was received with a royal chariot, and that Dionysius made public sacrifices to the gods in thankfulness for the great good fortune that had come to Syracuse. There was a general eagerness among the courtiers to study philosophy, and all Syracuse began to entertain hopes of a happy change of affairs. At first Dionysius was willing, even eager, to embark upon the program of reform that was laid before him. At one of the religious sacrifices, shortly after Plato's arrival, one of the priests prayed as usual for the long continuance of the tyranny, and Dionysius commanded him to cease praying for evil.[12] According to the testimony of the *Third Epistle* Dionysius declared his intention not only of "relieving Syracuse, by changing the tyranny into a kingship," but also of resettling the Greek cities in Sicily (315d, 316c). But there were influences at work to frustrate the plans of Plato and Dion.

One of the first acts of Dionysius was to recall the historian Philistus, who had formerly been a friend and ardent supporter of his father, but for some reason had incurred the displeasure of the court and had been banished to Italy. Philistus was a great admirer of absolutism in government ("He loved

12 Plut. *Dion* 13.

tyranny no less than the tyrants," says Nepos) and was therefore unalterably opposed to any weakening of the power the
elder Dionysius had built up. Though he himself had profited
by the new liberal policy, he set himself to oppose the plans
of Plato. Dion himself, because of the severity of his demeanor
and his own ascendancy with Dionysius, was probably not a
popular figure with the other courtiers and politicians; and
Philistus would find many to help him in undermining the
influence of Dion. Though Dionysius had a genuine admiration for Plato and Dion and an honest desire to reform his
government, he lacked the strength of character that the situation demanded. It seems also that Plato insisted that the reforms should be delayed until Dionysius had acquired some
education, and it is likely that the young tyrant's initial zeal
for reform cooled, as he began to tire of the strenuous study
which was required of him and the moral admonitions that
he received from Dion and Plato. Whether it was prudent to
hold Dionysius back in this way is a question we cannot very
well answer, knowing as little as we do of the circumstances.
It would seem, however, that under the conditions that prevailed at Syracuse, with the substance of constitutional government so long in abeyance, any change would have to be made
cautiously and kept carefully in hand until the new order
could gain some measure of stability. It may therefore have
been only prudent to insist that Dionysius keep a firm hold on
the reins of power until he had shown himself able by force
of character to exercise a moral ascendancy over his courtiers
and subjects. These considerations at least may have influenced Plato and Dion in the choice they actually made.
At the same time, their refusal to allow Dionysius to proceed
with some measure of reform may well have been a real
blunder, and a tragic one for Sicily and Syracuse.

All these circumstances made it easy for the opposition to
undermine the influence of Dion. They cautioned Dionysius
that Dion was secretly planning to seize the power himself and
that he hoped to accomplish this by engaging the young
tyrant's interest in philosophy. By force of repetition these

rumors produced their effect upon Dionysius, and the party of Philistus finally persuaded him that Dion had been guilty of treasonable negotiations with the Carthaginians. Dion's life was spared, but he was sent into exile. Plato's position at court was thus changed overnight from that of chief counselor and tutor to the king to that of political prisoner (*VII*, 329e); and the prospects of the philosophical conversion of Dionysius seemed indefinitely postponed. But Dionysius had no intention of doing violence to Plato. The situation was tense; there was talk of a revolution by the friends of Dion, and Dionysius saw that any further step would be dangerous (329cd). Besides this, he evidently had a warm admiration for Plato, and his personal vanity, as well as other motives, led him to desire Plato's friendship and loyalty in return (330a). He seems to have entertained the childish notion that he could supplant Dion in Plato's esteem. Plato, however, made every effort to bring about a reinstatement of Dion and still hoped that Dionysius could be won over to the political and moral principles which he regarded as fundamental (330b). But the opposition party continued pouring its insinuations into the ears of Dionysius and effectually prevented him from giving himself up to the study of philosophy, or yielding to Plato's appeals on behalf of Dion. Thus matters continued for some time, until the outbreak of war in Sicily, when Dionysius allowed Plato to return to Athens, promising that when the war was concluded he would recall both him and Dion (*VII*, 338a). This was in 367.

After his return to Athens, Plato may have maintained friendly relations with Dionysius for a time in the hope of bringing about a reconciliation between him and Dion. If the *Thirteenth Epistle* is genuine, it shows that their relations were frank and intimate, though based on no very deep community of interests. During this time Dion also was living at Athens and enjoying the revenue from his large property in Syracuse, which Dionysius had allowed him to retain. Then in 361 came another invitation to Plato to return to Syracuse (*VII*, 338b-339d). Reports had been coming in that the young tyrant, strange to say, had taken a new interest in philosophy; and Archytas of Tarentum, who was on friendly—perhaps intimate—terms with Dionysius as a result of Plato's former visit, wrote that Dionysius had made great progress. It was ominous that the invitation from Dionysius said nothing about the recall of Dion, and for this reason Plato was at first inclined to disregard it; but when another summons came from Dionysius, borne by one of Plato's especial friends among the Pythagoreans in Sicily, and accompanied by other messengers who brought the same good reports of the tyrant's interest and progress in philosophy, and containing, moreover, a veiled threat that unless Plato came Dion would be deprived of his property and all other rights in Sicily, Plato could do nothing but yield to the urging of Dion and his other friends. It was with misgiving, however, that he set forth on this third journey to Syracuse, knowing the instability of Dionysius' character and the strength of the opposition he would encounter. Yet he knew from his experience as a teacher that a young man may suddenly "wake up" to the intellectual and moral world and display interests and accomplishments that would formerly have been regarded as impossible, and he felt that, out of consideration for Dion and for himself, he ought not to give up the project of a reform of Syracuse without making further trial of Dionysius.

When he arrived at Syracuse, one of the first things he did was to make trial of the tyrant's reputed philosophy by means of a test which is described in the *Seventh Epistle* (340b-341a). The test consisted in presenting the nature of that quest for knowledge and being that absorbs the philosopher's interest, together with a hint of the ultimate principles that Plato thought could be attained if one is willing to undergo the laborious self-discipline and prolonged study required. He who is born to philosophy, says Plato, will have his ambition kindled immediately; he at once will want to hear more, and no labor will seem too great or beyond his powers. Whereas those who are not genuine philosophers, feeling that the task is beyond them, will persuade themselves that they understand these principles already, or else that there is nothing in them. Dionysius was content with this one exposition of Plato's philosophy, and thus stood self-condemned.

After this, Plato gave up his attempt to interest Dionysius in philosophy and devoted all his energies to bringing about a reconciliation between him and Dion. In this also he was unsuccessful. The party of Philistus was more powerful than ever, and the tyrant's reputed inclination for philosophy had also attracted to his court numbers of philosophers of various sects, some of whom no doubt lent their influence to discredit Plato. Among others we hear of Aristippus, Aeschines the Socratic, Eudoxus, and Helicon; so that philosophical jealousies contributed their part to the unpleasantness of the personal and political situation. Matters went from bad to worse. After numerous evasions and unfulfilled promises, Dionysius finally sold Dion's property outright and married his wife, Arete, to one of the court favorites; and Plato at once knew that the possibility of a reconciliation was gone. Plato himself eventually fell into disfavor with the tyrant because of his continued loyalty to Dion's interests and to the friends of Dion still remaining in Syracuse, and only by the intervention of the Pythagoreans at Tarentum was he allowed to come off safely and return to Athens.[13]

DION'S TRIUMPH AND DEATH

On Plato's return to Greece he met Dion at the Olympic games [1] and told him all that had occurred. Dion swore solemnly that he would seek to get revenge upon Dionysius, and called upon all his friends to join him in an expedition against Syracuse. Plato refused to take any active part in the expedition, but many members of the Academy energetically

[13] A graphic account of these last days in Syracuse is given in *Epistle VII*, 345c-350b.

[1] Evidently the games held in the summer of 360.

espoused Dion's cause. Speusippus, who it appears had accompanied Plato on his third journey to Syracuse, encouraged
Dion with reports as to the state of popular feeling in Syracuse. Besides members of the Academy there were many other
Athenians and Peloponnesians who joined the expedition, one
of them being Callippus, an Athenian whose friendship Dion
valued very highly, though it was to cost him dearly. There
were also in Greece about a thousand exiles from Syracuse,
only twenty-five of whom were bold enough to join the undertaking. It was a hazardous enterprise, and nothing can better
show the ardor that inspired these adventurers than the discrepancy between their own force and the resources of the tyranny they were attacking. When the expedition was finally assembled at the island of Zacynthus, it numbered only eight
hundred men and five vessels—a ridiculous force with which
to expect to overthrow a tyranny of fifty years standing,
"equipped with four hundred war ships, ten thousand horses,
a hundred thousand foot soldiers, besides great quantities of
food and arms, its stronghold the largest city in Greece, with
a harbor and acropolis." [2] But Dion declared (and it was his
spirit that gave the tone to the expedition) that even though
he died immediately after setting foot on Sicilian soil, it was
glory enough to have died in such a cause.[3] The almost miraculous success of the expedition was the marvel of all
Greece, and a favorite theme for later rhetoricians. As Nepos
says, no doubt quoting from one of these, the fall of Syracuse
showed that no authority is secure unless fortified by good will
(nullum esse imperium tutum nisi benevolentia munitum).

The details of this military triumph as recorded for us in
Plutarch are beyond a doubt from the letter which Timonides

[2] Diod. XVI, 9, 2; Nepos Dion 5.

[3] This declaration is preserved by Aristotle (Politics, 1312a35 ff.), who
makes several other references to Dion's expedition. It was an event that
deeply stirred the Academy. One of the lost dialogues of Aristotle,
Eudemus, was written in commemoration of a member of the Academy
who lost his life in the fighting. Other members who are known to have
been with the expedition are Miltas the Thessalian and Timonides of
Leucas, who later wrote an account of the events to Speusippus.

of Leucas wrote to Speusippus. Evading the fleet of Philistus stationed at Iapygia to head them off, the expedition sailed part way around the island of Sicily and with some difficulty landed on its southeastern coast at Minoa, a town in the control of the Carthaginians but commanded by a personal friend of Dion's. Dionysius was at the time absent from Syracuse, having sailed to Italy to reinforce the fleet of Philistus; and upon hearing this, Dion and his troops pressed on almost at once toward the city. On the way they were joined by troops from Acragas and other Sicilian cities under the power of Dionysius, as well as by numbers of the rural population, so that when Dion arrived within sight of Syracuse he had a force of not less than five thousand men. His entrance into the city was unresisted. The tyrant's forces were divided, part being stationed in Ortygia, the rocky islet which forms the north side of the Great Harbor, and on which was located the fortress and the acropolis, and the rest in Epipolae, the very opposite portion of the city. The commander of the troops in Epipolae, seeing the acclaim with which the populace received Dion, fled hastily from the city, spreading exaggerated reports as to the strength of Dion's forces. Dion thus became without a struggle master of the whole city, with the exception of Ortygia. He at once called an assembly of the people and announced that after fifty years of slavery the day of freedom had come; and the assembly with enthusiasm elected him and his brother Megacles generals with full powers. Their first act was to construct a barricade across the land approach to Ortygia; so that when Dionysius returned to his fortress seven days later he found himself in possession only of the fortress, all the rest of the city being in Dion's power. But the struggle was not over. By an unexpected sally of his garrison at a time when he had thrown Dion off his guard by professing to negotiate for peace, he almost succeeded in breaking through the barricade; but Dion's bravery and generalship saved the day, and the garrison was forced to retire within the fortress. But Dionysius still possessed a superiority of forces by sea. Fortunately at this juncture Heraclides, a former commander of his troops but now, like Dion, a political exile, arrived from the Peloponnesus with thirty triremes and immediately engaged the fleet of Philistus. In spite of his superior forces, Dionysius was once more defeated. Not only was his navy repulsed, but what was more calamitous for him, Philistus himself was captured and put to death; and Dionysius thereby lost his ablest and most faithful supporter.

Thus the hold of Dionysius upon Syracuse and Sicily was completely broken, and it was a question whether he could even remain longer in Ortygia, now that he had lost command of the sea. But the same naval victory which had crushed the hopes of Dionysius was the beginning of Dion's eventual ruin. The prestige which Heraclides had gained by his victory over Philistus, coupled with the very fact that he was commander of the navy, gave him a hold upon popular favor which made him a formidable rival of Dion. Nor was he any too scrupulous in making use of his opportunities to undermine the influence of Dion. Plutarch says that he had quarrelled with Dion in the Peloponnesus and had resolved to lead an independent expedition against Syracuse. For anyone interested in undermining Dion's influence with the people the circumstances were most favorable. Beside his own haughty and imperious demeanor—a fault of which Plato or some other member of the Academy reminds him in the *Fourth Epistle,* written about this time—Dion's connection with the Dionysian dynasty was a reason for suspecting that he had not altogether allied his interests with the democratic party. These natural grounds for popular distrust were still further increased by the intrigues of Dionysius, who, now that he was no longer able to offer any military resistance, turned to less open methods of combating Dion. By putting in circulation fictitious letters, by addressing overtures for peace to Dion personally rather than to the Syracusan assembly, he did everything in his power to arouse in the minds of the people grave suspicions of Dion's loyalty to their cause.

The events of this period are very much confused, and we see them through the eyes of later historians who were inclined to take sides against Dion. But it is important to get as clear an understanding of them as possible, because of the light they throw upon Plato's references to Dion in the *Seventh Epistle*. One incident that occurred at the very beginning of the rivalry between Dion and Heraclides is instructive. The Syracusan populace, out of gratitude to Heraclides, had elected him admiral with full powers. Dion called an assembly and pointed out that in so doing they were rescinding their previous action in giving himself full powers. The assembly was therefore compelled to cancel its appointment of Heraclides; whereupon Dion, after reproving Heraclides for arousing factional differences when their common cause was not yet secure, nominated him admiral and asked for the confirmation of the assembly, and the grant of a bodyguard for Heraclides. This act must be praised for its magnanimity, but hardly for its wisdom. The manner in which it was performed doubtless prevented its gaining for Dion the loyalty of Heraclides; whereas the granting of such power to Heraclides could not but arouse the apprehension of Dion's followers. And Dion's assumption of the power of nomination could not fail to displease the assembly. "We have only exchanged a drunken tyrant for a sober one," said the people.

The differences rapidly became acute between Heraclides and Dion. Shortly after the incident mentioned above, Heraclides proposed to the assembly a redistribution of property in the city, and other sweeping changes of a similar sort, all of which Dion opposed. The climax was reached the following summer when the assembly met and elected twenty-five new generals, Heraclides being among the number, but Dion's name being absent. Dion thereupon withdrew his mercenaries to Leontini, defending himself every step of the way from the attacks of the pursuing Syracusans. For this expulsion of Dion the city paid heavily. Shortly before this time Dionysius had eluded the ships of Heraclides and escaped from the fortress, leaving the garrison there in the charge of his son Apollocrates; and upon arriving in Italy in the portion of his empire which was still faithful, he dispatched naval reinforcements under the command of Nypsius. This fleet arrived upon the scene; though Nypsius was defeated in the initial engagement, he remained near the harbor of Syracuse, and by a sudden and unexpected night attack broke through the defenses of the city and put its defenders to flight. The demoralization of the city's forces was complete, and the city lay helpless, while the soldiers of Nypsius went about pillaging and setting fire to everything. In this extremity envoys were sent to Dion, begging him to forget his previous mistreatment and come to the rescue of the city. Once more Dion chose to be magnanimous, and by a fervent appeal he persuaded his own mercenaries and the troops of Leontini to march with him to the rescue of Syracuse. Upon arriving at the city they found the troops of Nypsius disorganized and demoralized after two days of pillaging, so that it was not long before they were cut down or driven back and the city was once more in the hands of Dion.

This second deliverance of the city should have made Dion's power supreme, as it did for a time, since the assembly immediately re-elected him general with full powers. But the same conflict of policies between himself and the democratic populace under the leadership of Heraclides soon reappeared. Dion's first act was to pardon Heraclides and the others who had formerly conspired to overthrow him, and to restore to Heraclides his command of the naval forces. It would have been better if Dion had recognized at this time, as he did later, that it was impossible for him to realize his plans as long as Heraclides remained a disturbing factor in the city. On at least two later occasions Heraclides provided Dion with a legitimate ground, if not for putting him to death, at least for sending him into exile; but on each occasion Dion preferred to deal leniently with him rather than to take any measures that might seem inspired by personal jealousy or dislike. But in spite of the activities of Heraclides, which at one time even included negotiations with Dionysius, Dion succeeded in frustrating all the efforts of Dionysius to regain the city; and the garrison in the acropolis finally surrendered, leaving Dion in full and secure possession of the city.

Now, at the height of his power, it seems that Dion should have been able to bring about those reforms which he and Plato had in mind. Probably a man of different temperament and training would have been able to realize them, at least partially. But Dion was proud and unyielding and little disposed to make concessions to popular clamors for the immediate restoration of the democracy. The very greatness of his aims doubtless suggested to him that he should keep a firm hold on the government until there was a good chance of setting up the kind of constitution he desired. That his ultimate aims were generous and disinterested and directed toward the welfare of Syracuse and the other Greek cities in Sicily, we have Plato's unhesitating and repeated testimony (*Ep. VII*, 335e-336b; 351a-e; *Ep. VIII*, 357ab); and I do not see that we are in a position to reverse Plato's judgment in the matter. In fact Plutarch tells us that Dion had already sent to Corinth for a delegation to assist him in devising a constitution for Syracuse.[4] It was Plato's opinion that a group of men of this sort would be necessary for drawing up laws that would be free from party spirit and would best represent the interests of the whole state. But however disinterested his motives and however lofty his aims, Dion's reign, we are told, became in time indistinguishable from the tyranny which he had overthrown. He not only refused to yield to the popular clamor and demolish the citadel and all other remnants of the tyranny, he not only kept his armed bodyguard and his mercenary troops, but he added to this parade of authority an act of flagrant injustice. Seeing that it was impossible to accomplish his aims as long as Heraclides lived, he contrived to have him put to death, thus doing secretly and with every appearance of injustice what could have been done earlier with perfect legality and propriety. Nepos further tells us [5] that in order to maintain his power and quell the popular disorders, he did not hesitate to use his mercenary troops against the citizens, and in order to keep the loyalty of his

4 *Dion* 53.
5 *Dion* 6-7.

troops he was forced to make them gifts derived in large part from the confiscated property of his political enemies, and sometimes also from that of his friends. How much truth lies imbedded in these statements of Nepos it is impossible for us to say. The account ultimately comes, it seems, from Athanis, who was one of the political opponents of Dion at Syracuse. Apart from the assassination of Heraclides, the charges against Dion are clothed in general terms, and could easily be a politically prejudiced account of administrative acts performed in carrying out a strong but disinterested policy. Plutarch rather significantly refrains from telling us much about this last period of Dion's life. The tribute at the close of the *Seventh Epistle* (351a-e) seems to admit that Dion was guilty of some highhanded acts; but Plato reiterates his confidence in his underlying motives and purposes.

At any event, popular opinion saw in Dion an enemy of liberty. Some of his own followers turned against him. Callippus, the Athenian friend who had entered the city at his right hand and who had remained throughout one of his most trusted followers, conceived the idea of using for his own advantage the popular feeling against Dion. By availing himself of the confidence which Dion reposed in him, he was able to organize a considerable conspiracy without attracting Dion's suspicions. One day when Dion was at dinner with some companions, the conspirators surrounded the room, while their collaborators inside, after an attempt to strangle Dion, stabbed him to death with a dagger handed in through a window.[6]

THE ADVICE TO DION'S PARTY IN 353

Plato's connection with Syracuse did not come to an end with the death of Dion. The friends and followers of Dion fled to Leontini, leaving Syracuse in the hands of Callippus.

6 Plut. *Dion* 57.

Before this, it seems, they had sent an appeal to Plato to which the *Seventh Epistle* is an answer. At Leontini the partisans of Dion entered into alliance with Hipparinus, the son of the elder Dionysius and half brother of Dionysius II, and by a joint attack upon Syracuse when Callippus was absent upon an expedition against Catana they succeeded in regaining the city.[1] Thus the tyranny of Callippus at Syracuse came to an early end. It was then that the party of Dion turned to Plato with the request for advice that resulted in the writing of the *Eighth Epistle*.

The situation for which Plato was asked to advise was not a promising one. Though the parties of Dion and Hipparinus were united for the time being and masters of the situation against the other factions at Syracuse, yet their alliance was most precarious. As events proved, it was far less effective in bringing them together for the common good than in uniting them against the common enemy. And beside the mutual jealousies of these two groups, there were other parties at Syracuse whose interests would have to be reconciled in some way in any stable and enduring arrangement. There was the monarchical party of Dionysius, whose followers in Syracuse were doubtless still considerable, and they might with some justice claim that he was now in unlawful banishment. And there was also the democratic party, formerly led by Heraclides, eager to regain for the people the powers they had enjoyed before the rise of the elder Dionysius. None of these parties was strong enough to enforce its will permanently upon the others, and there was no strong man in sight to bring them all into subjection.

The advice that Plato gives under these circumstances has a peculiar interest because of the realistic way in which he suggests concessions to each of these factions in order to win a general allegiance to the settlement he proposes. First of all he asserts that the only hope of peace lies in the willingness of the party temporarily in power to grant political amnesty to its opponents, establish laws for the common good, and

1 Polyaenus V, 4.

then set an example of thorough and disinterested devotion to these laws (*VII*, 336e-337a; cf. *VIII*, 352c-e). In the *Seventh Epistle* Plato does not seem very hopeful that this large-mindedness will be manifested by any of the contending factions; but between the writing of the *Seventh* and the *Eighth* he seems to have received more encouraging news; in any case the greater fullness of the advice given in the *Eighth* suggests that he was then more hopeful of a satisfactory settlement. As the best method of establishing a set of impartial laws Plato recommends summoning a group of eminent men from other cities in Greece and entrusting them with authority to draw up legislation for Syracuse. These should be "old men with wives and children at home, descended from a long line of illustrious ancestors, each of them possessing a fair amount of property"; and having been induced to come to Syracuse for this purpose, they are to take oath that they will consider the interests of the victors no more than those of the vanquished, and will legislate for the common good of all citizens without discrimination (*VII*, 337bc; cf. *VIII*, 356c). In both letters this primary advice is accompanied by impressive moral exhortation. The *Seventh Epistle* depicts the shame and misery of a life devoted to lawless enjoyment and the need of living in the Dorian fashion if Sicily is to be made free and prosperous (334e-335c, 336cd); the *Eighth* expounds the familiar doctrine of the superiority of soul to body and body to wealth, and urges that the laws recognize and enforce this scale of values (355bc).

The advice culminates in the outline of a constitution (*VIII*, 355d-356e) which Plato evidently thinks will provide the basis for a satisfactory compromise between the warring factions. Though the details of the plan he has in mind are not fully given—and are probably intended to be worked out by the arbitrators—the main lines are clear and throw considerable light upon his political views at this latest period of his thought. He proposes a wide distribution of powers and responsibilities, which will serve the double purpose of giving something to all parties and making it impossible for any one

of them to dominate the situation. To satisfy the claims of the
monarchical parties Plato suggests a triple monarchy, after
the fashion of the dual monarchy at Sparta, the three kings to
be Dion's son Hipparinus, Hipparinus the son of Dionysius I,
and Dionysius II. Plato seems to have some doubt whether
Dionysius will give up his claims to the tyranny, so a dual
monarchy may be what he expects will result from these suggestions. To make it easier for the other parties to accept
such a monarchy, the letter calls to mind the long period of
time during which the families of Dion and Dionysius (called
a "single family" in 353a) have held power in Syracuse, i.e.
since the beginning of the Carthaginian war at the end of
the preceding century, and reminds the Syracusans of the
genuine benefits these families have conferred upon Syracuse.
According to the proposed constitution the kings are to have
charge of the sacrifices and "whatever else is appropriate, considering their past services to the state." What powers they are
to have other than these religious functions Plato does not
say; but he suggests that they might be given the power of the
Spartan kings, with some limitations. This would mean at
most the command of the armies in the field, and the exercise
of some minor judicial functions. In short, their position is
to be one involving more honor and deference than actual
authority. The real power is to be vested in a body of thirty-
five guardians of the laws (νομοφύλακες), who are to govern
with a council and a popular assembly. How great are to be
the powers of the popular assembly and what are to be the
relations between these three governing bodies the *Eighth
Epistle* does not say. If we may judge from the *Laws,* with
which this sketch of a government has striking similarities,
both the council and the νομοφύλακες are to be elected by the
assembly of the citizens. In the *Laws* it is provided that the
council shall consist of an equal number of members from all
the four property classes in the state (VI, 756cd), and mem-
bership in the board of νομοφύλακες is not restricted to any
special class (VI, 755b). Thus if we are to interpret the constitution of the *Eighth Epistle* by the parallel constitution in

the *Laws*, it is evident that the scheme Plato proposes makes considerable concessions to the democratic party, even though the powers of the popular assembly are to be strictly limited.

Plato's chief concern seems to be with the courts of justice, and here, as in the *Laws*, he departs most noticeably from the favorite institutions of the Greek democracies. The constitution of the courts of justice would clearly be a matter of much importance during the first years of the new constitution, when there would be plenty of old grudges to be paid off, and Plato evidently does not propose to let them become the instruments of popular passion. All cases involving exile or death or imprisonment are to be brought before a special court composed of the thirty-five νομοφύλακες and those magistrates who were best in their respective offices during the preceding year. This is precisely the constitution of the highest court described in the *Laws* (VI, 767); and as this corresponding court in the *Laws* is to be a court of appeal, it is not too much to infer that it is to have this function here in the *Eighth Epistle*. Plato mentions other courts, but leaves their jurisdiction and the manner of their constitution unspecified. As a special precaution against the dangers of political reprisals in the period of transition, it is specified that the kings are to have no part in the administration of justice, since, like priests, they are "to remain undefiled by bloodshed or imprisonment or exile" (357a).

There are many striking resemblances between this sketch of a government and the more elaborate constitution described in the *Laws*. Both are "mixed constitutions," involving a union of monarchical and democratic elements. The most important magistrates here, as in the *Laws*, are the νομοφύλακες, and their number is strikingly similar, thirty-five in this letter, thirty-seven in the *Laws* (VI, 752). Both here and in the *Laws* Plato provides for a body of independent and specially qualified judges to have jurisdiction over cases involving the graver crimes, and possibly to serve as a court of appeal from the lower tribunals. Both constitutions recognize the legitimacy of the demand for freedom and both make concessions (not unwilling concessions, so far as the *Laws* is concerned) to the democratic sentiments of the period. There are no kings provided for in the *Laws*. But it must be remembered that the prescriptions of the *Eighth Epistle* are intended for a city with a monarchical party that could hardly be placated without some recognition of its special claims; whereas the constitution of the *Laws* is intended for a newly established colony, as yet unhampered by traditions or political parties. These general and specific agreements between the *Eighth Epistle* and the *Laws* are just what we should expect if, as seems to be the case, the two works were written by the same man at about the same time.

Plato's advice to the contending factions in Syracuse has been appraised in the most various fashions. The proposal of three co-ordinate kings has been termed "fantastic" and chimerical; but something like this had long existed at Sparta, and the limited powers they are given would seem much less fantastic to an ancient Greek than to a political thinker of modern times, familiar with the theory and practice of sixteenth- and seventeenth-century kings. The title of βασιλεύς was more often in Greece a symbol of dignity than of political power; and whatever power he had, a king was always subject to law in the exercise of it.[2] Perhaps, as Burnet says, the real defect of the advice was that it was too statesmanlike to be accepted by embittered party men.[3] Plato himself recognized that his proposals sounded somewhat like a pious wish, because they demanded a genuine and sincere abandonment of party interest in favor of the interests of Sicily and Greek civilization, and there was little reason to believe that this change of heart would occur. If this was the true state of affairs—and that it was, seems borne out by subsequent events —there would have been even less possibility of establishing the pure democratic form of government that was probably desired by the most numerous party in Syracuse. Plato did

---

[2] Cf. βασιλικοὶ νόμοι (*VIII*, 354c); ἀρχὴ ὑπεύθυνος βασιλική (*VIII*, 355e).

[3] *Greek Philosophy*, p. 300.

not, however, ignore the demands of this democratic party. He recognized the legitimacy of their desire for freedom, and one purpose of the letter is to persuade them that the government he proposed would provide the basis for a stable and enduring freedom and would avoid the weakness of "extreme" democracy. So far as we can see, therefore, this plan involved a genuine compromise involving mutual concessions; it was in general principles and in details so closely akin to the familiar Dorian tradition that it would easily become rooted in popular feeling, once partisan passions had subsided; and at the same time it made provision for correcting one of the greatest evils of Greek politics, the subservience of the courts of justice to political passions. For these reasons, then, it is not too much to say that this plan offered a feasible solution for the condition at Syracuse, and if partisan feelings had permitted it to be adopted, would probably have given Syracuse a stable and just government. The failure to reach a solution in 352 was due not to the lack of wisdom in Plato's proposals, but to the lack of willingness among the people and their leaders to lay aside factional bitterness and make mutual concessions for the common good, the very thing that Plato in both the *Seventh* and *Eighth Epistle*s lays down as the first condition of a settlement.

However sensible this advice, it was not taken by the warring factions, for the scanty information we have regarding the next seven or eight years of Syracusan history shows that it was a period of anarchy and violence. Hipparinus, the son of Dionysius, seems to have seized the power, and after a short and drunken career met his death at the hand of an assassin.[4] In the meantime Dionysius had installed himself at Locri, where he abrogated the constitution and gave himself over to all sorts of excesses.[5] We know little of the course of events; but we learn that Dionysius once more entered Syracuse about 346 and drove out his brother Nysaeus, who was

[4] Athen. 436a; Aelian *V.H.* II, 41.
[5] Strabo VI, i, 8.

then in power.[6] A brighter chapter begins with the advent
of Timoleon from Corinth in 344, resulting in the expulsion
of Dionysius and the restoration for a brief period of the
freedom and prosperity of Syracuse. Though the constitution
that Timoleon set up seems to have been more democratic
than anything that Plato or Dion would have liked,[7] yet it
seems to have been a "mixed constitution," like that sketched
in the *Eighth Epistle*; and in other respects Timoleon's aims
and policies, as measured by his accomplishments, were identical with those of Plato.[8] The proclamation read at his in-
terment in Syracuse, as preserved for us by Diodorus and
Plutarch, says that he "broke the power of the tyrants, defeated the barbarians, resettled the most important of the
Greek cities, and restored liberty to the people of Sicily." [9]
But when Plato died in 347 the outlook was anything but
bright; Syracuse was being laid waste by factional strife, and
Sicily lay helpless before the barbarians.

[6] Plut. *Timoleon* 1.
[7] Diod. XVI, 70, 4-5.
[8] Scheliha, *Dion*, pp. 96-99.
[9] Diod. XVI, 90, 1; Plut. *Timoleon* 39.

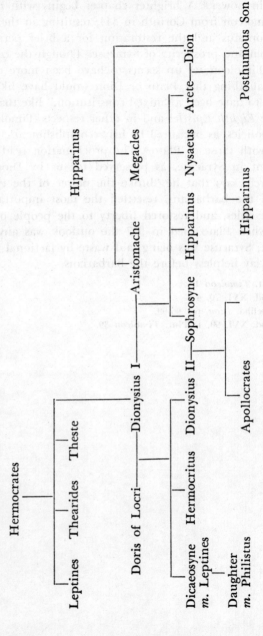

GENEALOGICAL TABLE OF THE FAMILIES OF THE DIONYSII AND DION

TRANSLATION OF THE EPISTLES

PLATO TO DIONYSIUS, WELFARE.[2]   309

During all the time that I was with you administering your
empire and enjoying your confidence above all others, you
got the benefits and I the slanders. But I endured them, griev-

[1] This letter is certainly spurious. The position it ascribes to Plato at
the court of Dionysius is irreconcilable with the account given in *III* and
VII. Plato is described as having been αὐτοκράτωρ at Syracuse for a considerable period of time and as having saved the city on numerous occasions. But we learn from *VII* that after the first four months Plato was
practically a prisoner at court during the whole of his first visit; and *III*
says that Plato had taken little part in Dionysius' government, and that
only "at the beginning" (316a). Again, this letter describes Plato as
having been abruptly dismissed, whereas *VII* shows us that Plato, on both
occasions, was only too eager to depart. These circumstances agree better
with Dion's position at court, and this is doubtless why there is a variant
tradition, dating from Ficinus, it seems, ascribing this letter to Dion. But
this alternative is likewise unsatisfactory, since the writer speaks as if he
were a foreigner.

How did this letter ever come into the collection? O. Immisch (*Philologus*, LXXII [1913], 1-41) thinks the editor of the *Epistles* extracted this
letter from Timaeus' account of the dismissal of the Spartan general
Dexippus, who had enjoyed considerable power under Dionysius I;
originally inserted merely as a fitting introduction to Plato's own
letters of political advice, it eventually came to be ascribed, like the rest,
to Plato. It is simpler, however, and perhaps as satisfactory to suppose
that this letter was originally a rhetorical exercise upon a well-known
historical theme. We know from *III* that the belief seems to have been
widely held that Plato did exercise considerable power at Syracuse (cf.
also *VII*, 329c, 333a, 350a).

[2] The salutation εὖ πράττειν, with its double meaning, "do right" and
"prosper," defies adequate rendering. The use of this formula, instead of
the more customary χαίρειν seems to have been characteristic of Plato
(cf. Diog. Laert. III, 61). Both the *Third* and the *Thirteenth Epistles* call
attention to this manner of salutation. Elsewhere Plato plays upon the
double meaning of the phrase: *Gorg.* 495e, 507c; *Charm.* 172a; *Rep.* 353e.

ous as they were, because I knew that men would not think me a willing accomplice in any of your more barbarous acts. For all who are associated with you in your government

b are my witnesses, many of whom I myself have defended and saved from no little injury. And although I have held the highest authority and have protected your city on numerous occasions, you have deported me with less consideration than you ought to show in sending away a beggar who had been with you for the same length of time. I shall therefore in the future consult my own interests with less trust in mankind, and you, tyrant that you are, will live without friends.

c   The bearer of this letter, Baccheius,[3] is bringing you the pretty gold that you gave for my departure. It was not enough for my traveling expenses, nor could I use it for any other need. The offer of it did you great dishonor, and its acceptance would do me almost as much, therefore I refuse it. No doubt it makes little difference to you whether you get or give such a trifle as this, so take it back and use it to serve some other friend as you have served me; I have had enough of your attentions.

d   A line of Euripides comes appropriately to my mind: "Thou'lt pray for such a helper at thy side."[4] Let me remind you also that most of the other tragic poets, when they bring in a tyrant who is being assassinated, make him cry out: "O

310 wretched me! for lack of friends I die." But no one has ever portrayed him as dying for lack of money. And these other lines, too, make sense to sensible men:

> It is not gold, though a shining rarity in mortals'
> hopeless life,
> Nor gems, nor silver couches, that brighten the eyes
> of men,

[3] Baccheius is otherwise unknown. Would Plato have mentioned the travel money in *VII*, 350b, if he had returned it, as this letter says?

[4] Translation by R. G. Bury, *Epistles*, in the Loeb Classical Library (Cambridge, Mass. and London, 1929). Cf. Nauck, *Trag. Frag.* Eur. No. 956. A writer genuinely indignant would be little likely to appeal to Euripides for effect.

Nor broad and self-sufficient fields laden with
    the harvest,
But the approving thought of upright men.[5]

Farewell. May you realize how much you have lost in me and b
so conduct yourself better toward others.

II

PLATO TO DIONYSIUS, WELFARE.

Archedemus [1] tells me you think that not only I but my
friends also should keep quiet about you and refrain from
saying or doing anything to your discredit, Dion alone ex-
cepted. This very statement, that you except Dion, shows that c
I have no power over my friends; for if I could control you
and Dion and the others as you suggest, it would be much
better for us, I maintain, and for all the other Greeks. As it is,
I am conspicuous in showing willingness to follow my own
precept. But I say this without implying that there is any
truth in the reports of Cratistolus and Polyxenus,[2] one of
whom told you, I hear, that while at Olympia he heard many d
of my companions speak ill of you. He must have much
sharper hearing than I, for I heard nothing of the sort. But
this is what you must do, I think, in the future: whenever
you hear anything like this said of one of us, write and inquire
of me, and I will tell you the truth without shame or hesitation.

So far as the relations between you and me are concerned

[5] The source of these verses is unknown. Perhaps the author of this
letter composed them. See Kaibel, in *Hermes*, XXV, 101.

[1] A pupil of Archytas, mentioned also in *Epistle VII*, 339a, 349d and
in *Epistle III*, 319a. We know nothing of him other than what these
letters say, and very probably the author of this letter knew no more.
According to *Epistle VII*, 339a, Plato had a very high opinion of him.

[2] Of Cratistolus we know nothing. On Polyxenus see *Ep. XIII*, 360c,
note.

the situation is this. We are both known to practically every
e Greek, and our connection with each other is no secret. Remember, too, that it will be no secret to future generations,
for those who hear of it will be as great in number as our
friendship has been long continued and open. What do I
mean by saying this now? Let me begin with a general truth.
It is a law of nature that wisdom and great power go together; they exert a mutual attraction and are forever seeking
to be united. And men love to converse with one another
about them, and to listen to what the poets say. For example,
311 when men talk of Hiero and Pausanias the Lacedaemonian,
they like to recall Simonides' connection with them and what
he said and did. Likewise they usually celebrate together
Periander of Corinth and Thales of Miletus, Pericles and
Anaxagoras, and again Croesus and Solon, as wise men, with
Cyrus, as ruler. In the same strain the poets couple Creon
b and Tiresias, Polyeidus and Minos, Agamemnon and Nestor,
Odysseus and Palamedes. And our early ancestors, if I am not
mistaken, linked Prometheus with Zeus in much the same
manner. Of these men some are sung about as coming together in conflict, others for friendship; and some as being
friends at one time and enemies at another, and agreeing in
some things and disagreeing in others. I say all this to show
c you that when we are dead, men will still talk about us, and
we must have a care for their opinions. It is necessary, I think,
that we should be concerned about the future, since it is the
nature of an utterly slavish man to give it no thought, whereas men of superior virtue do everything in their power to
have themselves well spoken of after they are dead. This very
attitude is to me an indication that the dead have some perception of what is going on here; for superior minds divine
d that this is so, while those of no account deny it; and of these
two the intimations of good men are the more worthy of
credence. It is my belief that the men whom I have mentioned above would be only too eager, if it were possible, to
rectify their associations with one another so as to have a
better account given of them than is now current. This is still

possible for us, please God; if there has been any fault in our past relations we can still correct it by our words and actions; for the account which will be given of true philosophy, and the reputation that it will enjoy, will be better or e worse, I say, according as we act nobly or basely. Indeed we can show no greater piety than to act always with this concern, nor greater impiety than to neglect it.

Shall I tell you then what we ought to do and what justice requires? When I came to Sicily my reputation was high among philosophers, and I came to Syracuse to make you my 312 witness, so that philosophy might gain favor with the multitude. In this I failed ingloriously, as is well known. But I deny that the cause was what many persons might think. Instead, it is because you showed that you did not quite trust me, but desired to send me away and summon others to find out from them what my purposes were, apparently mistrusting me. Many people thereupon bruited it about that you held me in contempt and were interested in other things. b This, as you know, was the general report. Hear now what in consequence you ought to do, and this will answer your question how you and I should behave towards each other. If you feel nothing but contempt for philosophy, then let it alone; or if from your own studies or from the teachings of others you have found better doctrines than mine, give them your allegiance. But if, as I think, you favor my principles, then you ought to honor them and me in particular. Now, as at the beginning, if you lead I will follow. If you honor me, I will honor you; if not, I will keep silent. Furthermore, if you c take the lead in honoring me, you will get the reputation of honoring philosophy; and the very fact that you once were considering other philosophers will bring you commendation from many persons as being yourself a philosopher. But if I pay you honor without any honor from you, it will look as if I had my eyes on your money, and we know that this attitude has an evil name among men. In short, if you honor me it will be a tribute to us both; if I honor you, it will bring us both disgrace.

d   Enough of these matters. The sphere [3] is not correct. Archedemus will explain it to you when he comes. And upon that
other question of weightier and more sublime import about
which you say you have difficulties, let him by all means en-
lighten you. According to his report, you say that the nature
of "the first" has not been sufficiently explained. I must speak
of this matter to you in enigmas, in order that if anything
should happen to these tablets "in the recesses of the sea or
land," whoever reads them may not understand our meaning.

e   It is like this. Upon the king of all do all things turn; he is
the end of all things and the cause of all good. Things of
the second order turn upon the second principle, and those
of the third order upon the third.[4] Now the soul of man longs
to understand what sort of things these principles are, and it
looks toward the things that are akin to itself,[5] though none

313   of them is adequate; clearly the king and the other principles mentioned are not of that sort. The soul thereupon
asks, What then is the nature of these principles? This is the
question, O son of Dionysius and Doris,[6] that causes all the
trouble; or rather, this it is that produces in the soul the pains
of childbirth, from which she must be delivered, or she will
never really attain truth. You yourself once told me, under
the laurel trees in your garden, that you understood this

b   matter, having found the answer yourself; and I replied that

     [3] To what does the σφαιρίον refer? There is an interesting parallel
between this passage and *Epistle XIII*, 363d (see note). The writer of this
letter, whether or not he is borrowing from *XIII*, probably intends to
suggest some problem or diagram connected with the mathematical study
of the heavenly bodies. But since the letter is almost certainly spurious
it is hardly worth while trying to clarify the writer's intentions.

     [4] On the interpretation of this enigma see above, p. 115. The difficulties
attending the inquiry into first principles are a clear echo of *Epistle VII*,
342-344; but the vagueness of the passage and its rhetorical coloring
indicate the hand of an imitator.

     [5] If one is to give a meaning to what the writer professes to state
too enigmatically for comprehension, the best clue is afforded by
τὸ φανταζόμενον in 313c. The images, or fancies, of the mind can
properly be called akin to it. Cf. *Laws* X, 892a.

     [6] Doris of Locri, one of the two wives of Dionysius I.

if you thought so, you had spared me many words. I said, however, that I had never met anyone who had discovered this truth, and that most of my own study was devoted to it. Perhaps you once heard something from someone and providentially started on the track of the answer, but then, thinking you had it safe, neglected to fix fast the proofs of it, which now dart here and there [7] about some object of your fancy, whereas the reality itself is quite different. You are not alone   c
in this experience; I assure you that everyone at first hearing is affected in just this way, and though some have more difficulty than others, there is almost no one who escapes with but little effort.

Considering thus our past and our present circumstances, we can fairly say we have found the answer to the question in your letter about our relations toward each other. For now that you are conversing with other philosophers and are testing my doctrines, both by themselves and by comparing them   d
with others, these teachings will take root this time, if your examination is sincere, and you will become attached both to them and to me.

Now how can this and all else that I have mentioned be brought about? It was quite proper of you to send Archedemus to me; do likewise in the future, for when he reaches you and gives you my answers you may still have difficulties. You will then send Archedemus back to me, if you are well advised, and he will return to you, like a good merchant. After you have done this two or three times and have thoroughly examined the answers I send to you, I shall be much surprised   e
if the matters which are now troubling you do not appear in an altogether different light. So be bold and inquire of me in this way; for you could not order, nor could Archedemus secure for you, any nobler or diviner merchandise.

Only take care that these letters do not fall into the hands   314
of uninstructed men. Nothing, I dare say, could sound more ridiculous to the multitude than these sayings, just as to

---

[7] Reading with Souilhé (*Lettres*) and Novotný (*Platonis Epistulae*) ἄττουσι instead of ἄττει σοι.

gifted persons nothing could be more admirable and inspir-
ing. One must talk about them and hear them expounded
again and again, perhaps for many years, and even then their
gold is with the utmost difficulty separated and refined. The
most surprising thing about it is this: many a man of able
b understanding and tenacious memory has become old in the
hearing of these doctrines and has told me that after more
than thirty years of hearing them expounded, after examining them and testing them in every way, those points which at
the beginning seemed most doubtful he now thinks to be the
clearest and most self-evident of all, while the matters he then
thought most credible are now quite the contrary. Keep this
in mind and take care that you have no occasion in the future
to feel remorse for now exposing these doctrines unworthily.
The best precaution is not to write them down, but to com-
c mit them to memory; for it is impossible that things written
should not become known to others. This is why I have never
written on these subjects. There is no writing of Plato's, nor
will there ever be; those that are now called so come from an
idealized and youthful Socrates.[8] Farewell and heed my warning; read this letter again and again, then burn it.

Enough of these matters. You were surprised that I sent
d Polyxenus to you; but about him as well as Lycophron [9] and
the other men now at your court, I repeat the opinion that I
have long had: you are far superior to them in dialectic, both
by natural aptitude and by your method of disputation; and
none of them lets himself be defeated intentionally, as some
people suppose, but only because he cannot help it. You seem,
however, to have dealt with them quite fairly and rewarded
them properly. But enough, and more than enough, about
e such men. As for Philistion,[10] if you still need him, by all

8 Or "an idealized and modernized Socrates" (Post, *Thirteen Epistles*).
For the meaning of this strange assertion see above, pp. 114 f.

9 Probably the Sophist of the school of Gorgias, mentioned frequently
by Aristotle (e.g. *Met.* 1045b10).

10 An illustrious physician of Syracuse; see Diog. Laert. VIII, 86 and

means keep him there; but if it is possible, release him and let Speusippus have his services. Speusippus joins me in this request, and Philistion also assured me that he would be glad to come to Athens if you would let him go. You did well to release the man from the rock quarries; and my petition about Hegesippus, the son of Ariston,[11] and his family is easy to grant, for you wrote me that if anyone ever tried to do him 315 or them an injury and you knew of it you would prevent it. The truth should be told about Lysiclides; he is the only man who has come from Sicily to Athens who has not given a distorted report of the relations between us; he continues, as always, to put the best interpretation upon what happened.

III

PLATO TO DIONYSIUS, JOY.

Is this the most appropriate way to address you, or should I wish you welfare, as I usually do in letters to my friends?[1] b You yourself, so I am told by those who were with you on the embassy to Delphi, addressed the god with this fawning expression, writing, they say,

> Joy to you! May you continue the pleasant life of the tyrant![2]

---

89. On the poor health of Speusippus in these years see Diog. Laert. IV, 3, and *Socratic Epistles* XXXIII and XXXIV.

[11] Hegesippus and Ariston, as well as the Lysiclides mentioned below, are otherwise unknown.

[1] On Plato's preference for the salutation $\varepsilon \hat{v} \ \pi \rho \acute{a} \tau \tau \varepsilon \iota v$ rather than the more usual $\chi a \acute{\iota} \rho \varepsilon \iota v$ see note on *Ep. I*, 309a. Compare the present passage with *Charm.* 164de, where Socrates explains that the Delphic inscription "Know thyself" is the god's greeting to his worshippers, taking the place of the trivial $\chi a \acute{\iota} \rho \varepsilon \iota v$.

[2] This exhortation appears to be, in true Delphic style, deliberately ambiguous; it may be a prayer that Apollo would preserve Dionysius in his tyranny, or a wish that the god would maintain his own enviable

c For my part I should not address such an exhortation even to a man, far less to a god. To God it would be enjoining something contrary to nature, since the divine has its seat far removed from pleasure and pain; and as for man, pleasure and pain more often do harm, by breeding stupidity, forgetfulness, folly, and insolence in his soul. But enough from me on the subject of salutations; read this and make whatever use you please of it.

Not a few persons have reported to me that you are telling
d it about among the ambassadors to your court that once, when I heard you announce your intention to resettle the Greek cities in Sicily and relieve Syracuse by changing your government from a tyranny to a kingship, I dissuaded you, you say, though you were very eager; but that now I am instructing Dion to do these very things, and thus we are using
e your own ideas to wrest your empire from you. You know best whether you gain anything by such tales; in any case you are doing me wrong in telling the exact opposite of what happened. I have been slandered enough by Philistides [3] and numerous other persons before the mercenaries and the people of Syracuse, because I was living in the citadel; and those outside, if any mistake was made, blamed it all on me, saying that you obeyed me in all things. You yourself know quite
316 well that on political matters I willingly labored with you on only a few things at the beginning, when I thought I could do some good. Besides other minor matters, I did considerable work on the preambles to the laws,[4] i.e. on those parts distinct

---

ascendancy. But what the writer (Plato?) obviously objects to most is the glorification of pleasure that is implied. For the inappropriateness of addressing such a wish to the gods, see *Phil.* 33b, and *Epin.* 985a.

[3] There can be no doubt that the Philistides here referred to is the same person as Philistus, the historian and loyal supporter of the Dionysii; see above, pp. 22 and 169 f. Proper names were often abbreviated in the manuscripts and hence variant readings could easily arise. Cf. Ritter, *Neue Untersuchungen*, p. 403; Meyer, *Geschichte des Altertums*, V, 502.

[4] In *Laws* IV, 719 ff., Plato maintains that the competent legislator in dealing with free citizens will use persuasion as well as command, and

from what you or someone else has added. For I hear that some of you have since been revising them; but which parts are mine and which yours will be obvious to anyone who is able to judge of my character.[5] But as I have just said, I don't need to be further misrepresented, either to the people of Syracuse or to anyone else whom these words of yours may influence; rather I need to be defended against those earlier b charges as well as against these graver and more malicious ones that have since appeared. Since, then, I am accused on two counts, I must make a twofold defense and show, first, that it was reasonable of me to avoid taking part in your affairs of state, and secondly, that it was not my advice that prevented you, as you say, and stood in your way when you were going to resettle the Greek cities. So now hear first my c defense on the former of these two points.

I came to Syracuse at the joint invitation of you and Dion. The latter was an old and well-tried friend of mine, of mature age and settled character;[6] and these qualities, as any man with a grain of sense can see, were absolutely necessary for advising upon problems as important as yours were at that time. You, on the contrary, were quite young, with almost no experience in the affairs with which you should have been acquainted, and were quite unknown to me. Shortly d after—whether it was a man, or God, or chance working through you that was responsible[7]—Dion was banished. Do you think that I could then co-operate with you in state affairs, when I had lost my wise colleague and saw the foolish one left, a ruler only in his own imagination, in reality being

---

will preface his laws with exhortation and explanation. What are the laws for which he is represented as writing prooemia in 367? See above, p. 92.

[5] Or "to recognize my style" ($\mathring{\eta}\theta o \varsigma$).

[6] Dion was then about forty years old and the younger Dionysius about twenty-five. See Grote, *History of Greece*, chap. 84 *ad init.*

[7] That human affairs are a mixture of providence, art, and chance is a familiar doctrine in the later dialogues. Cf. *Laws* IV, 709b; and *Ep. VIII*, 353b.

ruled by the crowd of unscrupulous men around him? What
was my duty under those conditions? Was it not to do what
e   I did, i.e. to let public affairs alone from that time on, protecting myself against the slanders of those who envied me,
and trying above all to make you [and Dion] friends again, if
possible, despite the differences that had arisen to separate
you? You yourself can testify that this is the end for which I
never ceased to labor. Eventually, though with difficulty, we
came to an agreement. Since you had a war on your hands, I
317 was to take ship for home; but after peace had been brought
about, both Dion and I were to return to Syracuse and you
were to summon us. These are the facts of my first visit to
Syracuse and my safe return home.

When peace had come you sent for me a second time, not,
however, in accordance with our agreement, for you invited
me only, promising to recall Dion later. On this account I
refused to come, much to Dion's displeasure, for he thought
b   it would be better for me to come as you commanded. A year
later a trireme arrived with letters from you, the main import
of which was that if I would come, Dion's affairs would be
settled in accordance with my desires, but the contrary if I
did not. I hesitate to say how many letters at that time came
from you and from others in Italy and Sicily who wrote at
c   your request, and to how many of my friends and acquaintances they were sent, all urging in the strongest terms
that I accede to your request and go. Thus it seemed to everyone, beginning with Dion, that I ought to take ship without
hesitation. I kept protesting to them that I was old,[8] and in-
sisting that you would not be strong enough to resist those
who were slandering me and wished to make us enemies. For
I saw then as I see now that a great and swollen fortune,
whether the possessor be a private person or a monarch, gen-
d   erally produces an equally numerous and mighty progeny of
talebearers and companions in shameless pleasures; this is the

8 Plato was nearing seventy at this time.

worst result of wealth or power of any sort.[9] Nevertheless I
dismissed all these thoughts and came to you, determined that
no friend of mine should ever be able to claim that he had
lost all his goods when they could have been saved by my
efforts. Upon my arrival (you know, of course, all that hap-   e
pened thereafter) I demanded, in accordance with the
promises made in your letters, first that you recall Dion and
make him your friend—urging that friendship which, if you
had then listened to me, would probably have been better
for you and for Syracuse and for the rest of Greece than what
we now have, or so my inner oracle tells me. In the second
place I asked that Dion's property be held by his family, instead of being apportioned among the executors whose names   318
I need not mention. Furthermore, I thought that my presence
with you made it more rather than less obligatory upon you
to continue the annual revenues you had been sending to
Dion.[10] Failing in each of these requests, I asked permission
to depart. Your next move was to urge me to remain for the
year, saying that you would sell the whole of Dion's property
and send half the proceeds to Corinth, retaining the other
half there in Syracuse for Dion's son. I could mention many   b
promises that you made and did not keep, but they are numerous and I must be brief. After you had sold all his property and without Dion's consent (though you had said you
would not sell it without his consent), then, my fine friend,
you put the colophon on all your broken promises. You hit
upon a scheme that was neither honorable nor fitting, nor
just nor advantageous, to frighten me into ignoring what was

[9] This passage is characteristically Platonic, both in thought and
manner. For similar employment of parentheses see *Ep. VII*, 325d, 326a,c,
328b, 334a, 344d. For the thought see *Rep.* VIII, 559d ff.

[10] The text of this passage is in a very uncertain state, as the numerous variant readings testify, and its meaning is correspondingly uncertain.
I have accepted Burnet's text, and take $\mu\hat{a}\lambda\lambda o\nu$ . . . $\kappa a\grave{\iota}$ $o\mathring{v}\chi$ $\mathring{\eta}\tau\tau o\nu$
as modifying $\delta\epsilon\hat{\iota}\nu$, rather than as implying that Plato proposed to in-
crease rather than diminish the annual revenues sent to Dion. But see
Pavlu, *Mitteilungen*, VIII, 23.

going on so that I would not even ask for the dispatch of
c Dion's money. After you had banished Heraclides [11] (an act
which neither I nor the people of Syracuse thought just), the
fact that I had joined with Theodotes and Eurybius in begging you not to do this you took as a sufficient pretext and
said that it had long been clear that I cared nothing for you,
but only for Dion and his friends and followers; and that now
when accusations had been made against Heraclides and
Theodotes, who were friends of Dion, I was doing all in my
d power to keep them from being punished.

But enough of our partnership in political affairs. If you
noted in me any other evidences of estrangement from you,
you may rightly explain them in the same way. What would
you expect? Any reasonable man would properly think me a
knave if I had been seduced by the greatness of your power
to desert an old comrade and guest-friend in the distress that
you had brought him to (and a man in no way inferior to
e you, if I may say so) and had chosen you who were the cause
of his wrongs, and had fallen in with all your plans, evidently
for the sake of money; for no one would have thought there
was any other reason for such a change in me, if I had so
changed. It is these events, brought about by you as I have
described, that are responsible for the estrangement and wolf-
friendship between us.

And now comes, almost as an immediate consequence of
the foregoing, my statement on the second point on which I
said I should have to defend myself. Attend carefully and see
319 if you can detect any falsehood or untruth in what I say. I
declare that about twenty days before my departure from
Syracuse for home, when Archedemus [12] and Aristocritus were
with us in the garden, you brought against me the same re-
proach that you now make, that I cared more for Heraclides

[11] One of Dionysius' generals. See above, pp. 175 ff., and for a fuller
account of this incident, *Ep. VII*, 348b-349c.
[12] See note on *Ep. II*, 310b. Aristocritus is mentioned in *Ep. XIII*,
363d. We infer that he was close to Dionysius.

and all the rest than I did for you. In their presence you
asked me whether I remembered advising you, when I first
arrived, to resettle the Greek cities. I admitted that I remem-   b
bered it, and said I still thought that was the best policy. And
I must remind you, Dionysius, of what was said immediately
afterwards. I asked, as you remember, whether this was all
my advice, or whether there was something more; and you
replied, with considerable anger and derision, as you thought
(whence it has come about that what you then derided is no
longer a dream but a reality),[13] and said, with a very forced
laugh, "I remember well; [14] you told me to get an education,   c
or leave all these projects alone." I replied that your memory
was excellent. "And this education," you said, "was to be in
geometry, was it not?" I refrained from giving the reply that
occurred to me, fearing lest a little word might narrow my
prospect of sailing home, to which I was then looking forward
with confidence.

Now the reason for all I have said is this: don't slander me
by saying that I would not allow you to resettle the Greek
cities destroyed by barbarians, or to relieve the people of   d
Syracuse by changing your tyranny into a kingship. No lie
you could possibly tell about me would be less appropriate;
and there is more and even clearer evidence that I could
submit for examination, if ever there should be a competent
inquiry into the matter, that it was I who urged you to these
projects and you who refused to undertake them. And it is
not hard to show that they were the best things that could
have been done for you and the people of Syracuse and all
Sicily.

And now, my friend, if you deny that you have said any of   e
these things that you said, that is all the justice I ask; but if

[13] Dionysius' contempt for the ideal of a philosophical ruler brought
about the victory of Dion and the triumph (or so it seemed at the time)
of Plato's political ideals.

[14] Reading, with Pavlu, εὖ μέμνημαι (instead of εἰ μέμνημαι) and taking
it as a part of the tyrant's reply.

you agree that you said them, then follow the wise example of Stesichorus, imitate his recantation, and change your lies to truth.

IV[1]

PLATO TO DION OF SYRACUSE, WELFARE.

320   I think my good will towards your enterprise has been evident from the beginning, as well as my earnest desire to see it brought to completion, for no other reason than admira-
b   tion for noble deeds. For I deem it right that the men who

---

1 This letter, if genuine, was written sometime between the first victories of Dion in Syracuse in 357 and his death in 354. This we may infer from the reference to "having put Dionysius out of the way" (ἀναιρεθέντος Διονυσίου) and the rivalry between Dion and Heraclides (320e). The writer expresses his ardent interest in Dion's enterprise and his hope that it may terminate successfully; but warns him of dangers ahead and cautions him not to adopt too severe and uncompromising an attitude toward his opponents and followers in Syracuse. The zeal expressed here for the success of Dion's expedition has been regarded as inconsistent with Plato's attitude toward the expedition in the *Seventh Epistle* (350cd). There is no real inconsistency, however. The *Seventh Epistle* merely says that Plato refused to take a personal part in Dion's enterprise; he did not attempt to restrain Dion from sailing against Syracuse nor his friends from joining the expedition. And since Plato's sympathies were wholly on the side of Dion as the injured party, there can be no doubt that once Dion had committed his life and reputation to the success of the expedition, Plato's attitude would be exactly that expressed by the writer of this letter. Besides, Plato looked upon the expedition not merely as an attempt to right a private wrong, but also as an undertaking that might bring much good to the Greeks (351a-e). Finally, it must be remembered that the *Seventh Epistle* was written in the depression following the failure of the enterprise, and naturally its tone would be much different from that of the present letter, written during the excitement of the initial successes.

The contents of this letter then seem to be above suspicion, and its purpose and manner are not unworthy of Plato. Nor do its style and diction offer any grounds for questioning its authenticity. But three or

really possess virtue and exemplify it in their conduct should receive the glory that is due them. All has gone well so far, thank God, but the greatest contest lies ahead. Strength, courage, and cleverness are qualities in which others also may win distinction; but to be pre-eminent above others in truthfulness, justice, high-mindedness, and the grace of conduct which these virtues express—this is what would by general c consent be expected of those who profess to honor these traits of character.[2] What I say is obvious; nevertheless we must keep reminding ourselves that these men (you know whom I mean) ought to stand out so that the rest of mankind will be as children in comparison. We must make it manifest that we are really the sort of men we say we are, particularly since, by God's help, it can easily be done. Other men have to d travel far and wide if they are to become known; but the events of which you are the center are such that the whole world, to speak somewhat boastfully, has its eyes upon one place, and upon you especially in that place. You are the object of universal interest; make ready, then, to eclipse Lycurgus and Cyrus and anyone else deemed pre-eminent in character and statesmanship,[3] especially since many people (indeed most people) here are saying that with Dionysius out e

four lines at the beginning are identical with the opening of a supposed letter of Speusippus (*Socratic Epistles* XXXIV), and Ritter (*Neue Untersuchungen*, pp. 374 ff.) is inclined to attribute it to Speusippus; but Souilhé (*Lettres*, p. lxviii), finding also in 321a an imitation of a passage in Isocrates' *Evagoras* (79-80), concludes that it is the work of a rhetorician.

2 This seems to be a reference to the Academy, or possibly to a select group within the circle of the Academy, who were expected to exemplify the Platonic ideals of conduct. The virtues of truthfulness, justice, and high-mindedness by which these men are said to place great store are Platonic enough; and the prominence given to truthfulness (or steadfastness) in this list has an interesting parallel in *Laws* V, 730c. Likewise the coupling of courage with boldness and strength as scarce deserving special praise accords with the description of courage in the *Laws* as the lowest part of virtue (I, 630c, 631c; XII, 963e).

3 Cf. *Ep. VIII*, 354b. Plato's admiration for Lycurgus and Cyrus is also strongly expressed in the *Laws;* see III, 691e (a clear reference to Lycurgus), and 694a.

of the way your cause will in all likelihood come to ruin through your ambitions and those of Heraclides, Theodotes, and the other notables. May no such dissension arise; but if it does, you must show that you can heal it and all will be well.

321   You will no doubt smile at my saying this, for you are yourself aware of the danger. But I have noticed that competitors in the games are spurred on by the shouts of the children, and still more by those of their friends, when they think that the cheering springs from sincerity and good will. Be you then the contestants, and write us when we can help you.

Matters here are almost the same as when you were with b   us. Write us also what you have done or are doing, since we hear many reports but know nothing surely. Letters have just now come to Lacedaemon and Aegina from Theodotes and Heraclides,[4] but as I said, though we hear many rumors from the people here,[5] we know nothing. Remember that some persons think you are not sufficiently obliging; don't forget that one must please men if one would do anything with c   them, whereas self-will is fit only for solitude.[6] Good luck!

---

[4] Heraclides and Theodotes are also mentioned in *Ep. VII*, 348b ff., and *Ep. III*, 318c. On Heraclides see above, pp. 175 ff.

[5] Accepting the emendation of Pavlu (*Mitteilungen*, IX, 54, n. 2) of ἀκούοντές περ τῶν τῇδε for ἀκούοντες περὶ τῶν τῇδε.

[6] Plato regards the ability of a man to gain and retain loyal followers as a sure indication of his virtue. Compare this warning to Dion with the condemnation of Dionysius I in *Epistle VII*, 331e-332c. Cf. also *Ep. VI*, 322d. The austerity for which Dion is gently reproached here is well described by Plutarch (*Dion* 8), together with the unfortunate effects it had upon those around him.

V

Plato to Perdiccas,[1] Welfare.

I have advised Euphraeus, as you wrote me, to look studiously after your interests, and it is right that I should give you also the proverbial "holy counsel" of a friend on the various matters you mention, and particularly as to the use   d

1 This is Perdiccas III, elder brother of Philip and king of Macedon from 364-359. The Euphraeus whom the letter recommends for the position of political adviser was a native of Oreus in northern Euboea and a member of the Academy. Athenaeus tells us (506e) that while he was at the court of King Perdiccas he persuaded the monarch to divide his kingdom and give a portion of it to his younger brother Philip. Euphraeus was thus instrumental in starting Philip upon his career of power. Later, however, Euphraeus became the leader of the anti-Macedonian party in his native city and committed suicide when the sympathizers with Philip finally triumphed in 343 (Athen. 508e; Dem. *Phil. III*, 59 ff.). This letter, therefore, accords accurately enough, so far as we can discover, with the historical circumstances to which it refers. Likewise the interest the writer shows in the types of constitutions and the laws appropriate to each agrees with Plato's political views and interests. This is the sort of inquiry we find presented dramatically in the *Republic*, Books VIII and IX, and more prosaically in the *Laws*. But the metaphor of the various constitutions, each speaking with its own voice, like so many animals, is hardly a felicitous one. The defense of Plato's political inactivity at Athens is irrelevant to the main purpose of the letter, and it is also strange that Plato should defend himself in this fashion to Perdiccas, a young and to him comparatively unknown king. On the other hand, the language is Platonic enough and possesses many points of similarity with the language of the genuine letters (Ritter, *Neue Untersuchungen*, p. 397; Hackforth, *The Authorship of the Platonic Epistles*, p. 75).

Various theories have been advanced as to the authorship of this letter and the motive of its composition, assuming that it is not from Plato himself. It is natural to connect it with the rivalry between the Academy and the school of Isocrates, in the decade after Plato's death, for the favor of Philip. Possibly it was written during this period by some Academic sympathizer to support the claims of the Academy upon the gratitude of Philip. On the other hand, it may have been put in circulation, as Post suggests (*Thirteen Epistles*, p. 133), by an opponent of

you should now make of Euphraeus.[2] The man can be of
service to you in many ways, but most of all in supplying
what you now lack, for you are young and there are not
many who can counsel young men about it. Constitutions, like
species of animals, have each their own language—democracy
one, oligarchy another, and monarchy still another. Many
e persons would say they know these languages, but for the most
part, and with rare exceptions, they fall short of understanding them. The constitution that speaks its own language to
gods and men, and suits its actions to its words, always pros-
pers and survives; but it goes to ruin if it imitates another.
Now in this Euphraeus can perhaps be of most use to you,
though he will be a manly aid in other respects as well; I
322 believe that he can search out the words appropriate to monarchy as well as any man in your service. Use him, then, for

Plato, as a subtle means of connecting him with Philip's rise to power
and thus discrediting the Academy in Athenian public opinion. But in
either case it would have been irrelevant to introduce a defense of Plato's
political inactivity, for it is not clear how this would serve either to
discredit Plato with the democracy or endear him to Philip. Some of the
difficulties of the letter are explained by supposing that it was written
to Perdiccas by one of Plato's friends—Dion, as Ficinus suggested, or
Speusippus, according to Ritter. Dion was intimate with the Academy
during these years and might well have written in behalf of Euphraeus.
We know also that Speusippus had close relations with the court of
Macedon (Diog. Laert. IV, 1); and since he was one of the ranking members of the Academy, his recommendation would doubtless have weight.
Again, if Dion or Speusippus wrote this letter, we can understand why
the defense of Plato is in the third person rather than in the first, as
would be more natural if Plato had written it himself. And on general
grounds, this defense would seem to come more naturally from one of
them than from Plato. But why introduce this defense of Plato at all?
The lack of connection between the two subjects suggests that the letter
is a bit of romantic fiction; but if so, its writer must have been well
informed, and it is probable that he is relying, as G. F. Dümmler argued
(*Kleine Schriften* [Leipzig, 1901], I, 121 ff.), upon the letter of Speusippus
which we hear about through Athenaeus (506e ff.).

[2] This proverb is referred to also in *Theages*, 122b. Cf. Xen. *Anab.* V,
vi, 4.

this, and you will not only profit yourself but confer upon him a very great benefit.

If anyone hears this and says, "Plato apparently claims to know what is good for a democracy, but though he is at liberty to speak in the assembly and give it his best advice, he has never yet stood up and said a word," you can answer by saying, "Plato was born late in the life of his native city, and he found the demos advanced in years and habituated by   b former advisers to many practices incompatible with the advice he would give. Nothing would be sweeter to him than to give advice to the demos as to a father, if he did not think he would be risking danger in vain and accomplish nothing. He would do the same about advising me, I know. If we seemed to him incurable, he would bid us a long farewell and refrain from advising about me or my affairs." [3] Good luck!   c

VI

PLATO TO HERMEIAS AND ERASTUS AND CORISCUS, WELFARE.

It is evident to me that some god has graciously and gener-ously prepared good luck for you, if you receive his gift properly. For you are living as neighbors to one another and each of you needs what the others can best supply. Hermeias [1]   d

---

[3] I have followed Hackforth (p. 73) in regarding the whole passage from Πλάτων ὀψέ to συμβουλῆς as the reply it is suggested that Perdiccas should make to Plato's critics. Thus Πλάτωνα is to be supplied as the subject of δρᾶσαι ἄν; and τὴν ἐμὴν συμβουλήν means "the advice Plato would give me [Perdiccas]."

[1] Hermeias, tyrant of Atarneus and Assos in the Troad, was one of the most remarkable men of the fourth century. Probably of barbarian origin, formerly a slave of Eubulus, tyrant of Atarneus and Assos, he later became associated with his master in the government of these cities, and on the death of Eubulus in 351 succeeded to his power. He was afterwards betrayed into the hands of the Persian king, and according to

should know that his power for all purposes has its greatest support not in the number of his horses or other equipment of war, nor in the gold he adds to his treasury, but in stead-fast friends of solid character.[2] And to Erastus[3] and Coriscus I say, "old as I am,"[4] that they need to supplement their knowledge of the Ideas—that noble doctrine—with the knowl-
e edge and capacity to protect themselves against wicked and unjust men. They are inexperienced, since they have spent a great part of their lives with us, among men of moderation

---

some accounts met his death by crucifixion when he would not divulge the plans of his ally and confederate, Philip of Macedon. The character of the man is well attested by the fact that he was an intimate friend of Aristotle and Xenocrates, both of whom retired to his court after the death of Plato and resided there for several years. Aristotle married his adopted daughter Pythias. In the fragments of Didymus' work on Demosthenes there is an excerpt from a eulogy of Hermeias by Cal-listhenes, the nephew of Aristotle. Callisthenes praises his steadfastness and loyalty to his friends, as shown in particular by the circumstances of his death. Of him it could be said, says Callisthenes, that he had done nothing unseemly nor unworthy of philosophy (Didymus, *Kommentar zu Demosthenes*, ed. Diels-Schubart, p. 25). His death must have been an event of tragic interest to Aristotle and the Academy. Aristotle was moved by it to write a paean to Hermeias, and had a statue erected to him at Delphi (Diog. Laert. V, 6 and 7).

[2] The emphasis on the value of friendship as a support for political power is unquestionably Platonic. See especially *Ep. VII*, 331d ff.

[3] Erastus and Coriscus are known to us from Diogenes Laertius as members of the Academy (III, 46); and the above-mentioned fragments of Didymus show that Theopompus, in his letter to Philip, coupled the name of Erastus with that of Hermeias. This Erastus is doubtless the one mentioned in *Ep. XIII*, 362b. Coriscus was the father of Neleus, a pupil of Aristotle and Theophrastus, and the recipient of Aristotle's library after the death of Theophrastus.

[4] Few translators or editors have been able to interpret this passage to their satisfaction. Post (*Class. Rev.*, XLIV [1930], 116) has suggested that the writer is quoting the opening words of a distich from Sophocles' *Thyestes*:

καίπερ γέρων ὤν· ἀλλὰ τῷ γήρᾳ φιλεῖ
χὠ νοῦς ὁμάρτειν καὶ τὸ βουλεύειν ἃ δεῖ.
Fr. 239, Nauck

The writer of this letter assumes that the reader will complete the lines. I have followed this happy suggestion in my rendering.

and good will; this is why I said they need some power to
protect them, that they may not be forced to neglect the true
wisdom and concern themselves more than is fitting with that
which is worldly and necessary. Now this power that they need
Hermeias apparently possesses, both as a natural gift (so far
as one may judge without knowing him),[5] and as an art
perfected by experience.

323

What is the point of these remarks? To you, Hermeias,
since I have known Erastus and Coriscus longer than you
have, I solemnly declare and bear witness that you will not
easily find more trustworthy characters than these neighbors
of yours, and I therefore advise you to make it a matter of
central importance to attach yourself to them by every honorable means. Coriscus and Erastus in their turn I advise to
hold fast to Hermeias and to try to develop this mutual
alliance into a bond of friendship. If ever any one of you   b
should seem to be weakening this union (for nothing human
is altogether secure), send a letter to me and my friends declaring the grievance; for unless the injury be very grave, I
believe your sense of justice and your respect for us will
make the words that we may send more efficacious than any
incantation would be in binding up the wound and causing
you to grow together again into friendship and fellowship as
before. If all of us, you and we alike, according to our sev-   c
eral abilities and opportunities, apply our wisdom to the
preservation of this bond, the prophecies I have just uttered

[5] There is a contradiction here with Strabo's assertion (XIII, i, 57) that
Hermeias had studied under both Plato and Aristotle at Athens; see A.
Boeckh, *Kleine Schriften* (Leipzig, 1858-1872), VI, 185. But A. Brinkmann
has shown (*Rheinisches Museum*, LXVI [1911], 226-30) that this passage
of Strabo dealing with the fate of Aristotle's library contains numerous
inaccuracies. Furthermore, the name of Hermeias does not appear in the
Index Herculanensis (33 ff. Mekler) nor in that given by Diogenes Laertius
(III, 46). Both these sources, however, confirm Strabo's assertion of
Hermeias' close connection with Aristotle and Xenocrates after the death
of Plato (*Index* 22 ff., Diog. Laert. V, 3 and 9). This letter, then, assuming it to be genuine, may have been the first direct contact between the
Academy and the tyrant of Atarneus.

will come true. What will happen if we do not, I will not say, for I am prophesying only what is good, and I declare that with God's help we shall bring all these things to a good issue.

Let this letter be read, if possible, by all three of you gathered together, otherwise by twos, and as often as you can in common. Adopt it as a just and binding law and
d covenant, taking a solemn oath—in gentlemanly earnest, but with the playfulness that is the sister of solemnity—in the name of the divine leader of all things present and to come, and in the name of the lordly father of this governor and cause, whom we shall all some day clearly know, in so far as the blessed are able to know him, if we truly live the life of philosophy.[6]

[6] Suspicion has been aroused by this concluding passage. Ritter (*Neue Untersuchungen,* pp. 366 f., 373 f.) goes so far as to class it with the "riddle" passage of the *Second Epistle.* But the objection to the latter lies in its deliberate mystification; here there is no mystification, though it is difficult to determine the precise meaning intended. The "father" is probably to be identified with the "father and maker" of the *Timaeus* (28c, 37c, 41a); and it would seem reasonable to identify the "governor" with one of the created deities of the *Timaeus,* possibly the world-soul, as Raeder believes ("Über die Echtheit der Platonischen Briefe," *Rheinisches Museum,* N. F. LXI [1906], 536), or the sun (according to Apelt in *Platons Briefe*). The fact that the writer is speaking half playfully makes it scarcely worth while to try to fix his meaning too precisely. In any event there is nothing in its import to prevent our accepting the letter as Plato's.

The mingling of playfulness and solemnity in this concluding passage, the figure of the wounded friendship being "bound up" so that the friends may "grow together again" as before, the mellowness and the deeply religious tone of the whole composition—these are traits that suggest Plato, particularly the Plato of the *Laws.* If the letter is genuine it gives us an intimate and charming picture of the friendship that existed among the members of the Academy and served to link them together even when scattered far over the Greek world. Most students now regard it as an authentic letter of Plato, though Hackforth, Souilhé, and Maddalena (*Platone: Lettere* [Bari, 1948]), reject it, as did Ritter.

VII

PLATO TO THE FRIENDS AND FOLLOWERS OF DION, WELFARE.

You have written me that I must consider your aims as
identical with those that Dion had, and you therefore urge me
to co-operate with you as much as I can, both in word and in   324
deed. My answer is that if your views and purposes are really
the same as his, I agree to join with you; if not, I shall have
to consider the matter further. What his principles and ambitions were I can tell you, I may say, not from conjecture,
but from certain knowledge. For when I first came to Syracuse, being then about forty years of age, Dion was of the age
that Hipparinus is now; [1] and it was then that he came to the
opinions which he continued to hold until the end; the Syra-   b
cusans, he thought, ought to be free and live under the best of
laws. It would not then be surprising if some divine power
should bring Hipparinus also to the same mind that Dion had
about government. To learn the way in which these convictions come about is instructive to young and old alike; and
since the present occasion seems appropriate, I will try to
describe how they originated in my own case.

When I was a young man I had the same ambition as many
others: I thought of entering public life as soon as I came of
age. And certain happenings in public affairs favored me, as   c
follows. The constitution we then had, being anathema to
many, was overthrown; and a new government was set up con-
sisting of fifty-one men, two groups—one of eleven and another
of ten—to police the market place and perform other necessary
duties in the city and the Piraeus respectively, and above them

[1] On the identity of this Hipparinus see pp. 85 f. Why would it not be
surprising if Hipparinus should come to the same opinion as Dion had?
Because twenty is an impressionable age? Or because Hipparinus has been
influenced by the memory of his father? During the preceding eight or
nine years he has been the ward of his uncle Dionysius.

d   thirty other officers with absolute powers.[2] Some of these men
     happened to be relatives and acquaintances of mine,[3] and they
     invited me to join them at once in what seemed to be a proper
     undertaking. My attitude toward them is not surprising, be-
     cause I was young. I thought that they were going to lead the
     city out of the unjust life she had been living and establish
     her in the path of justice, so that I watched them eagerly to
     see what they would do. But as I watched them they showed
     in a short time that the preceding constitution had been a
e   precious thing. Among their other deeds they named Socrates,
     an older friend of mine whom I should not hesitate to call the
     wisest and justest man of that time, as one of a group sent to
     arrest a certain citizen [4] who was to be put to death illegally,
325 planning thereby to make Socrates willy-nilly a party to their
     actions. But he refused, risking the utmost danger rather than
     be an associate in their impious deeds. When I saw all this and
     other like things of no little consequence, I was appalled and
     drew back from that reign of injustice.[5] Not long afterwards
     the rule of the Thirty was overthrown and with it the entire
     constitution; and once more I felt the desire, though this time
b   less strongly, to take part in public and political affairs. Now
     many deplorable things occurred during those troubled days,
     and it is not surprising that under cover of the revolution too
     many old enmities were avenged; but in general those who re-
     turned from exile [6] acted with great restraint. By some chance,
     however, certain powerful persons brought into court this same

   [2] The numbers given here are strikingly corroborated by Xenophon
(*Hell.* II, iv, 58) and Aristotle (*Const. of Ath.*, xxxv). Aristotle also describes the favorable beginning of the rule of the Thirty and the disillusionment that followed.

   [3] Critias, leader of the Thirty, was a paternal cousin of Plato's mother
Perictione; and Charmides, one of the group administering the Piraeus,
was her brother.

   [4] Leon of Salamis. See Plato's *Apol.*, 32cd.

   [5] Or "from those evil men" ($\dot{\alpha}\pi\dot{o}$ $\tau\hat{\omega}\nu$ $\tau\acute{o}\tau\epsilon$ $\kappa\alpha\kappa\hat{\omega}\nu$). Plato's "withdrawal"
does not imply that he had at first been a member of the government;
he was only twenty-three, too young by Athenian standards for any official
post.

   [6] I.e. Thrasybulus and the democrats.

friend Socrates, preferring against him a most shameless accu- c
sation, and one which he, of all men, least deserved. For the
prosecutors charged him with impiety, and the jury condemned and put to death the very man who, at the time
when his accusers were themselves in misfortune and exile,
had refused to have a part in the unjust arrest of one of
their friends.

The more I reflected upon what was happening, upon what
kind of men were active in politics, and upon the state of our
laws and customs, and the older I grew, the more I realized
how difficult it is to manage a city's affairs rightly. For I saw
it was impossible to do anything without friends and loyal d
followers; and to find such men ready to hand would be a
piece of sheer good luck, since our city was no longer guided
by the customs and practices of our fathers, while to train
up new ones was anything but easy. And the corruption of
our written laws and our customs was proceeding at such
amazing speed that whereas at first I had been full of zeal for e
public life, when I noted these changes and saw how unstable
everything was, I became in the end quite dizzy; and though
I did not cease to reflect how an improvement could be
brought about in our laws and in the whole constitution, yet 326
I refrained from action, waiting for the proper time. At last
I came to the conclusion that all existing states are badly governed and the condition of their laws practically incurable,
without some miraculous remedy and the assistance of fortune; and I was forced to say, in praise of true philosophy,
that from her height alone was it possible to discern what the
nature of justice is, either in the state or in the individual,
and that the ills of the human race would never end until b
either those who are sincerely and truly lovers of wisdom come
into political power, or the rulers of our cities, by the grace
of God, learn true philosophy.[7]

Such was the conviction I had when I arrived in Italy and
Sicily for the first time. When I arrived and saw what they

[7] For the expression of this doctrine in the *Republic* see V, 473d, VI,
487e, 499b, **501e**.

call there the "happy life"—a life filled with Italian and Syracusan banquets,[8] with men gorging themselves twice a day and never sleeping alone at night, and following all the

c other customs that go with this way of living—I was profoundly displeased. For no man under heaven who has cultivated such practices from his youth could possibly grow up to be wise—so miraculous a temper is against nature—or become temperate, or indeed acquire any other part of virtue. Nor could any city enjoy tranquillity, no matter how good its laws, when its men think they must spend their all on ex-

d cesses, and be easygoing about everything except the feasts and the drinking bouts and the pleasures of love that they pursue with professional zeal. These cities are always changing into tyrannies, or oligarchies, or democracies,[9] while the rulers in them will not even hear mention of a just and equitable constitution.

These, plus the conviction previously mentioned, were my

e thoughts on coming to Syracuse—a coming which may have been mere coincidence, but which seems to have been the work of some higher power [10] laying then the foundation for what has since come to pass with respect to Dion and Syracuse; and for still further misfortunes, too, I fear, unless you now obey the advice which I am giving for the second time.[11] How

327 can I say that my coming to Sicily then was the beginning of it all? In my associations with Dion, who was then a young

8 Syracusan tables were proverbial; cf. *Rep.* III, 404d; Athen. 527d. Apelt remarks that the literature of cookery seems to have had its origin in Sicily; cf. *Gorg.* 518b. Cicero refers twice to this passage, i.e. *Tusc. Disp.* V, xxv, 100; *De Fin.* II, xxviii, 92.

9 I.e. into one of the lawless forms of constitution enumerated in *Polit.* 291d ff., 302c ff.

10 For this meaning of οἱ κρείττονες see *Soph.* 216b, *Laws* IV, 718a. There are echoes of this passage in Plutarch *Dion* 4. The recognition that human events are always exposed to the influence of higher powers is a recurrent theme in the *Epistles* and the *Laws*. See, e.g., *Ep. VII*, 324b, 327c,e, 336e; *VIII*, 353b, 355e, 357a, 357d; *Laws* IV, 709b; VII, 798a; IX, 875c.

11 Doubtless a reference to the attempt in 367 and 361 to influence the young Dionysius. Cf. 331d.

man, I imparted to him my ideas of what was best for men and
urged him to put them into practice; and in doing so I was
in a way contriving, though quite unwittingly, the destruction
of the tyranny that later came to pass. For Dion was in all
things quick to learn, especially in the matters upon which I
talked with him; and he listened with a zeal and attentiveness
I had never encountered in any young man, and he resolved   b
to spend the rest of his life differently from most Italians and
Sicilians, since he had come to love virtue more than pleasure
and luxury. For this reason his way of life was more than
annoying to those who guided themselves by the practices of
tyranny, until the death of Dionysius.[12] After that event he
conceived that these convictions which he himself had got
from proper instruction might arise in others beside himself;   c
and observing that they were in fact making their appearance
in the minds of some, at least, of his associates, he thought
that by the help of the gods Dionysius himself might be
counted among this number; and if this should happen, it
would mean an incalculably blessed life for the tyrant himself
and the other Syracusans. Furthermore, he thought that by all
means I should come to Syracuse as soon as possible and become a partner in his plans, for he recalled our conversations   d
together and how effectively they had aroused in him the desire for a life of nobility and virtue. If now he could arouse
this desire in Dionysius, as he was attempting to do, he had
high hopes of establishing throughout the land a true and
happy life, without the massacres and deaths and the other
evils that have come to pass. With this just purpose in mind
Dion persuaded Dionysius to send for me, and he himself
wrote urging me by all means to come at once before certain   e
others [13] came in contact with Dionysius and diverted him to

12 The strange periphrasis here—μέχρι τοῦ θανάτου τοῦ περὶ Διονύσιον
γενομένου—is doubtless a hint of the mysterious circumstances surrounding the death of Dionysius I. See pp. 28 f.

13 Does this refer to Philistus, who was recalled from exile shortly
after Dionysius II came into power, or to some of the other philosophers
and sophists, such as Aristippus, who seem to have gathered like flies
around the wealthy young tyrant?

a less worthy ideal of life. His petition, though too long to give in full, was as follows: "What better opportunity can we expect," he said, "than the situation which Providence has presented us with?" He mentioned the empire in Italy

328 and Sicily, his own power in it, the youth of Dionysius, and the eager interest he was showing in philosophy and culture; Dion's nephews and other relatives, he said, could be easily persuaded to accept the life and doctrine that I have always taught, and would be a very strong additional influence upon Dionysius; so that now, if ever, might we confidently hope to accomplish that union, in the same persons, of philosophers and rulers of great cities.

b These and many other like arguments he addressed to me. For my own part I felt a certain anxiety, since one never knows how young men will turn out, for their desires arise quickly and often change to their contraries;[14] but Dion's character, I knew, was steadfast by nature and he had already reached middle age. Consequently I weighed the question and was uncertain whether or not to yield to his urging and undertake the journey.[15] What tipped the scales eventually was the thought that if anyone ever was to attempt to realize these

c principles of law and government, now was the time to try, since it was only necessary to win over a single man[16] and I should have accomplished all the good I dreamed of. This, then, was the "bold" purpose I had in setting forth from home, and not what some persons ascribed to me.[17] Above all

[14] For a parallel to this comment see *Laws* XI, 929c.

[15] No doubt many persons felt that Plato's going to Syracuse had done more harm than good, that the venture was a hopeless one from the start. So Plato takes pains to emphasize (1) the favorable elements in the situation which might really lead one to hope for the reform of Syracuse, (2) his friendship for Dion and his unwillingness to refuse aid to his friend, and (3) the fear that he would lose his self-respect if he hesitated to make the most of this opportunity to put his political principles to the trial.

[16] Cf. *Rep.* VI, 502b.

[17] This shows that there was some criticism not only of Plato's judgment, but also of his motives in going to Syracuse. What these imputed

I was ashamed lest I appear to myself as a pure theorist, un-willing to touch any practical task—and I saw that I was in danger of betraying Dion's hospitality and friendship at a   d time of no little real danger to him. Suppose he should be killed or banished by Dionysius and his other enemies and should come to me in his exile and say, "Here I am, Plato, a fugitive, not because I lacked hoplites or horsemen to ward off my enemies, but only for need of the persuasive words by which, as I well know, you are always able to turn young men towards goodness and justice and make them friends and comrades of one another. This weakness which you could   e have remedied is the cause of my being here in exile from Syracuse. But my own misfortune is a small part of your dis-honor. You are always praising philosophy, and saying she is held in little esteem by the rest of mankind; but in betraying me now have you not, by neglecting this opportunity, also betrayed her? If we had happened to be living in Megara you   329 would certainly have come as a helper in answer to my call, or you would consider yourself the most trifling of men. And now do you think you can escape the charge of cowardice by pleading the length of the journey, the greatness of the voyage and its fatigue? Far from it." To words of this sort what re-spectable answer could I give? None. And so from motives as rational and just as is humanly possible I departed, giving up   b for those reasons my occupations here, which are not without dignity, to live under a tyranny seemingly unsuited both to my doctrines and to me. In so going I discharged my obliga-tion to Zeus Xenios [18] and cleared myself of reproach from philosophy, which would have been dishonored if I had in-curred disgrace through softness or cowardice.

When I arrived—to make the story short—I found the court of Dionysius full of faction and of malicious reports to the tyrant about Dion. I defended him as well as I could, but I   c

motives were we can can only conjecture; but see above, pp. 46 ff. These criticisms rankle a little, as the following pages show.

[18] Zeus the protector of strangers, the guardian of the obligations of hospitality.

was able to do very little; and about the fourth month Dionysius, charging Dion with plotting against the tyranny, had him put aboard a small vessel and exiled in disgrace. Thereupon we friends of Dion were all afraid that one of us might be accused and punished as an accomplice in Dion's conspiracy. About me there even went abroad in Syracuse a report that I had been put to death by Dionysius as the cause of

d all that had happened. But Dionysius, seeing how we all felt, and apprehensive lest our fears might lead to something even graver, treated us all kindly, and me especially he reassured, telling me to have no fear and earnestly begging me to remain; for there was no honor for him in my leaving, he said, but only in my remaining. For this reason he made a great pretense of begging me, but we know that the requests of tyrants are mingled with compulsion. He devised a means for

e preventing my departure by bringing me inside the citadel and lodging me there, whence no ship's captain would have dared to take me away without a messenger sent from Dionysius himself commanding him to do so, still less if Dionysius had forbidden it. Nor would any merchant or guard along the roads leading out of the country have let me pass alone, but would have taken me in charge at once and brought me back to Dionysius, especially since another report had already got

330 abroad, contrary to the earlier one, that Dionysius was wonderfully fond of Plato. What in fact was the situation? With the passage of time Dionysius, I must truly say, did become more and more attached to me as he became more familiar with my manner and character; but he wanted me to praise him more than I did Dion and value his friendship more highly, and he was marvellously persistent towards this end. How this could best have come about, if at all, was through

b his becoming my disciple and associating with me in discourse about philosophy; but he shrank from this, for the intriguers had made him fear that he would be entrapped, so that Dion would have accomplished his purposes. I put up with all this, however, holding fast to the original purpose for which I had

come, hoping that he might somehow come to desire the
philosophic life; but I never overcame his resistance.

These, then, were the circumstances that account for my
first [19] visit to Sicily and occupied the time of my sojourn   c
there. Afterwards I came home, only to return again at the
urgent summons of Dionysius. Why I returned and what I
did, with the explanation and justification of my actions, I
will go into later for the benefit of those who wonder what
my purpose was in going a second time. But in order that
these incidental matters may not usurp the chief place in my
letter,[20] I will first advise what is to be done in the present
circumstances. This, then, is what I have to say.

When one is advising a sick man who is living in a way in-
jurious to his health, must one not first of all tell him to   d
change his way of life and give him further counsel only if
he is willing to obey? [21] If he is not, I think any manly and
self-respecting physician would break off counseling such a
man, whereas anyone who would put up with him is without
spirit or skill. So too with respect to a city: whether it be
governed by one man or many, if its constitution is properly
ordered and rightly directed, it would be sensible to give advice to its citizens concerning what would be to the city's ad-   e
vantage. But if it is a people who have wandered completely
away from right government and resolutely refuse to come
back upon its track and instruct their counselor to leave the

[19] I.e. the first to Dionysius II.

[20] These incidental matters (πάρεργα) are not really irrelevant, despite
this rather formal transition. What has gone before serves as a necessary
propaedeutic to the understanding of the advice which Plato now proceeds to give. This second part of the letter extends to 337e. The narrative of Plato's third journey to Sicily which begins at that point and
occupies the remainder of the letter, except for a defense of Dion's motives at the end, becomes not only an apologia for Plato's actions, but also
a dramatic demonstration of the difficulties facing Dion's party in putting
Plato's principles into effect.

[21] Plato is evidently not very sure of the sincerity of the professed followers of Dion, nor of their willingness to carry out his suggestions. See
the opening sentence of this letter.

331 constitution strictly alone, threatening him with death if he
changes it,[22] and order him instead to serve their interests and
desires and show them how they can henceforth satisfy them
in the quickest and easiest way—any man, I think, who would
accept such a role as adviser is without spirit, and he who refuses is the true man. These are my principles; and whenever
anyone consults me on a question of importance in his life,
b   such as the making of money, or the care of his body or soul,
if it appears to me that he follows some plan in his daily life
or is willing to listen to reason on the matters he lays before
me, I advise him gladly and don't stop with merely discharg-
ing my duty. But a man who does not consult me at all, or
makes it clear that he will not follow advice that is given him—
to such a man I do not take it upon myself to offer counsel;
nor would I use constraint upon him, not even if he were my
own son. Upon a slave I might force my advice, compelling
him to follow it against his will; but to use compulsion upon
c   a father or mother is to me an impious act,[23] unless their
judgment has been impaired by disease. If they are fixed in
a way of life that pleases them, though it may not please me,
I should not antagonize them by useless admonitions, nor yet
by flattery and complaisance encourage them in the satisfaction of desires that I would die rather than embrace. This is
the principle which a wise man must follow in his relations
towards his own city. Let him warn her, if he thinks her con-
d   stitution is corrupt and there is a prospect that his words will
be listened to and not put him in danger of his life; but let
him not use violence upon his fatherland to bring about a
change of constitution. If what he thinks is best can only be
accomplished by the exile and slaughter of men, let him keep
his peace and pray for the welfare of himself and his city.

In this way, then, I venture to advise you, as Dion and I

[22] Cf. *Rep*. IV, 426c.

[23] "Father or mother"; cf. *Crito* 51c. Plato is doubtless thinking of
Athens here. Compare this explanation of his political inactivity at
Athens with that implied in *Rep*. VI, 496b-e. Cicero no doubt refers to
the present passage in *Fam*. I, 9, 18.

used to advise Dionysius, first of all to make his daily life such as to give him the greatest possible mastery over himself and win him loyal friends and followers. In so doing, we said, he might avoid his father's experience when, after taking over many great cities in Sicily that had been laid waste by the barbarians, he was unable at their resettlement to establish loyal governments in them. For he had no comrades to head these governments, neither among foreigners, nor among his own brothers whom he had trained in their youth (since they were younger than himself) and raised from private to royal station and from poverty to great wealth.[24] None of these was he able, either by persuasion or by teaching, by benefits conferred or by ties of kinship, to make an associate in his empire. In this respect he was seven times weaker than Darius, who had neither brothers to rely upon, nor persons trained by himself, but only those who helped him to overthrow the Mede and the Eunuch. He distributed among them seven provinces, each one greater than all Sicily, and he found them to be loyal, for they did not attack him or one another; and in so doing he set an example of what a good lawgiver and king should be, for he established laws that have kept the Persian empire to this day.[25] We have another example in the

[24] On the importance of friends and loyal followers see 325d; also Xen. *Cyr.* VIII, vi, 12, vii, 13. Dionysius had two brothers, Leptines and Thearides, both of whom seem to have been loyal adjutants, and Plato's remarks about them here are hard to understand.

[25] This is the point of the comparison Plato makes between the achievements of Darius and Dionysius. The Persian empire as organized by Darius had maintained itself for almost two centuries, whereas the much smaller empire of Dionysius became progressively weaker during its founder's own lifetime and fell apart within less than ten years after his death. This difference is due, Plato thinks, to the superior character of Darius, who had loyal and high-minded collaborators, viz. the Persian nobles who had helped him to overthrow the "Eunuch," i.e. the usurping pretender Smerdis. There is a similar eulogy of Darius in *Laws* III, 695c ff., where mention is again made of "the seven" (Darius himself apparently being counted as one of the number) who brought the empire again under Persian control. The evidence of the Behistun inscription, and of Herodotus, confirms Plato's statement about the six helpers of

Athenians, who took over the protection of a number of Hellenic cities threatened by barbarians. Though the Athenians had not themselves settled these cities but took them over already established, yet they maintained their power over
c them for seventy years because of the friends they made in each of them.[26] But Dionysius, though he united all Sicily into a single city (for he knew that he could trust no one), was scarcely able to survive, for he was poor in friends and loyal followers, and the possession or lack of these is the best indication of a man's virtue or vice.

This is the advice that Dion and I gave to Dionysius, since
d his father's neglect had resulted in his being without culture and unused to associations appropriate to his position. We said that once embarked upon the course just mentioned [27] he should induce others among his relatives and companions to become friends and partners in the pursuit of virtue; but above all to become a friend to himself, for in this respect he was incredibly deficient. We did not say it thus openly, for that would not have been safe, but made veiled references to his weakness, striving by our words to show him that everyone must do this who would save himself and the people over
e whom he rules, whereas any other course will accomplish his ruin and theirs. Let him take the path we pointed out and perfect himself in wisdom and self-control; then if he should resettle the deserted cities of Sicily, and bind them together with such laws and constitutions as would make them friendly to himself and to one another and a mutual help against the barbarians, he would have an empire not twice but actually

Darius; but Plato is strangely mistaken in asserting that Darius divided the empire into seven parts; both the Behistun inscription and Herodotus say he divided it into twenty or more satrapies, the organization which it had in Plato's day and of which he could hardly have been ignorant.

[26] Round numbers, i.e. from the establishment of the Confederacy of Delos about 477 to the end of the Peloponnesian War in 404. This is a distinctly more favorable interpretation of the Athenian Empire than we should have expected from Plato; cf. 351b.

[27] Omitting Burnet's lacuna in the text and reading, with Souilhé and Novotný, πρῶτον ἐπὶ ταῦτα.

many times as powerful as his father's had been; he would be   333
ready to inflict upon the Carthaginians a far heavier defeat
than they had suffered in the days of Gelon,[28] instead of paying tribute to these barbarians as he was doing at present
under the agreement his father had made.

These were the words of exhortation we addressed to Dionysius—we who were conspiring against him, according to the
reports that were current on all sides. These reports finally
prevailed with Dionysius, as you know, bringing exile to Dion
and fear to us his friends. But—to jump to the end of the   b
many events of this short time—when Dion returned from
the Peloponnesus and Athens he indeed taught Dionysius a
lesson. And then when he had delivered the people of Syracuse and twice restored their city to them,[29] they felt towards
Dion exactly as Dionysius had. For at the time when Dion was
endeavoring to educate Dionysius and form him into a king
worthy of the office, making himself thus a partner in all Dionysius' life, Dionysius was giving ear to the slanderers who
said that Dion was conspiring against the tyrant in all that   c
he was doing. The studies he enjoined were obviously intended, they said, to bewitch the mind of Dionysius so that
he would neglect his kingdom and entrust it to Dion, who
would then make it his own and treacherously banish Dionysius from power. These suspicions against Dion prevailed
then as they did later when circulated among the Syracusans;
but their triumph was an unnatural one and puts to shame
those who were the cause of it. What sort of triumph it was
you ought to hear, you who have asked for my help in the
present crisis. I, an Athenian citizen,[30] a friend of Dion and   d

28 This is a reference to the crushing defeat of the Carthaginians at
Himera in 480. It was seventy years before the Carthaginians again attacked the Greek cities in Sicily.

29 First when on his expedition from the Peloponnesus he took Syracuse from Dionysius, and again when he was recalled from Leontini and
defeated the army of Nypsius that was pillaging the city.

30 Plato emphasizes the fact that he is an Athenian citizen because he
feels that his own loyalty to Dion, as well as the treachery of Callippus,
ought to be remembered by the critics of Athens.

his ally, came to the tyrant in order to bring about friendship, not war, between them; but the slanderers worsted me in this contest. And when Dionysius tried by honors and gifts to persuade me to take his side and affirm that his banishment of Dion had been proper, he failed utterly, as you know. Later

e Dion came home bringing with him two brothers from Athens, friends whom he had acquired not through philosophy, but by way of that facile comradeship which is the basis of most friendship, and which is cultivated by hospitality and mystic rites and initiation into secrets; because of these associations and the service they had rendered Dion in returning to Syracuse, these two men who came with him had become

334 his comrades. But when they arrived in Sicily and saw how Dion was being slandered among the people of Syracuse whom he had liberated, and was being accused of plotting to become a tyrant, not only did they betray their comrade and host, but they became as it were his murderers, since they stood by with arms in their hands to assist his assassins. The shame and impiety of their action I mention only, without dwelling upon it; many others will make it their theme both now and in

b time to come. But I cannot pass over what is said about Athens, that these men brought dishonor on their city. Remember that he also was an Athenian who refused to betray this same Dion when by doing so he could have had money and honors in abundance. He had become Dion's friend not through vulgar fellowship, but through common liberal culture; and this alone should a sensible man trust, rather than kinship of soul or body.[31] Therefore I say that these two who

c murdered Dion were not worthy of bringing their city into discredit, for they were never men of any consequence.

I have said all this for the purpose of advising Dion's friends and relatives; and to all that has been said I add the same advice and the same doctrine that I have given twice be-

[31] Three bases of friendship are implied here: vulgar fellowship (βάναυσος φιλότης), kinship (συγγένεια ψυχῶν καὶ σωμάτων), and fellowship in liberal culture (ἐλευθέρας παιδείας κοινωνία). Cf. Aristotle's discussion of friendship in *Nic. Eth.* VIII and IX.

fore. Do not subject Sicily nor any other state to the despotism of men, but to the rule of laws; this at least is my doctrine. For despotic power benefits neither rulers nor subjects, but is an altogether deadly experience for themselves, their children,   d
and their children's children; and no one grasps at the prizes it offers except petty and illiberal souls who know nothing of the divine and human goods that are now and for all time good and just. This is the doctrine that I endeavored to bring home, first to Dion, next to Dionysius, and now for the third time do so to you. Listen to me then, in the name of Zeus the Savior, to whom this third libation belongs.[32] Consider Dionysius and Dion, of whom one was deaf to my teachings and now lives ignobly,[33] and the other listened to me and died   e
nobly; for it is altogether noble and right to suffer whatever may come while aiming at the highest for oneself or one's city. None of us can avoid death, nor if any man could would he be happy, as people think; for there is nothing worth mentioning that is either good or bad to creatures without souls,   335
but good and evil exist only for a soul, either joined with a body or separated from it.[34] And we must always firmly believe the sacred and ancient words declaring to us that the soul is immortal, and when it has separated from the body will go before its judges and pay the utmost penalties.[35] Therefore

[32] We learn from a fragment of Aeschylus (Fr. 55, Nauck) that it was a custom at banquets to make the third libation to Ζεὺς Σωτήρ. The proverb τὸ τρίτον τῷ σωτῆρι occurs also at 340a, *Charm.* 167a, *Phil.* 66d, *Rep.* IX, 583b. Cf. *Laws* III, 692a.

[33] At the time of this letter Dionysius was in Locri, whither he had fled after being expelled from Syracuse. He abrogated the constitution of the Locrians and conducted himself in such a cruel and licentious manner that when he left, the populace fell upon his wife and children and put them to an ignominious death. Strabo VI, i, 8; Plut. *Praec. Ger. Rei.* xxviii, 821d; Athen. 541d.

[34] The thought seems to be as follows: Nothing that possesses a soul can avoid death; people are wrong therefore in thinking that we should be happy if we did not have to die, for that would mean that we were creatures without souls and hence incapable of experiencing either good or evil.

[35] On these "sacred words" see *Laws* XI, 927a; *Meno* 81a; *Phaedo* 70c.

we must count it a lesser evil to suffer great wrongs and injustices than to do them, though this is a saying that the
b avaricious man, who is poor in the goods of the soul, will not give ear to; or if he does, laughs it into silence, as he thinks, and goes about like a wild beast snatching from every quarter whatever he thinks will furnish him meat or drink or the satisfaction of that slavish and graceless pleasure incorrectly called after Aphrodite.[36] He is blind and does not see what defilement his plunderings involve, nor how great an evil attaches to each wicked act—a defilement which the evildoer necessarily drags with him as he goes up and down the earth and follows his dishonorable and utterly wretched path to
c the world below.[37]

Now Dion had accepted this and other similar teachings of mine, and I may rightly be as indignant at his murderers as at Dionysius. Both parties have done infinite wrong to me and, I may say, to all mankind—the first two in striking down a man whose purpose was to realize justice, the other in refusing to have anything to do with justice, though he pos-
d sessed every resource for making it prevail throughout his domain. If in his empire there had been brought about a real union of philosophy and power, it would have been an illustrious example to both Greeks and barbarians, and all mankind would have been convinced of the truth that no city nor individual can be happy except by living in company with wisdom under the guidance of justice, either from personal achievement of these virtues or from a right training and education received under God-fearing rulers. This is the center
e of my grievance against Dionysius; the other injuries that he has done to me are trivial in comparison. And he who mur-

---

36 Construing this sentence after Wilamowitz (*Platon*, II, 409) as follows: ὅτιπερ ἂν οἴηται πορειεῖν αὑτῷ φαγεῖν ἢ πιεῖν κτλ. On the slander against Aphrodite see *Phil.* 12b.

37 I prefer to follow Burnet's reading of this possibly corrupt passage, despite the plausible emendations of Post (*Am. Jour. Phil.*, LVII [1936], 206) and Bluck (*Class. Rev.*, LX [1946], 7 f.). It seems to me an instance rather of the writer's original negligence than of later corruption.

dered Dion has unknowingly produced the same result. For
of Dion I know, as surely as a man can know anything about
his fellow men, that if he had held the power he would not
have been diverted from using it for the following purposes.
First of all, with regard to Syracuse,[38] his native city, after
having cleansed her of her servitude and put on her the
garment of freedom, he would have made every effort to
adorn her citizens with the best and most suitable laws. Then
he would have turned with ardor to the next task, that of resettling all Sicily and liberating her from the barbarians,
driving out some of them and subjugating others, a thing he
could have done more easily than Hiero.[39] Such deeds accomplished by a man of justice and courage and temperance and
philosophy would have produced in the multitude the same
respect for virtue which, if Dionysius had listened to me,
would have made its saving appearance, one may say, among
all mankind. But now some daemon or avenging deity has
fallen upon us, and through disrespect for law and the gods,
and worst of all, through the audacity of ignorance—that soil
in which all ills are rooted and grow, to produce in the end
a bitter fruit for those who have planted them [40]—such ignorance has a second time overturned all our plans and
brought them to naught.

But on this our third trial let us avoid saying anything of
ill omen. In spite of previous misfortunes, I advise you, the
friends of Dion, to imitate his love for his country and his
sober way of living and to try to carry out, under better aus-
pices, these plans of his; and what they were you have clearly
heard me explain. If there is anyone in your number who is
incapable of living in the Dorian fashion like your fathers

336

b

c

38 Reading with Egermann (*Die Platonischen Briefe VII und VIII*, pp.
44 f.) ἢ ἐπὶ τόδε. Συρακούσας κτλ.

39 The brother of Gelon and his successor as tyrant of Syracuse (478-
466). He saved Locri from destruction by Rhegium, defeated the Etruscans
in their attack on Cumae, and refounded Catana under the new name
of Aetna.

40 It was ἀμαθία, according to *Laws* III, 688c ff., that brought about
the downfall of the early kingdoms of Argos and Messene.

d   and follows the "Sicilian life" of the slayers of Dion,[41] do not
     ask his help nor imagine that he will act loyally or depend-
     ably. But summon others to help you in resettling all Sicily
     and equalizing her laws. Summon them not only from Sicily
     herself, but from the whole of the Peloponnesus; and do not
     fear even Athens, for Athens also has citizens pre-eminent in
     virtue who abhor the shameless audacity of those who slay
     their hosts. But if these projects I have mentioned must be
     deferred, because you are now hard pressed by the many and
e   diverse factions daily sprouting in your midst, then anyone to
     whom the gods have given a modicum of right opinion must
     know that there can be no end to the evils of faction until
     the party that has gained the victory in these battles and in
     the exiling and slaughtering of fellow citizens forgets its
337 wrongs and ceases trying to wreak vengeance upon its enemies.
     If it controls itself and enacts laws for the common good, con-
     sidering its own interests no more than those of the van-
     quished, the defeated party will be doubly constrained, by
     respect and by fear, to follow the laws—by fear because the
     other party has demonstrated its superior force, and by re-
     spect because it has shown that it is able and willing to con-
     quer its desires and serve the law instead. In no other way
b   can a city that is rent by factions bring its disorders to an end,
     but it will continue to be divided within itself by strife and
     enmity, hatred and distrust.
         Whenever, then, the victors desire to save their city, they
     must enter into counsel with themselves and first of all select
     the most eminent Greeks they can discover—old men, with
     wives and children at home, descended from a long line of
     illustrious ancestors and each of them possessing a fair amount
c   of property (fifty such men will be enough for a city of ten
     thousand)—and these they must induce, by personal entreaties
     and by all the honors at their disposal, to leave home and
     come to their aid; and when they have come they must direct
     them to make laws, binding them upon oath to award no
     more to the victors than to the vanquished, but to consider

41 Syracuse was founded by Dorians from Corinth.

only the equal and common good of the whole city. And then
when the laws have been laid down everything depends upon
this. If the victors show themselves more eager than the vanquished to obey the laws, then everything will be safe, happi-   d
ness will abound, and all these evils will take their flight.
But let no one who refuses to abide by these principles call
upon me or anyone else for support. These proposals are akin
to those that Dion and I tried to accomplish for the benefit of
Syracuse, but second best. The best were those that we earlier
tried to effect with the aid of Dionysius himself [goods to be
common to all].[42] But fortune is mightier than men and shat-
tered our plans. Now it is for you to try to bring them about   e
with better luck, and may divine favor attend your efforts.

This, then, is my advice and admonition, and the account
of my first visit to Dionysius. As to my later journey across
the water, whoever is interested can learn from what follows
that it was a reasonable and proper venture. The early part
of my first stay in Syracuse passed as I have described it above   338
before giving my advice to the relatives and friends of Dion.
After the events described, I made every effort to persuade
Dionysius to let me depart, and we came to an agreement that
when peace was restored (war was then going on in Sicily)
and when Dionysius had made his empire more secure, he
would recall both Dion and me. He also asked Dion to consider himself not as having been exiled, but only banished.[43]   b
On these conditions I promised that I would return. After
peace was restored he sent for me, but Dion he asked to wait
another year; me, however, he urged most strongly to come.
Dion consented, and even entreated me to set sail; in fact
there were many reports coming from Sicily that Dionysius
had now once more conceived a great desire for philosophy,
and this was why Dion persistently urged me not to disobey
the summons. But as for me, though I knew that philosophy
often affects young men in this way, yet it seemed to me safer,   c

---

[42] For the interpretation of this passage, see pp. 160 ff.

[43] Μετάστασις, as distinct from φυγή, both technical terms in Greek
law, did not involve the confiscation of the condemned person's property.

for the present at least, to say farewell to my plans and let Dion and Dionysius alone; and I offended both of them by replying that I was an old man, and that what they were doing now did not at all accord with the agreement we had made. Now it seems that after this, Archytas visited Dionysius (for before my departure I had established relations of friendship and hospitality between Archytas and his Tarentine

d friends and Dionysius), and that there were certain other persons who had learned something from Dion, and others who had learned from them; and being full of these half-understood doctrines, they were apparently trying to converse with Dionysius about them as if he had mastered all my thought. Now he is not without natural capacity for learning, and besides is extraordinarily vain; and no doubt he was pleased to have these questions addressed to him, and ashamed to have

e it discovered that he had learned nothing during my stay. For these reasons he came to desire a clearer understanding, and at the same time his ambition spurred him on. (Why he did not learn from me during my first visit, I have described above.) When, therefore, I had got safely home and had, as I have just said, disregarded his summons to return, Dionysius' chief ambition, I think, was to prevent anyone from supposing that I had refused to come to his court because I had a con-

339 tempt for his nature and character and was displeased with his way of living. I must tell the truth, and put up with it if anyone, after hearing what happened, despises my philosophy and esteems the tyrant's intelligence.[44] Dionysius summoned me a third time, sending a trireme to ease the journey for me, and with it certain Sicilian acquaintances of mine, among them Archedemus, one of the associates of Archytas and a man

b whom, as he knew, I valued the most highly of all men in Sicily. These all brought me the same story of the marvellous progress Dionysius was making in philosophy. He knew of my feelings towards Dion and of Dion's desire to have me embark and go to Syracuse; so he wrote me a very lengthy

[44] Another indication of the sort of criticism that had been directed at Plato.

letter, evidently composed with these facts in view. The beginning of it was about as follows: "Dionysius to Plato," then the customary salutations, and immediately afterwards, "If you come at once to Syracuse as we have requested, first of all the issues that concern Dion will be settled in whatever way you desire (for I know you will desire only what is fair and I agree to this); but if not, none of these questions, whether touching Dion's person or any other matter, will be settled to your liking." Such were his words; to give the rest of the letter would take too much space and would not be pertinent here. Other letters kept coming to me from Archytas and the Tarentines praising Dionysius' philosophy and saying that if I did not come now the friendship I had brought about between them and Dionysius, a friendship which was of no little importance to their state, would be broken off. Now when the summons had taken on this character, with my friends in Sicily and Italy pulling me and those at Athens almost pushing me away with their urging, the same consideration occurred to me as before, that I ought not to betray my friends and followers in Tarentum. Besides, I thought, it is not an unusual thing that a young man of native intelligence who has overheard some talk of lofty matters should be seized by a love for an ideal of life. I ought then to test the situation clearly to see on which side the truth lay, and by no means to give up in advance and expose myself to the blame that would rightly fall upon me if these reports should really be true. I set off, therefore, under cover of this reasoning, though with many fears and forebodings of evil, as can well be understood. "The third time to the Savior," runs the proverb; [45] and my third journey at least confirmed its truth, for by good luck I again came off safely; and next to God I thank Dionysius for it, because there were many determined to destroy me, but he prevented them and showed a certain respect for me and my position.

When I arrived, I thought my first task was to prove whether Dionysius was really on fire with philosophy, or

[c]

[d]

[e]

[340]

[b]

45 See n. 32 above.

whether the many reports that came to Athens were without
foundation. Now there is a certain way of putting this to the
test, a dignified way and quite appropriate to tyrants, especially to those whose heads are full of half-understood doctrines, which I saw at once upon my arrival was particularly
the case with Dionysius. You must picture to such men the
extent of the undertaking, describing what sort of inquiry

c it is, with how many difficulties it is beset, and how much
labor it involves. For anyone who hears this, who is a true
lover of wisdom, with the divine quality that makes him akin
to it and worthy of pursuing it, thinks that he has heard of a
marvellous quest that he must at once enter upon with all
earnestness, or life is not worth living; and from that time
forth he pushes himself and urges on his leader without ceas-
ing, until he has reached the end of the journey or has become capable of doing without a guide and finding the way

d himself.[46] This is the state of mind in which such a man lives;
whatever his occupation may be, above everything and always
he holds fast to philosophy and to the daily discipline that
best makes him apt at learning and remembering, and capable of reasoning soberly with himself; while for the opposite
way of living he has a persistent hatred. Those who are
really not philosophers but have only a coating of opinions,
like men whose bodies are tanned by the sun, when they see
how much learning is required, and how great the labor, and

e how orderly their daily lives must be to suit the subject they
are pursuing, conclude that the task is too difficult for their
powers; and rightly so, for they are not equipped for this

341 pursuit. But some of them persuade themselves that they have
already heard enough and need make no further effort. Now
this is a clear and infallible test to apply to those who love
ease and are incapable of strenuous labor, for none of them
can ever blame his teacher, but only himself, if he is unable
to put forth the efforts that the task demands.

It was in this fashion that I then spoke to Dionysius. I did

[46] Compare this description of the genuine philosopher with that in
Rep. VI, 490ab.

not explain everything to him, nor did he ask me to, for he claimed to have already a sufficient knowledge of many of   b the most important points because of what he had heard others say about them. Later, I hear, he wrote a book on the matters we talked about, putting it forward as his own teaching, not what he had learned from me. Whether this is true I do not know. I know that certain others also have written on these same matters; but who they are they themselves do not know.[47] So much at least I can affirm with confidence about any who have written or propose to write on these   c questions, pretending to a knowledge of the problems with which I am concerned, whether they claim to have learned from me or from others or to have made their discoveries for themselves: it is impossible, in my opinion, that they can have learned anything at all about the subject. There is no writing of mine about these matters, nor will there ever be one. For this knowledge is not something that can be put into words like other sciences; but after long-continued intercourse between teacher and pupil, in joint pursuit of the subject, suddenly, like light flashing forth when a fire is kindled, it is born in the soul and straightway nourishes it-   d self. And this too I know: if these matters are to be expounded at all in books or lectures, they would best come from me. Certainly I am harmed not least of all if they are misrepresented. If I thought they could be put into written words adequate for the multitude, what nobler work could I do in my life than to compose something of such great bene-

[47] This cryptic sentence has baffled interpreters. If the ellipsis in the Greek text is to be filled as suggested in my translation, there is obviously a reference to the Delphic maxim, "Know thyself," and therefore an implied criticism of the "certain others" who have so far forgotten themselves as to try to put into writing doctrines heard orally from Plato (cf. 344d). Simplicius in his commentary on Aristotle's *Physics* (151, 6 and 453, 25) reports that Plato's lectures on the Good were written down by Aristotle, Speusippus, Xenocrates, Heraclides, Hestiaeus and others of Plato's auditors, and it may be that Plato's criticism is directed at some of these fellow members of the Academy. For a survey and discussion of the various interpretations of this sentence, see Novotný *ad loc.*

fit to mankind and bring to light the nature of things for all
e   to see? But I do not think that the "examination," as it is
called,[48] of these questions would be of any benefit to men,
except to a few, i.e. to those who could with a little guidance
discover the truth by themselves. Of the rest, some would be
filled with an ill-founded and quite unbecoming disdain, and
some with an exaggerated and foolish elation, as if they had
learned something grand.

342   Let me go into these matters at somewhat greater length,
for perhaps what I am saying will become clearer when I
have done so. There is a true doctrine that confutes anyone
who has presumed to write anything whatever on such subjects, a doctrine that I have often before expounded, but it
seems that it must now be said again. For every real being,
there are three things that are necessary if knowledge of it is
to be acquired: first, the name; second, the definition; third,
b   the image; knowledge comes fourth, and in the fifth place we
must put the object itself, the knowable and truly real being.
To understand what this means, take a particular example,
and think of all other objects as analogous to it. There is
something called a circle, and its name is this very word we
have just used. Second, there is its definition, composed of
nouns and verbs. "The figure whose extremities are everywhere equally distant from its center" is the definition of
precisely that to which the names "round," "circumference,"
c   and "circle" apply. Third is what we draw or rub out, what
is turned or destroyed; but the circle itself to which they all
refer remains unaffected, because it is different from them.
In the fourth place are knowledge ($\epsilon\pi\iota\sigma\tau\eta\mu\eta$), reason ($\nu o\hat{v}s$),
and right opinion (which are in our minds, not in words or

---

48 Taking $\lambda\epsilon\gamma o\mu\acute{\epsilon}\nu\eta\nu$ as modifying $\acute{\epsilon}\pi\iota\chi\epsilon\acute{\iota}\rho\eta\sigma\iota\nu$. This noun here seems
to have some special meaning such as it has in Aristotle's *Topics* (111b16,
139b10), i.e. dialectical examination. But the present context and the
sequel show that what the writer is disparaging is not the dialectical
examination of a question by teacher and pupil (this is indeed essential),
but a public exposition of the results of such an examination, i.e. an
$\acute{\epsilon}\pi\iota\chi\epsilon\acute{\iota}\rho\eta\mu a$ (cf. *Topics* 162a16). Doubtless the two terms were often used
interchangeably.

bodily shapes, and therefore must be taken together as something distinct both from the circle itself and from the three
things previously mentioned); of these, reason is nearest the   d
fifth in kinship and likeness, while the others are further
away. The same thing is true of straight-lined as well as of
circular figures; of color; of the good, the beautiful, the just;
of body in general, whether artificial or natural; of fire, water,
and all the elements; of all living beings and qualities of
souls; of all actions and affections.[49] For in each case, whoever does not somehow grasp the four things mentioned will   e
never fully attain knowledge of the fifth.

These things, moreover, because of the weakness of language, are just as much concerned with making clear the particular property (τὸ ποιόν τι) of each object as the being (τὸ ὄν)
of it. On this account no sensible man will venture to express   343
his deepest thoughts in words, especially in a form which is
unchangeable, as is true of written outlines. Let us go back
and study again the illustration just given. Every circle that we
make or draw in common life is full of characteristics that
contradict the "fifth," for it everywhere touches a straight
line, while the circle itself, we say, has in it not the slightest
element belonging to a contrary nature. And we say that
their names are by no means fixed; there is no reason why   b
what we call "circles" might not be called "straight lines,"
and the straight lines "circles," and their natures will be none
the less fixed despite this exchange of names. Indeed the same
thing is true of the definition: since it is a combination of
nouns and verbs, there is nothing surely fixed about it. Much
more might be said to show that each of these four instruments is unclear, but the most important point is what I
said earlier: that of the two objects of search—the particular
quality (τὸ ποῖον τι) and the being (τὸ ὄν) of an object—the soul   c
seeks to know not the quality but the essence (τὸ τί), whereas
each of these four instruments presents to the soul, in discourse and in examples, what she is not seeking, and thus

49 For the relevance of this passage to the understanding of Plato's
later theory of Ideas, see p. 76.

makes it easy to refute by sense perception anything that may
be said or pointed out, and fills everyone, so to speak, with
perplexity and confusion. Now in those matters in which, because of our defective training, we are not accustomed to look
for truth but are satisfied with the first image suggested to us,
we can ask and answer without making ourselves ridiculous

d   to one another, being proficient in manipulating and testing these four instruments.[50] But when it is "the fifth" about
which we are compelled to answer questions or to make explanations, then anyone who wishes to refute has the advantage, and can make the propounder of a doctrine, whether
in writing or speaking or in answering questions, seem to
most of his listeners completely ignorant of the matter on
which he is trying to speak or write. Those who are listening
sometimes do not realize that it is not the mind of the speaker
or writer which is being refuted, but these four instruments
mentioned, each of which is by nature defective.

e   By the repeated use of all these instruments, ascending and
descending to each in turn, it is barely possible for knowledge to be engendered of an object naturally good, in a man
naturally good; but if his nature is defective, as is that of
most men, for the acquisition of knowledge and the so-called

344 virtues, and if the qualities he has have been corrupted, then
not even Lynceus could make such a man see.[51] In short,
neither quickness of learning nor a good memory can make a
man see when his nature is not akin to the object, for this
knowledge never takes root in an alien nature; so that no
man who is not naturally inclined and akin to justice and
all other forms of excellence, even though he may be quick at
learning and remembering this and that and other things, nor
any man who, though akin to justice, is slow at learning and

[50] Since the roles of questioner and respondent are interchangeable in
the dialectical exercises to which Plato is referring, it seems unnecessary in
translating this passage to adhere strictly to the agreement of δυναμένων
with ἐρωτώντων.

[51] Lynceus, one of the Argonauts, was proverbial for his keenness of
vision. Cf. Aristoph. *Plutus* 210; Lucian *Timon* 25.

forgetful, will ever attain the truth that is attainable about
virtue.[52] Nor about vice, either, for these must be learned b
together, just as the truth and error about any part of being
must be learned together, through long and earnest labor, as
I said at the beginning. Only when all of these things—names,
definitions, and visual and other perceptions—have been
rubbed against one another and tested, pupil and teacher asking and answering questions in good will and without envy
—only then, when reason and knowledge are at the very extremity of human effort, can they illuminate the nature of
any object.[53]

For this reason anyone who is seriously studying high mat- c
ters will be the last to write about them and thus expose his
thought to the envy and criticism of men. What I have said
comes, in short, to this: whenever we see a book, whether the
laws of a legislator or a composition on any other subject, we
can be sure that if the author is really serious, this book does
not contain his best thoughts; they are stored away with the
fairest of his possessions. And if he has committed these serious thoughts to writing, it is because men, not the gods, d
"have taken his wits away." [54]

To anyone who has followed this discourse and digression
it will be clear that if Dionysius or anyone else—whether more
or less able than he—has written concerning the first and
highest principles of nature, he has not properly heard or
understood anything of what he has written about; otherwise
he would have respected these principles as I do, and would
not have dared to give them this discordant and unseemly
publicity. Nor can he have written them down for the sake of
remembrance; for there is no danger of their being forgotten e
if the soul has once grasped them, since they are contained

[52] That there must be a kinship between the mind of the inquirer and
the ultimate objects of philosophic study is asserted repeatedly in the
Republic, e.g. 486d, 487a, 494d, 501d.

[53] Reading with Egermann συντεινόντων instead of the unintelligible
συντείνων (b7) of Burnet's text.

[54] Homer *Iliad* VII, 360.

in the briefest of formulas. If he wrote them, it was from un-worthy ambition, either to have them regarded as his own ideas, or to show that he had participated in an education of which he was unworthy if he loved only the reputation that would come from having shared in it. Now if Dionysius did indeed come to understand these matters from our single conversation, how that happened, "God wot," [55] as the Thebans say. For as I said, I went through the matter with him once only, never afterwards. Whoever cares to understand the course of subsequent events should consider why it was that we did not go over the matter a second or a third time, or even oftener. Was it that Dionysius, after this one hearing, thought he understood well enough and really did understand, either because he had already found these principles himself or had previously learned them from others? Or did he think that what I said was of no value? Or, a third possibility, did he realize that this teaching was beyond him, and that truly he would not be able to live in constant pursuit of virtue and wisdom? If he thought my teachings of no value he contradicts many witnesses who say the opposite and who are probably much more capable judges of such matters than Dionysius. And if he had already discovered or learned these doctrines and regarded them as fitted for educating a liberal mind, how—unless he is a very strange creature indeed—could he have so lightly brought ignominy upon their teacher and guardian? But this is what he did, as I shall now tell you.

Shortly after the above occurrence, although Dionysius had previously allowed Dion to retain possession of his property and to enjoy its revenues, he gave orders to Dion's stewards not to send anything more to the Peloponnesus, as if he had completely forgotten his letter, saying that this property belonged not to Dion but to Dion's son, who was his nephew and under his legal guardianship. Matters then had come to this, in so short a time. From this action I saw precisely the character of Dionysius' desire for philosophy, and in spite of

[55] Cf. *Phaedo*, 62a.

myself I was indignant, and with good reason. It was summer
at the time, and ships were leaving the port. Though it was
clear to me that I ought not to be more angry with Dionysius
than with myself and the others who had compelled me to
come a third time to this strait of Scylla, "To measure again   e
the length of deadly Charybdis," [56] yet I thought I ought to
tell Dionysius that it was impossible for me to remain after
this scurvy treatment of Dion. He tried to placate me and
begged me to remain, thinking it would not go well with him
if I should set out immediately as the personal bearer of this
news; but when he could not persuade me, he said that he
would himself make the preparations for my departure. For   346
in my anger I thought of going on board one of the vessels
ready to set sail and suffering the consequences, whatever they
might be, of being detained, since it was clearly evident that
I had done no wrong but was the victim of wrongdoing. Seeing that nothing could induce me to remain, he devised a
scheme for keeping me until the ships could no longer leave
port. The following day he came to me with this persuasive
speech: "Let us dispose of this matter of Dion and Dion's
property which has been the cause of frequent disagreement   b
between you and me. For your sake I will do this for Dion.
Let him have his property and live in the Peloponnesus, not
as an exile, but as one permitted to return here as soon as he
and I and you his friends have come to an understanding—
all this upon condition that he is not to conspire against me;
you and your relatives and the relatives of Dion here shall be
sureties to me, and he shall give you pledges of good faith.
Let the property he takes be deposited in the Peloponnesus
and at Athens in the keeping of any persons you please, and   c
let Dion enjoy the revenues from it, but be without power to
dispose of the principal without your consent. For it will be a
large sum and I have little faith that if he had this wealth at
his disposal he would act justly towards me; but in you and
your friends I have more confidence. See now whether these

[56] Homer *Odyssey* XII, 428.

proposals please you, and if they do, stay for the year on these
d terms and when spring comes depart with this property. Dion,
I know, will be very grateful to you if you do this for him."

I was angered when I heard this proposal, nevertheless I
said I would consider the matter and bring him my opinion
on it the following day. This then was agreed upon. Later,
when I had got to my own quarters and was thinking the
matter over, I found myself in great perplexity; but this was
e the dominant thought in my deliberations: "Beware! Dionysius may not intend to keep a single one of his promises; but
what if he should write to Dion after I have gone, telling him
what he has just said to me? And should persuade a number
of Dion's friends to write also, intimating plausibly that it
was not his refusal but mine that prevented his doing what
he promised, and making me out altogether indifferent to
Dion's interests? Besides this, if he does not want to see me go
and, without issuing definite orders to any ship's captain,
347 should let it be generally known, as he easily could, that he
was unwilling for me to sail, would any captain take me as a
passenger, even if I could get out of the palace of Dionysius?"
For besides the other disadvantages of my situation, I was living in the garden surrounding the palace, and the gatekeeper
would not have let me out without an express command from
Dionysius. "But if I remain for the year, I can write to Dion
what my situation is and what I am doing; and then if
Dionysius keeps any part of his promises, what I have done
b will not seem altogether ridiculous," for the property of Dion,
if estimated rightly, was probably worth not less than a
hundred talents. "On the other hand, if the contrary comes to
pass,[57] as is most likely, I don't see what course I can then
take. Nevertheless, it seems that I must probably hold out one
more year and put these schemes of Dionysius to the test of
events."

Having come to this decision, I told Dionysius the next day
c that I had decided to remain. "But," I said, "you must not
think that I can bind Dion. Let us send him a joint letter ex-

[57] Reading with Post ἀπεμφαίνοντα instead of ὑποφαίνοντα in b3.

plaining the agreement we have just made and ask whether its terms satisfy him, telling him that if he is not satisfied and wishes to modify them in any way to write us at once; and in the meantime I ask that you take no new steps affecting him." These were my words and these were the terms we agreed upon, almost exactly as I have stated them. Now the boats had set sail and it was no longer possible for me to leave, when Dionysius mentioned to me that half the property d should be Dion's and half his son's. He said he was going to sell it and give me half the proceeds to take to Dion; the other half he would keep here for the son, for this was clearly the most equitable procedure. I was stunned by this statement, but thought it foolish to make any further protest; yet I did say that we should await the letter from Dion and advise him of these new conditions. Immediately thereafter he sold the whole of Dion's property in the most audacious manner, sell- e ing it on whatever terms and to whomever he pleased, and said not a word to me about it. And likewise I refrained from saying anything more to him about Dion's affairs, for I thought any further effort would be useless.

This then was the result of my efforts in aid of philosophy and my friends. From this time on Dionysius and I lived, I like a bird looking out of its cage and longing to fly away, he 348 scheming how to frighten me [58] without turning over any of Dion's property; yet before all Sicily we professed to be friends.

Now Dionysius, contrary to the practice of his father, tried to reduce the pay of his older mercenaries. The soldiers, infuriated, gathered in a mob and declared they would not permit it. He tried to hold out against them by closing the b gates of the citadel, but they straightway moved against the walls, chanting a barbarian war cry; and this so frightened Dionysius that he yielded and granted even more than they

[58] The writer of *Epistle III*, whether Plato or someone else, appears to have given the only possible interpretation of ἀνασοβήσοι μὲ μηδὲν ἀποδοὺς τῶν Δίωνος, i.e. "to frighten me into ignoring what was going on so that I would not even ask for the dispatch of Dion's money" (318b).

demanded to the peltasts assembled there. Now a rumor
quickly got about that Heraclides [59] had been the cause of all
this disturbance. Upon hearing it, Heraclides took flight and
concealed himself; and Dionysius, being at a loss how to
c apprehend him, summoned Theodotes [60] to the palace garden, where I happened to be walking at the time. I do not
know what else they talked about, for I could not hear them;
but I know and recall what Theodotes said to Dionysius in
my presence. "Plato," he said, "I am trying to persuade
Dionysius here that if I can bring Heraclides before us to
answer the charges that have just been made against him, and
if in consequence it seems necessary for him to leave Sicily,
to let [61] him take his wife and child and sail to the Pelopon-
d nesus and live there, enjoying the revenue from his property
so long as he does no harm to Dionysius. I have already summoned him and will do so now again, and one or the other of
these messages should bring him. And I ask and beseech
Dionysius, if he should happen upon Heraclides anywhere,
either here or in the country, to do nothing more than banish
e him from the land during his present displeasure.[62] Do you
consent to this?" he asked, turning to Dionysius. "I consent,"
he said; "even if he should be found in your own house he
will suffer nothing beyond what you have said." The evening
of the following day Eurybius and Theodotes came to me in
haste, greatly troubled. Theodotes spoke for them. "Plato,"
he said, "you were a witness yesterday to the promise
Dionysius made to you and me about Heraclides?" "Indeed I
was," I replied. "But now," he continued, "there are peltasts
running all about trying to take Heraclides, and it is likely
that he is somewhere near here. You must with all speed go
349 with us to Dionysius," he said. So we set out, and when we
came into his presence the two men stood weeping silently,

[59] On Heraclides see pp. 175 ff.

[60] Theodotes is mentioned also in *Epistles III* and *IV*, 318c, 320e, 321b.

[61] Reading, with Post, ἀξιοῦν in c9 instead of ἀξιῶ.

[62] What they asked was μετάστασις for Heraclides, instead of death or
ἀειφυγία. See n. 43 above.

and I said: "They are afraid that you have changed your
mind regarding Heraclides and are acting contrary to what
was agreed upon yesterday. For it appears that he has taken
refuge nearby." At this he became angry and turned various
colors, as is the way with an angry man. Falling before him,
Theodotes seized his hand and implored him, with tears in   b
his eyes, not to do such a thing. "Cheer up, Theodotes," I
interrupted, trying to encourage him; "Dionysius will not pre-
sume to do anything contrary to the promise he made yesterday." And Dionysius looked at me and, like a true tyrant,
"To you," he said, "I made no promise whatever." "By the
gods," I replied, "you at least made a promise, not to do what
Theodotes is now imploring you not to do." With these words
I turned and went out. After this Dionysius continued to hunt
for Heraclides, while Theodotes sent messengers warning him   c
to flee; and though Tisias and a band of peltasts were sent in
pursuit, Heraclides, it was reported, having a few hours the
start of them, got safely into Carthaginian territory.

After this, Dionysius conceived that my resistance to his
long-standing plot not to restore Dion's money could now be
plausibly made the ground for enmity toward me. His first
step was to send me out of the citadel on the pretext that the
women were to hold a ten-day sacrifice in the garden where I   d
dwelt, and directed me to live outside during this period at
the home of Archedemus. While I was there Theodotes sent
for me and poured out his complaints and his anger against
Dionysius for what he had done. When Dionysius heard that
I had visited Theodotes he used this as another pretext,
similar to the earlier one, for quarreling with me. He sent to   e
inquire whether I had in fact visited Theodotes at his invitation. "Certainly," I replied. "Then he bade me say," said the
messenger, "that you are not doing right in always preferring
Dion and Dion's friends to himself." After this message he
never again summoned me back to the palace, it being now
clear that I was the friend of Heraclides and Theodotes, and
consequently his enemy, and he knew also that I was not
pleased at the complete dissipation of Dion's goods. From that

350 time on, then, I lived outside the acropolis among the mercenaries. Some of the rowers in the fleet were from Athens
and fellow citizens of mine; they and others came to me with
the report that I had an evil name among the peltasts and
that some of them were threatening to kill me if they ever got
hold of me.[63] I began then to plan the following means of
escape. I sent letters to Archytas and my other friends in
Tarentum telling them of my plight, and they found some
pretext for an embassy from their city, dispatching Lamiscus,
b one of their number, with a thirty-oared vessel. When he
arrived he besought Dionysius on my behalf, saying that I
wished to depart and begging him not to prevent it. Dionysius
complied and released me, giving me travel money; but for
Dion's property I made no further demand, nor did anyone
deliver it to me.

Upon my return to the Peloponnesus I encountered Dion
among the spectators at Olympia and recounted to him what
had occurred. Calling upon Zeus to witness, he straightway
summoned me and my relatives and friends to prepare for
c vengeance against Dionysius, demanding satisfaction to me
for breach of hospitality (these were his words and this is
what he thought), and to himself for his unjust dismissal and
exile. When I heard this I told him to call upon my friends,
if they wished to help him. "But as for me," I said, "you and
the others compelled me, in a way, to become a guest at the
table and hearth of Dionysius and a participant in his sacrifices; and he perhaps believed, from the many reports circulated against me, that I was plotting with you against him
and the tyranny—yet he did not put me to death, but respected
d my person. Nor am I any longer at the age for helping anyone carry on war,[64] though I am with you if ever you desire

---

[63] Clearly the mercenaries would have no love for Plato, whose program, if realized at Syracuse, would have meant their dismissal. Possibly
there were reports connecting Plato with Dionysius' attempt to reduce
their pay. This seems to be implied in διαβεβλημένος.

[64] Plato was sixty-seven years old at this time. His refusal to take part
in Dion's expedition does not mean that he remained neutral in the

one another's friendship and wish to accomplish something good. But as long as you are intent on harm, look elsewhere for your allies." I said this in disgust at my Sicilian "adventure" [65] and its lack of success. But they did not listen to me; and in failing to heed my attempts at reconciliation they are themselves responsible for all the misfortunes that have come upon them. None of them would ever have occurred, humanly speaking, if Dionysius had restored his property to   e
Dion or become fully reconciled with him, for I would have been willing and easily able to restrain Dion; but as it is they have attacked one another and brought about universal disaster.

Dion's purpose, however, with respect to his native city and   351
to the power he sought for himself and his friends, was exactly what I should say any moderate man, myself or anyone else, ought to have; such a man would think of enjoying great power and honor only because he is conferring great benefits. I do not mean such benefits as are conferred by an impecunious agitator, lacking in self-control, the weak victim of his passions, who enriches himself and his partisans and his city by organizing plots and conspiracies, and puts to death the men of wealth on the pretext that they are enemies, and dis-   b
tributes their property, and charges his fellow conspirators and followers not to blame him if they are poor; nor do I mean the honors enjoyed by a man who "benefits" his city in this way, by dividing the goods of the few among the many by public decree, or who, as head of a great city ruling over many lesser ones, unjustly assigns the wealth of the smaller ones to his own city. Neither Dion nor anyone else in his right mind   c
would seek power for these ends, power that would be a plague to himself and his family for all time; but rather would seek it for the purpose of creating, without murder or bloodshed,

---

struggle; he would inevitably be, and be thought of, as Dion's ally. Cf. *Ep. IV;* Cicero *De Oratore* III, 34; Aelian, *V. H.* III, 17.

[65] πλάνη, literally "wandering." This is quite probably intended, as Bury and Souilhé suggest, to recall the adventures of Odysseus. The same parallel is implied in the quotation from the *Odyssey* in 345e.

the best and most just constitution and system of laws. This is what Dion was aiming at, preferring to be the victim of wickedness rather than the agent of it, though he endeavored to protect himself. In spite of all this he fell, just as he had come to the summit of triumph over his enemies. There is
d nothing surprising in what he experienced. For although a good man who is also prudent and sagacious cannot be altogether deceived about the character of wicked men, it would not be surprising if he should suffer the misfortune of the skilled captain who, though not unaware of the approach of a storm, may not foresee its extraordinary and unexpected violence, and be swamped by its force. This is the mistake that Dion made. Those who caused him to fall were men whom he well knew to be villains, but he did not suspect the depths of
e their ignorance and villainy and greed. By this error he is fallen, and Sicily is overwhelmed with grief.
352 The advice I have to offer you in the present state of affairs has mostly been given, and let that suffice. Why I undertook the second voyage to Sicily I thought I ought to explain, because of the strange and improbable nature of these events. If then they appear more plausible as I have described them, and if it has been made evident that there were sufficient motives for what happened, this account will have properly accomplished its purpose.

VIII

b PLATO TO THE RELATIVES AND FRIENDS OF DION, WELFARE.

What principles you must follow if you are really to fare well I will do my best to explain to you. And I hope that my advice will be of advantage not only to you (though to
c you, of course, first of all), but secondly to everyone in Syracuse, and thirdly even to your enemies and adversaries—ex-

cept anyone of them who has done an unholy deed; [1] for such
acts are irremediable and a man can never wash away their
stain. Give your thought, then, to what I say.

Since the fall of the tyranny you have had nothing but
dissension throughout all Sicily, one party desiring to get its
power back, the other to make final the suppression of the
tyranny. In such circumstances the multitude always think   d
the right counsel is to recommend those measures that will
do their enemies the most harm and their friends the most
good. But it is by no means easy to do great harm to others
without bringing many other evils upon oneself. We have a
clear example of this close at hand. Only look at what has
happened right here in Sicily, with one party attempting to
act upon that principle and the other defending itself against
their actions; the story of these events, if you should tell it to   e
others, would give them many useful lessons, though of such
instruction there is hardly any need. On the other hand, a
policy that would benefit all concerned, friends and foes
alike, or do as little harm as possible to both—this is not easy
to see, nor to carry out when it is seen; and to counsel such a
policy, or attempt to explain it, seems like making a prayer.
By all means, then let it be a prayer—for the gods should be   353
first in every man's words and thoughts—and may it be fulfilled when it declares unto us some such word as follows.

Now you and your enemies have been ruled almost con-
tinuously from the beginning of the war by a single family,[2]
a family that your ancestors put in power at a time when they
were in the direst peril and there was imminent danger that

[1] Clearly a reference to Callippus and his associates; in *Epistle VII*,
334a, the murder of Dion is called ἀνόσιον.

[2] The "single family" was the united families of Dionysius and Dion:
Dionysius married Dion's sister Aristomache, and Dion married Arete,
the daughter of Dionysius and Aristomache. See the Genealogical Table,
p. 188. Furthermore, the two other sisters of Dion were married to
Dionysius' brothers, Leptines and Thearides. Except for the short reign
of Callippus, this "family" had been continually in power since the
beginning of the war with Carthage in 404.

all of Hellenic Sicily would be overrun by the Carthaginians
and become barbarian territory. For then it was that to save
Sicily they chose Dionysius, a young and brilliant warrior, to
b   take charge of the military actions for which he had an aptitude, and Hipparinus as his elder and counselor, making
them, as they say, "generals with full powers." [3] Was it God
and divine chance that saved the city? Or the valor of these
leaders? Or both luck and leadership together with the efforts
of the citizens? Think what you will; in any case, the city was
c   saved for that generation. It is right that everyone should feel
gratitude to these saviors for the qualities they displayed; and
if in later times the tyrants misused in any way the gift the
city had bestowed upon them, for these misdeeds they have in
part paid the penalty and should make even further atone-
ment. But what penalties would it necessarily be right to impose in the present state of their affairs? If you were able to
get rid of them easily, and without great toil and danger, or
if they could easily regain their power, there would be no
occasion for offering the advice that I am going to give. As it
d   is, however, both of your factions ought to reflect and call to
mind how often each party has been in high hopes, and has
thought almost always that it lacked only a little of being able
to do what it liked, and that this little has repeatedly turned
out to be the cause of great and innumerable disasters. The
limit is never reached; but what seems to be the end of an old
difficulty always involves the beginning of a new one, and in
this endless round there is danger that both the tyrannical
e   party and the democratic party will be completely destroyed;
and eventually, if things take their natural course (which God
forbid!), the whole of Sicily will have practically lost the
Greek language and will have come under the empire and
dominion of the Phoenicians or the Opici.[4]

3 Reading, with Souilhé, στρατηγούς in b3, instead of τυράννους,
obviously a scribal error.

4 The Opici, or Oscans, were tribes of central Italy and one of the chief
sources of Dionysius' mercenaries. Some of them had been settled in
Sicily by Dionysius. See pp. 146, 152.

This is a prospect which should incite every Hellene to search for a remedy with all his might. If anyone has an apter or a better plan than the one I am going to offer, let him bring it forth and he will rightly be called a loyal Hellene. 354 What now appears best to me I will try to explain in all frankness and set it forth with just and impartial reasoning. I am speaking in the fashion of an arbitrator between two parties at law, the one a former tyrant, the other his former subject, and proffering to each of them my well-known counsel. Now, as always, I advise the tyrant to shun his name and the reality it stands for, and to change his government to a kingship if he can. That he can is shown by the action of that b wise and good man, Lycurgus, who, seeing that his own relatives in Argos and Messene were becoming tyrants instead of kings and in both cases destroying both themselves and their cities, was filled with apprehension both for his house and his native city, and instituted as a remedy the office of the Elders and that of the Ephors as the saving bond of the kingly power.[5] By such means this kingship has been signally secure through all these generations, since law became the lord and c king of men, not men tyrants over the laws.

Now this is the point of my present recommendation to you all: let those who are aiming at tyrannical power shun and flee from what senseless and insatiate men call happiness; let them try to change into the form of kings and subject themselves to kingly laws, thus acquiring the highest honors from their willing subjects and from the laws. Likewise I advise those who cherish the ways of freedom and shun the yoke of d slavery as something evil, to beware lest by an excessive and ill-timed thirst for freedom they fall into the affliction of their ancestors, the excessive anarchy they experienced as a result of their unmeasured passion for liberty. For the Sicilians before the reign of Dionysius and Hipparinus lived happily, as they thought, faring sumptuously and ruling their rulers; they it was who, without any legal judgment, stoned to death the

[5] For the apparent inconsistency between the role ascribed to Lycurgus here and the account in *Laws* III, 691e, see pp. 87 f.

e   ten generals who preceded Dionysius, in order not to be subject to any master, not even justice and the law, but to be
altogether and absolutely free. This is why tyranny came upon
them. Both servitude in excess and liberty in excess are very
great evils, but in due measure both are great goods. Due
measure is found in obedience to God, the absence of measure
in obedience to men. And the god of wise men is the law; of
foolish men, pleasure.[6]

355   Since this is so, I call upon the friends of Dion to say to all
Syracusans that what I advise is his and my joint counsel. I
shall be the interpreter of what he would say if he were alive
and able to speak to you now. Well, then, someone may say,
what words does Dion's counsel contain for us about our
present situation? These: [7]

"First of all, men of Syracuse, accept laws that you think
b   will not arouse your desires and turn your thoughts toward
money-making and wealth. Of the three goods—soul, body,
and wealth [8]—your laws must give the highest honor to the
excellence of the soul, the second place to that of the body, as
subordinate to the excellence of the soul, and the third and
lowest rank to wealth, since it serves both body and soul. The
c   sacred tradition that ranks them in this order might rightly be
made a positive law among you, since it makes truly happy
those who live by it; whereas the doctrine that the rich are
the happy ones is a foolish saying of women and children, a
miserable doctrine in itself, bringing misery upon all who
follow it. Put to trial these words about law and you will see

[6] The doctrine of moderation between unbridled liberty and despotism
is the heart of the political theory of the *Laws*. See especially III, 701e.
For law as the god of wise men, see *Laws* IV, 713a ff.

[7] The use of Dion as spokesman here is probably more than a rhetorical
device; it suggests, what is altogether possible and even probable, that
these recommendations rest upon a plan worked out by Plato and Dion
jointly.

[8] On this threefold classification of goods see *Laws* III, 697bc; V, 727-
729, 743e. Aristotle (*Nic. Eth.* 1098b13-18) says that this ranking of goods
was ancient and agreed upon by the philosophers.

by the event that my advice is sound; experience seems to be the truest test of any matter.

"Having received laws of this sort, then, since Sicily is in grave danger and neither you nor your adversaries are clearly   d
superior in force, it would without question be just and expedient for all of you to strike a compromise—both for those of you who wish to avoid the rigor of absolute rule and for those who are bent on regaining their power. It was their ancestors, remember, who in their time saved the Hellenes from the barbarians and made it possible for us now to be discussing a constitution; for if the Greeks had been defeated then, there would be no opportunity for deliberation nor any basis for hope. So now let the one party have the freedom they desire, but under the government of a king; and let the other have their office, but let it be a responsible kingship, the   e
laws punishing kings and citizens alike if they disobey.

"Now with a steadfast and wholehearted adherence to all these conditions, and with God's help, appoint [three] kings: first, my son,[9] in double gratitude for my father's services and my own (as my father in his time saved the city from the barbarians, I have twice freed it from tyrants, as you your-   356
selves can bear witness); secondly, him who has the same name as my father and is the son of Dionysius, in gratitude for the help he has just rendered your cause,[10] as well as because of his upright character; for though he is the son of a tyrant, he is voluntarily liberating the city and gaining for himself and his house undying honor in place of an ephemeral and unjust tyranny. Thirdly, invite him who is now head of the army of your enemies—Dionysius the son of Dionysius—to become king   b
of the Syracusans as willing king of a willing city, if, through fear of misfortune and pity for his native city and its neglected

9 On the identity of this son see pp. 83 ff.

10 Meyer's interpretation of this clause is now generally accepted: it refers to Hipparinus' assistance in taking Syracuse from Callippus, an event which took place in 353, thirteen months after Callippus had seized power.

temples and tombs, he shows himself willing to exchange his power for that of a king, in order that his city may not be completely ruined by this civil strife and fall a rich prize to the barbarians.

"Let these then be your kings, three in number. Whether you invest them with the authority of the Spartan kings [11] or agree upon some more limited powers for them, install them in something like the following manner. I have already said
c this to you on a former occasion, but it is well that you hear it again.[12] If the family of Dionysius and Hipparinus is willing to end the present disorders for the salvation of Sicily and gain enduring honors for themselves and their houses on these terms, then, as I have said, summon ambassadors with full authority to effect a reconciliation. Let these ambassadors be whoever and as many as they please, chosen from persons here, or abroad, or both. When they have come together, let
d them begin by drawing up laws and a constitution providing that the kings shall have authority over religious and all other matters appropriate to former benefactors of the city, but that matters of war and peace shall be under the control of five-and-thirty guardians of the laws ruling in conjunction with the assembly and council. There should be various courts of justice for various offenses, but offenses involving death or exile should be judged by the thirty-five, in conjunction with other select judges chosen each year from the officeholders of

[11] This shows the source of Plato's inspiration. In the third book of the *Laws* he pictures the dual kingship at Sparta as a feature which, by dividing the kingly office, prevented it from overriding the other elements in the state and becoming despotic (691e). Viewed in its historical context the proposal for three co-ordinate kings at Syracuse is by no means as fantastic as some modern critics have thought.

[12] The proposal to summon commissioners from abroad to draw up a constitution and laws is put forward in *VII*, 337bc; but according to Plutarch (*Dion* 53) Dion had himself proposed to invite legislators from Corinth for this purpose. The present passage then need not be taken as referring to *Epistle VII*; indeed, since it is presented as coming from Dion's mouth, it may perhaps more naturally be taken as referring to proposals that Dion had made in his own person. Cf. 357a.

the preceding year (one from each office, namely that officer   e
who showed himself the best and justest); these should for the
ensuing year judge all cases involving the death or imprisonment or exiling of citizens. But a king should not be permitted to act as judge in such cases, since like a priest he is
to remain undefiled by bloodshed or imprisonment or exile.   357

"This is what I planned to accomplish for you when I was
alive, and this is still my earnest desire. If avenging deities in
the guise of friends had not prevented me, I should have
carried out this plan, after conquering my enemies with your
help. Then, if everything had gone as I desired, I should have
resettled the rest of Sicily and driven out the barbarians that
now possess it, with the exception of those who made common
cause with us in fighting for freedom against the tyranny, and   b
I should have restored to their ancient and ancestral homes
the former inhabitants of those Hellenic regions. So now I
advise all parties to adopt these same purposes as your common aims, and to work and summon everybody to work with
you for their realization, and to regard anyone who refuses as
your common enemy. These aims are not impossible of accomplishment, for what is already in two minds, and readily
appears the most feasible to those who have reflected upon it,
can hardly be called impossible by any man of understanding.
By the "two minds" I mean that of Hipparinus, the son of   c
Dionysius, and that of my own son; when these two have come
to an agreement, I think all others in Syracuse who care for
their city will give their assent.

"Now offer honor and prayers to all the gods and to all
other beings to whom, with the gods, honor belongs, per-
suading and exhorting friends and opponents gently but un-
ceasingly, until the plans that I have just described, like the
dreams that God sends to waking men,[13] have been brought   d
to visible and happy realization."

13 Cf. *Soph.* 366c.

IX[1]

PLATO TO ARCHYTAS OF TARENTUM, WELFARE.

e

358

Archippus and Philonides[2] and their companions have
come to me with the letter you gave them and have brought
me news of you. Their mission to the city they accomplished
with no difficulty, since it was not a burdensome matter. But
as to you, they reported that you think it a heavy trial not to
be able to get free from the cares of public life. It is indeed
one of the sweetest things in life to follow one's own interests,
especially when they are such as you have chosen; practically
everyone would agree. But this also you must bear in mind,
that none of us is born for himself alone; a part of our
existence belongs to our country, a part to our parents, a
part to our other friends, and a large part is given to the

[1] There is nothing in the circumstances presupposed by this letter to
arouse suspicion. Archytas was seven times strategos of his native city,
although the law and precedent seem to have been against re-election to
that office (Diog. Laert. VIII, 79). Plato visited Tarentum sometime
shortly before 388 (Diog. Laert. III, 18; Nepos *Dion* 2), and the intimacy
between him and Archytas was probably maintained without interruption
from that date. During Plato's second visit to Sicily in 367, he brought
about a friendly alliance between Archytas and the young Dionysius (*Ep.
VII*, 338c), and it was Archytas who intervened to secure Plato's safe departure from Syracuse in 361 (*Ep. VII*, 350a). From these facts we may
well assume that there was friendly correspondence between Plato and
his eminent friend in southern Italy. On the other hand, the advice to
Archytas is quite gratuitous, and the theme of the letter, the duty of
entering public office, is a trite one. The vague reference to the mission
of Archippus and Philonides (357e) is a suspicious touch. Cicero's citation of the letter (*De Fin.* II, 14; *De Off.* I, 7), and his evident belief that
the letter comes from Plato, do not prove its authenticity. Like *Epistles
I, II,* and *XI,* it is probably a product of the schools of rhetoric.

[2] An Archippus and a Philonides are mentioned in Jamblichus' list of
Pythagoreans (*Vita Pythag.* xxxvi) as coming from Tarentum. Archippus
is said to have been one of the two Pythagoreans who survived the
disaster at Croton in the later fifth century.

circumstances that command our lives. When our country calls us to public service it would, I think, be unnatural to refuse; especially since this means giving place to unworthy b men, who enter public life for motives other than the best.

Enough of this. As for Echecrates,[3] I am taking care of him and will do so in the future, both for your sake and the sake of his father Phrynion as well as for the young man himself.

X[1]

PLATO TO ARISTODORUS, WELFARE.

I hear from Dion that you are one of his most trusted fol- c lowers and have been so from the beginning, manifesting the most philosophical of the philosophical virtues; for to be steadfast, loyal, and dependable—this, I say, is true philosophy; whereas all other learning, and all cleverness directed to any other end than this, I call—and I think rightly—mere ornaments. Farewell; hold fast to these virtues that you have thus far manifested.

[3] This may be Echecrates of Phlius, the auditor of the narrative of the *Phaedo*, himself a Pythagorean and a pupil of Philolaus and Eurytus, who in their later life taught at Tarentum; or it may be the less-known Echecrates of Tarentum, mentioned in Jamblichus' list of Pythagoreans.

[1] There is nothing to arouse suspicion in this brief note of commendation to one of Dion's faithful followers, written probably during the later period of Dion's life when some of his former adherents were turning against him. The thought is certainly Platonic. The emphasis upon steadfastness, or "unforgetfulness" (ἀλήθεια) is especially characteristic of Plato's later moral teaching, as is also the scorn for mere refinements, as compared with the more solid culture of the character (*Theaet*. 176c; *Laws* I, 644a). The Aristodorus to whom this note is addressed is otherwise unknown. The extraordinary brevity of this epistle is striking, and Ritter (*Neue Untersuchungen*, p. 415) suggests that it may have been enclosed in a letter to Dion.

XI

d PLATO TO LAODAMAS,[1] WELFARE.

I have written you before that the matters you have mentioned will all be greatly advanced if you yourself can come to Athens; but since you say that is impossible, the next best thing would be, as you write, that I or Socrates[2] should come

[1] We know nothing of the Laodamas to whom this letter is addressed, nor are the circumstances which it presupposes at all clear. Diogenes Laertius (III, 24) mentions a certain Leodamas as a Thasian and a pupil of Plato, and this may be the individual to whom this letter is addressed. The date at which the letter is supposed to have been written cannot be easily made out. The reference to the dangers of traveling (358e) has been taken to indicate the period between 361 and 359 when Alexander of Pherae was blocking the land route to Thrace and also carrying on a piratical warfare on Athenian commerce. Again Plato is said to be an old man, which would accord very well with the date 360. We may further suppose that the colony for which Laodamas seeks Plato's assistance is Crenidae (as Raeder suggests, *Rheinisches Museum,* p. 440), founded in 360-359, or Datos (according to Meyer, *Geschichte des Altertums,* V, 481, 503), founded in 360. But the vagueness of the letter on these points is ground for suspicion. Neither is it made clear just what Laodamas wanted Plato to do. We may infer that he was merely asking aid in drawing up laws for his colony. Why then the marked reluctance of Plato to have anything to do with the project? Members of the Academy had on numerous occasions in the past performed similar services for various Greek communities, and we must assume that their activity had Plato's approval and co-operation. Ritter (*Neue Untersuchungen,* p. 398) thinks the advice to pray to the gods and await better times is not truly Platonic, but a distorted version of *Epistle VII,* 330d ff. The naming of Socrates' illness looks like an attempt at verisimilitude; and the appeal to the experience of "almost all earlier cities" to show that Laodamas cannot hope to accomplish anything smacks of the school exercise. In short, this is just such a letter as a student in the schools of rhetoric could have written, and I see no reason for ascribing it to Plato.

[2] The Socrates referred to is of course the younger Socrates, who figures as one of the personages in the *Politicus,* and who must have been a person of some importance in the Academy. Aristotle cites his opinion in one passage of the *Metaphysics* (1036b25).

to you, if we can. But Socrates is ill with strangury, and it e
would be unseemly for me to come and not accomplish what
you summoned me for. For my part I have little hope that it
can be done, though to explain why would require another
and longer letter giving all the reasons; and besides, at my
time of life I have not the bodily strength for travel and for
all the dangers that one encounters both by land and by sea,
and at present all the circumstances of travel are full of
danger. I can, however, give you and the leaders of your colony
a piece of advice which, when I have spoken it, "may seem   359
trifling," to quote Hesiod, but is hard to take.[3] If they think [4]
that a constitution can ever be well established by the enact-
ment of laws, of whatever sort they may be, without some authority in the city to look after the daily life of the citizens
and to insure that both free men and slaves live in a temperate and manly fashion, they are thinking wrongly. This
could be done, however, if you have at hand men worthy of
exercising such authority; but if you lack an educator, then   b
you have neither teachers nor learners, as I see it, and no
course is left but to pray to the gods. Indeed most cities in
the past have been similarly established and later attained
good government under the force of circumstances brought on
by war or other enterprises of the city, when a man of nobility
and character has appeared and exercised great power. In the
meantime you must and should ardently desire this to happen;
but reflect on what I have said and do not act lightly, think-   c
ing that success is within your grasp. Good luck!

[3] The source of this quotation is unknown and its meaning uncertain.
[4] I have followed Souilhé in reading οἴονται instead of the οἷόν τε
of Burnet's text. The subject of this verb (the "they" of the translation) I
take to be the leaders of the proposed colony.

XII [1]

PLATO TO ARCHYTAS OF TARENTUM, WELFARE.

d   I am overjoyed at receiving the treatises that have come
from you and am filled with admiration for their author, who
seemed to me a man worthy of his ancient ancestors. These
ancestors are said to have been Myrians, and to have been
among the Trojans who emigrated under Laomedon. Good
men they were, according to the accepted legend. As to the
writings of mine about which you wrote, they are not yet
completed, but I am sending them to you as they are. We are
e   agreed that they ought to be guarded,[2] so I need not ad-
monish you on that point.

(Some have contended that this letter is not Plato's.) [3]

[1] According to Diogenes Laertius (VIII, 80-81) this letter is a reply to
one from Archytas, in which Archytas says he is sending Plato certain
writings of Ocellus. This Ocellus was a Pythagorean of Lucania and
probably an older contemporary of Archytas. It is generally believed
(following H. Diels, *Doxographi Graeci* [Berlin, 1879], pp. 187 ff.), that the
so-called Ocellus writings are not older than the beginning of the first
century B.C. Both the letter of Archytas, then, and the answer which is
Epistle XII in our collection, seem to have been composed for the purpose of authenticating these writings; and if so they did not come into
existence until more than a century and a half after Plato's death.

[2] This injunction to keep Plato's writings secret looks suspicious. How
it misrepresents Plato's real attitude as expressed in *Epistle VII* has been
shown above, pp. 112 ff.

[3] This notation is found in our best manuscripts, and may go back to
Thrasyllus.

XIII

PLATO TO DIONYSIUS, TYRANT OF SYRACUSE, WELFARE.   360

Let this beginning of my letter be likewise a sign to you that it comes from me.[1] Once when you were feasting the young men from Locri[2] you arose and came over to me (your couch being at some distance from mine) and greeted me with a phrase that was both friendly and neatly turned, as it seemed to me. The man lying next to me (and a fair youth he was)   b thought so too, for he said: "I suppose, Dionysius, that you have got much wisdom from Plato?" "And much else besides," you said; "for from the very minute I sent for him, and by the very fact that I had sent for him, I was the gainer."[3] So let us preserve this opinion and endeavor always to increase our usefulness to one another. It is for this very purpose that I am sending you some Pythagorean writings and some *Divisions,*[4] and also a man whom we thought, you remember, that both you and Archytas, if Archytas comes to you, could use   c

[1] On this reference to the salutation see notes on *I,* 309a and *III,* 315a.

[2] The Epizephyrian Locrians, a Dorian city close to the tip of southern Italy, were friends or allies of Syracuse. The young tyrant's mother was a Locrian. Very possibly the young men had come to observe or take part in athletic contests.

[3] The reputation of Dionysius was enhanced as soon as it was known that he had summoned Plato; and why should it not have been?

[4] It is tempting to assume, with Apelt (*Platons Briefe*) and others, that by these πυθαγόρεια the writer of this letter means the *Timaeus* and by the διαιρέσεις the *Sophist* and *Politicus.* But if the letter is genuine and this interpretation is accepted, it would follow that these dialogues were written prior to 366, which can hardly have been the case. There is no need to assume that any of the known dialogues are referred to here. Any metaphysical-mathematical inquiry might be called *Pythagoreia.* Aristotle refers to "written divisions" (γεγραμμέναι διαιρέσεις), i.e. exercises in classification (*De Part. Animalium* 642b12). Cf. also the verses of the comic poet Ephippus ridiculing the διαιρέσεις in the Academy (Athen. 59d-f).

to advantage. His name is Helicon,[5] his family is of Cyzicus, and he is a disciple of Eudoxus [6] and well versed in all that eminent man's doctrines. Moreover he has been associated with one of the pupils of Isocrates and with Polyxenus,[7] one of the followers of Bryson.[8] But, what is rarer with such men, he is pleasant to meet, seemingly not difficult, but easy and

d mild mannered. I put it thus cautiously, for it is a man I am giving my opinion of; and though man has his good qualities, he is, with rare exceptions and in the greater part of his actions, quite changeable. I had my fears and doubts even about this man, so I not only conversed with him myself but also made inquiry among his fellow citizens, and nobody had anything to say against him. But look him over yourself and be on your guard. Above all, if you can in any way find leisure for it,[9] take lessons from him as part of your studies

e in philosophy. If not, have him instruct someone else so that when you do have leisure you can learn and thereby add to your character and your good name. In this way I shall continue to be of help to you. But enough of this.

361   As for the things you wrote me to send you, I have had the Apollo executed and Leptines [10] is bringing it to you, the

[5] Very little is known of Helicon other than what is told here. Plutarch (*Dion* 19) says that while in Syracuse he predicted an eclipse of the sun and was rewarded with a talent of silver.

[6] Eudoxus of Cnidos, one of the foremost mathematicians of the fourth century, had moved his school from Cyzicus to Athens and merged it with the Academy at a time shortly before Plato's visit to Syracuse in 367. See G. F. Unger, in *Philologus*, L (1891), 191 ff.

[7] Polyxenus is referred to in Alexander's commentary on Aristotle's *Metaphysics* (84, 16) as a Sophist and the inventor of the "third man" argument. For other references to him see *Epistle II*, 310c, 314cd; Diog. Laert. II, 76.

[8] Bryson, a pupil of Eucleides of Megara, was a noted Sophist, referred to by Aristotle as author of an attempt to square the circle (*Post. An.* 75b40; *Soph. El.* 171b16, 172a4).

[9] Dionysius was busy with the Lucanian War; this was the reason why Plato was given permission to return to Athens (*Ep. VII*, 338a).

[10] Cf. 361b and 363c. Can this trusted messenger be the Athenian against whom Demosthenes delivered his *Leptines* in 354? For other guesses as to his identity see Apelt and Novotný *ad loc.*

work of a good young sculptor whose name is Leochares.[11]
There was another piece in his shop that I thought very
charming, and I therefore bought it to give to your wife, for
she looked after me, both in health and in sickness, in a
manner that did honor both to me and to you. Give it to
her, then, if you think it fitting. I am also sending twelve jars
of sweet wine and two jars of honey for the children. I arrived
too late for the fig harvest, and the myrtle berries that were   b
laid by have spoiled. We shall look after them better next
time. Leptines will tell you about the plants.

The money for these purchases and for certain payments to
the city I procured from Leptines, telling him (what I thought
was quite proper as well as true) that the money we spent in
fitting out the Leucadian ship, about sixteen minae, came
from my funds. So I got this sum from him, have made use of
it, and have sent these objects to you.[12] Now hear how it   c
stands with respect to your funds here at Athens, and mine.
I will make use of your money, as I told you, just as I do
that of my other friends; but I am using it as sparingly as
I can, and only so much as seems necessary or just or proper,
not to me only, but to your agent. My own situation is this.
Four daughters were left by my nieces (who died at the time
when you bade me wear a crown, you remember, but I re-   d
fused), one of marriageable age, another eight years old, another a little over three, and the other not yet one. My friends
and I must provide dowries for them, at least for those who
are married during my lifetime; the others we may leave out
of account. Nor need I provide for those whose fathers may
become richer than I am; but at present I am the wealthiest,
and it was I who, with the help of Dion and other friends,   e
provided dowries for their mothers. The oldest of these girls

[11] Leochares was a well-known sculptor at Athens. His artistic activity
seems to have extended from some time before 356 to about 320, and the
reference to him here as a "young" artist is consistent enough.

[12] No doubt Plato is putting this and other financial dealings he has
had with Dionysius in the light most becoming to the tyrant. We would
give much to know the full truth.

is to marry Speusippus, whose sister's daughter she is. For her I will require at most thirty minae; that is a reasonable wedding portion for us to give. Moreover, if my mother should die I should need almost ten minae for building her tomb. These are about all my obligations at present. If any other private or public expense comes up because of my visit to you, I will endeavor to make the expenditure as little as possible; but what I cannot avoid will have to be at your

362 charge, as I told you must be the case.

Now a word regarding your funds at Athens and their expenditure. In the first place, if it should ever be necessary for me to fit out a chorus or anything of the sort, you have no guest-friend here who would advance the money, as we thought.[13] Furthermore, if some matter of great importance to you should arise such that you would be benefited immediately if an expenditure were made but injured if it were not made or were delayed until word had come from you, the situation would be not only damaging but humiliating for

b you. I found this out myself when, wishing to send you some other and more costly articles that you had written for, I sent Erastus to Andromedes the Aeginetan,[14] upon whom, as your guest-friend, you told me to draw if I needed money. He replied, as was only human and natural, that he had formerly advanced money for your father but had had difficulty in collecting it; so now he would give a small sum, but no more. And so I got it from Leptines, who deserves to be praised, not because he gave, but because he gave willingly; and in all else

c that he has done and said about you he has shown the quality of his friendship. I ought to report such things, as well as matters of an opposite sort, to show how I think this or that man is disposed towards you. And so I shall be frank with you about your money; since it is only right, and since moreover I can speak from experience of the men who surround you.

[13] Cf. Plutarch *Dion* 17, where it is said that Dion bore the expense of a choregia for Plato.

[14] Andromedes is otherwise unknown. Perhaps Erastus is the same as the Erastus of *Epistle VI*.

Whenever your men bring in their reports, they hesitate to mention any matter that they think involves expense, for fear of your displeasure. You must therefore compel them to form   d
the habit of speaking about these things as well as other matters; for it is your duty to know everything, so far as possible, and pass judgment and not shrink from any facts. This will be the best of all ways of enhancing your authority. To make expenditures rightly and to repay debts properly is a good thing in many ways, and even furthers the acquisition of money, as you yourself will see more and more. Then do not allow those who profess to be looking out for your interests to give you a bad name; for there is no advantage nor honor in being known as difficult in money matters.   e

And now I would say something about Dion. About the other matters at issue I can say nothing as yet, until the letters come which you say you are sending me; but on the subject which you forbade me to mention to him,[15] though I have not mentioned nor spoken about it, I have tried to find out how he would take it if you carried out your design, and it seemed to me he would be not a little indignant. In every other respect Dion's attitude toward you, as shown in his words and actions, is quite temperate.

To Cratinus,[16] the brother of Timotheus and my friend, let   363
us give a hoplite breastplate, one of the light kind for foot soldiers; and to the daughters of Cebes three full-length [17] chitons, not the expensive Amorgian ones,[18] but linen ones of Sicilian make. You are probably familiar with the name of Cebes, for he figures in the Socratic writings as taking part with Simmias in a discussion with Socrates about the soul. He is an intimate friend and well disposed towards us all.

[15] See pp. 105 f.

[16] Cratinus is otherwise unknown; but can his brother Timotheus be the famous Athenian general, the protégé of Isocrates?

[17] "Full-length," literally "seven cubits long" (10′ 6″).

[18] On the "expensive Amorgian" chitons, see the interesting article by Miss G. M. A. Richter, which Post has called to my attention, in *Am. Jour. Arch.*, XXXIII (1929), 27-33.

b   You no doubt recall the sign that distinguishes the letters I
write that are seriously intended from those that are not. Still
I would have you attend carefully and keep it in mind; for
there are many who ask me to write whom it is not easy to
refuse openly. Those that are seriously meant begin with
"God"; those less seriously with "gods." [19]

The ambassadors also asked me to write you, and quite
properly; for they have everywhere been sounding your praises
and mine, not least of all Philagrus,[20] the one who had a sore

c   hand, you remember. Philaides, who has just returned from
the Great King,[21] also spoke of you. If it had not required too
long a letter I should have written you what he said; but as
it is you must ask Leptines.

If you send the breastplate or anything else that I have
mentioned, and have no one you wish to send it by, give
it to Tyrillus; for he is always traveling back and forth,
and is a friend of mine, accomplished in philosophy and other
matters. He is the son-in-law of Teison, who was civic magis-
trate [22] at the time when I set sail.

[19] Is this little device incompatible with what we know of Plato's
character? The puzzling thing is that there is no evidence of its employment in the letters that we have. Perhaps it was designed solely for
letters of recommendation written to Dionysius. Plato may have been
besieged with requests for such letters, because of his known connection
with the rich young tyrant. It is unlikely that there is any hidden meaning behind the choice of these terms; Plato seems to use "God" and "the
gods" interchangeably in the dialogues.

[20] Philagrus and those names following—Philaides, Tyrillus, Teison,
Iatrocles, Myronides—are mere names to us. Aristocritus is mentioned in
Epistle III, 319a.

[21] Cavaignac suggests, in *Rev. des Études Grecques*, XXXIX (1926),
247, that Philaides was one of the ambassadors sent to Persia in 367 to
solicit the arbitration of the Great King in the war between Sparta and
Thebes.

[22] Ἐπολιανόμει. The office of πολιανόμος was not known at Athens.
But it is found in inscriptions from Heracleia on the Siris, in southern
Italy, a colony of Tarentum; and there may well have been such an
office in Syracuse, another Dorian state. See G. Gilbert, *Handbuch der
griechischen Staatsaltertümer* (Leipzig, 1888, 1893), II, 246.

Farewell, study your philosophy, and try to interest the
other young men in it. Give my greetings to your fellow stu-   d
dents of the spheres.[23] Instruct Aristocritus and the rest that
if any book or letter comes from me, they are to have it
brought at once to your attention and to remind you to pay
heed to its contents. And now do not neglect to repay Leptines the money he advanced, but do it promptly so that
others, seeing your treatment of him, may be more willing
to oblige you.

Iatrocles, whom I set free at the same time as Myronides,   e
is traveling with the things I am now sending you. Put him
in your pay, since he bears you good will, and use him for
any service you wish. Preserve this letter, or an abstract of it,
and take it to heart.[24]

---

[23] Apelt translates συσφαιριστάς by "Ballspielgenossen"; similarly Post,
"the group who join you at ball play," though in his notes he admits the
possibility of the rendering given here. Since Plato is sending to Dionysius
a certain Helicon who is well versed in the doctrines of Eudoxus, and
since we know that Eudoxus was the author of an astronomical theory of
the heavenly spheres, I think this rendering is the more likely. The
σφαιρίον of Epistle II, 312d, may be borrowed from this passage, and if
so it shows the way in which the writer of that letter interpreted it.

[24] Reading, with Novotný, αὐτὸς ἴσθι. The admonition to preserve this
letter, or an abstract of it, is no reason for suspecting its genuineness; see
above, p. 107.

SELECTED BIBLIOGRAPHY

Adam, Rudolf. *Die Echtheit der Platonischen Briefe.* Berlin, 1906.

——. "Über die Platonischen Briefe," *Archiv für Geschichte der Philosophie,* XXIII (1910), 29–52.

Andreae, W. "Die Philosophischen Probleme in den Platonischen Briefen," *Philologus,* N.F. XXXII (1922), 75–87.

——. *Platons Staatsschriften. Erster Teil: Briefe.* Jena, 1923.

Apelt, O. *Platons Briefe.* Leipzig, 1921.

Bluck, R. S. *Plato's Seventh and Eighth Letters.* Cambridge, 1947.

Bury, R. G. Greek text and English translation of the *Epistles.* Loeb Classical Library (Plato, Vol. VII). Cambridge, Mass., 1929.

Egermann, Franz. *Die Platonischen Briefe VII und VIII.* Berlin, 1928.

Gomperz, Heinrich. *Platons Selbstbiographie.* Berlin and Leipzig, 1928.

Hackforth, Reginald. *The Authorship of the Platonic Epistles.* Manchester, 1913.

Harward, J. *The Platonic Epistles.* Cambridge, 1932.

Heidel, W. A. *Pseudo-Platonica.* Baltimore, 1896.

Hell, G. *Untersuchungen und Beobachtungen zu den Platonischen Briefen.* Berlin, 1933.

——. "Zur Datierung des 7. und 8. Platonischen Briefes," *Hermes,* LXVII (1932), 295–302.

Howald, E. *Die Briefe Platons.* Zürich, 1923.

Karsten, H. T. *Commentatio Critica de Platonis Quae Feruntur Epistolis.* Utrecht, 1864.

Maddalena, Antonio. *Platone: Lettere.* Bari, 1948.

Novotný, F. *Platonis Epistulae Commentariis Illustratae.* Brno, 1930.

Pasquali, Giorgio. *Le Lettere di Platone.* Firenze, 1938.

Pavlu, Josef. *Mitteilungen des Vereins Klassischer Philologie in Wien,* VIII (1931), 1–35; IX (1932), 53–61; X (1933), 77–94.

Post, L. A. *Thirteen Epistles of Plato.* Oxford, 1925.

————. *The Vatican Plato and its Relations.* (Publications of the American Philological Association.) Middletown, Conn., 1934.

Raeder, Hans. "Über die Echtheit der Platonischen Briefe," *Rheinisches Museum,* N.F. LXI (1906), 427–71, 511–42.

Reinhold, H. *De Platonis Epistulis Dissertatio.* Quedlinburg, 1886.

Richards, H. *Platonica.* London, 1911.

Ritter, C. *Platon.* 2 vols. Munich, 1910, 1923.

————. *Platons Gesetze.* Leipzig, 1896.

————. *Neue Untersuchungen über Platon.* Munich, 1910.

————. *Untersuchungen über Platon.* Stuttgart, 1888.

Scheliha, Renata von. *Dion: die Platonische Staatsgründung in Sizilien.* Leipzig, 1928.

Souilhé, Joseph. *Platon: Lettres.* Vol. VIII, Pt. 1, of the Budé edition. Paris, 1926.

Steinhart, K. and H. Müller. *Platons Sämmtliche Werke.* Vol. VIII. Leipzig, 1873.

Stenzel, Julius. *Platon der Erzieher.* Leipzig, 1928.

————. "Über den Aufbau der Erkenntnis im VII. Platonischen Brief," in *Kleine Schriften.* Darmstadt, 1956.

Taylor, A. E. "The Analysis of ʼΕΠΙΣΤΗΜΗ in Plato's *Seventh Epistle,*" *Mind,* N.S. XXI (1912), 347–70.

————. *Plato: the Man and his Work.* New York, 1927.

Wilamowitz-Moellendorff, Ulrich von. *Platon.* Berlin, 1919–**1920.**

INDEX

A. ENGLISH[1]

[1] Numbers in parentheses following page numbers refer to the marginal numbering in the *Epistles*.

B. GREEK [1]

[1] Italicized figures refer to marginal numbering in the *Epistles* (pp. 191-269).

The Library of Liberal Arts